The Family Baker

THE
Family Baker

150 NEVER-LET-YOU-DOWN
BASIC RECIPES

Susan G. Purdy

Illustrated by the author

BROADWAY BOOKS   NEW YORK

Broadway Books titles may be purchased for business or promotional use or for special sales. For information, please write to: Special Markets Department, Random House, Inc., 1540 Broadway, New York, NY 10036.

BROADWAY BOOKS and its logo, a letter B bisected on the diagonal, are trademarks of Broadway Books, a division of Random House, Inc.

Blueberry Shortcakes recipe was previously published in *Fine Cooking* magazine, September 1998.

Library of Congress Cataloging-in-Publication Data

Purdy, Susan Gold
    The family baker : 150 never-let-you-down basic recipes / Susan G. Purdy.
    — 1st ed.
        p.   cm.
    Includes index.
    ISBN 0-7679-0261-0 (hardcover)
    1. Baking   I. Title.
TX763.P96   1999
641.8'15—dc21   99-20469
                                                         CIP

FIRST EDITION

Designed by Vertigo Design
Illustrations by Susan G. Purdy

99 00 01 02 03 10 9 8 7 6 5 4 3 2 1

This book is dedicated with love

to my daughter, Cassandra,

for the delicious times we have shared

in the kitchen

Contents

Acknowledgments

This book is a celebration of families baking together and sharing the pleasures of the table. To my family, then, I owe the greatest thanks. To my husband, Geoffrey, for cheerfully but critically taste-testing; to our daughter, Cassandra—the real family baker—for helping develop as well as test recipes; to my mother, Frances Joslin Gold, for her inspiration, insight, and the sharing of a lifetime of recipes; and to my father, the late Harold Gold, who loved pound cakes. I also want to thank my extended family: my sister, Nancy, and her sons, David and Scott; my aunts; uncles; cousins; and grandparents. Some are present here in their recipes; others are vividly present in my memory because of recipes, or meals, shared in the past. These taste memories are a very real legacy that I want to pass on, not only because they are tasty but also in order to perpetuate the traditions of our family.

In the preparation of this manuscript, I was fortunate to have the help of many capable people. I thank my expert baking assistants, Kristin Eycleshymer (cake chapter) and Ann Martin (cookie chapter), as well as my extraordinary recipe testers, Rose Sinkins and Mary Ann Havron (and her husband, Bill, and son, Matthew) and their friends, who shared a running commentary on the items tasted.

For contributing recipes, testing material, or for sharing culinary tips and techniques, I want to thank Elmira Ingersoll, Mary Muhlhausen, Charley (Susan) Kanas, Steve Keneipp, Lora Brody, Florence Bloch, Diane Cordial, David DeJean, Elizabeth and Pirie MacDonald, Jacquie Colman Manley and her son Jesse Colman, Carol Fyfield, Ginnie Sweatt Hagan, Anne Maidman, Claire Rosenberg, Jerry Allford and his mother, the late Louvene Allford, Mrs. Marilyn Ober, Erik Landegger, Robin von Reyn, Jesse Nelson, Phoebe Joslin Vernon, Irra Gellin, Lucille Purdy, Amelia Robinson-Fritz and her daughter Mollie Fritz, Kathy Jarrett, Delores Custer, Patsy Jamieson, Chef John George of Boston's Tremont 647 Restaurant, Martha Sloan, Janet James Purdy, Lisa and Pearl Sandone, Tracy Glaves Spalding, April Crumrine, Greg Bonsignores, and the late Anna Olson, Lauren Lieberman, and Gladys Martin.

For her careful critique of my introduction, as well as her moral support and friendship, I thank noted writer Hila Colman. For their expert knowledge of culinary chemistry and help with eleventh-hour baking dilemmas, I thank food chemist and author Shirley O. Corriher and her husband, Arch Corriher. For their interest in this project as well as for information about Diamond walnuts, I thank Noreen Griffee and Bill Hosie.

I wish to thank my literary agent, Olivia Blumer, for her friendship, confidence, and creative management of this project, and my editor at Broadway Books, Harriet Bell, for her enthusiastic support and skillful editing. For transforming my manuscript into a handsome finished book, I am indebted to Karen Fraley, copy editor; Alison Lew, designer; Roberto de Vicq de Cumptich, art director (and his adorable niece, Ginger Cutler, who appears on the book jacket); as well as Quentin Bacon, photographer, and stylist Darienne Sutton.

Introduction

The creativity of cooking, and especially baking, has always been an important part of my life. From the time I was old enough to reach the counter, my mother let me help her cook and bake. As a painter and creative artist, she loved (and still does) to use her hands and to show me how to make things. I loved watching her roll out pie pastry and decorate cakes. I clearly remember the first time she helped me tentatively push the plunger of a metal decorating tube to squeeze out a wildly sloping "Happy Birthday Daddy" on a tall chocolate cake. I was hooked. From that moment, I became the family cake decorator. My Grandmother Clara was dazzled, and never tired of telling the story of Susan baking her first "two-egg cake by herself and decorating it, too." The fine points are mercifully lost in history (surely I had help baking), but it became one of those dreadful family stories that stuck; to my ears it never seemed as adorable, or as hilarious, as it did to others. In fact, it is still embarrassing, though the truth is I can still remember how happy I was with that cake and the story makes a point about the importance of a young child's sense of achievement.

When my own daughter, Cassandra, was about two, she pulled her chair up to the kitchen table to help me stir cake batter and, with just a little coaching, learned how to separate eggs by tipping them out into her hand. A few years later, she was just the right age to help me test cookie recipes for my children's cookbooks. It is no accident that she earns her living as a chef, baker, and restaurant consultant. And as children's skill and confidence grow, so do their accomplishments. Above my desk I have her photo, age five, gluing jelly beans on the sagging roof of a heavily-sugared gingerbread house we had made together. Hanging nearby is a "Best Cake" blue ribbon from the local Bridgewater Country Fair, which she won at age eleven for baking Anna Olson's Swedish Almond Butter Cake (see page 148).

Anna's cake had by then been in our family a long time and had taken on a life of its own. It was the first cake I taught Cassandra to bake, and was our favorite recipe for every special occasion. Anna herself had been an important figure in my childhood. She was a family friend who stayed with my sister, Nancy, and me when our parents went on vacation. We couldn't wait for the treats that accompanied her arrival. She was an incomparable baker; I can still smell the perfume of butter and almonds that permeated the kitchen while she was baking and see her pink cheeks dusted with a touch of flour.

Many years ago, I published one of Anna's recipes in my first children's cookbook. Nearly ten years after that book appeared, I received a phone call at Christmas from Lisa, one of Anna's daughters. Her mother had recently passed away, and Lisa, as she related the story, was trying to lift herself from a deep depression by collecting her mother's recipes. One recipe in particular eluded her; she could not find Anna's spritz cookies. Lisa was sharing this search for baking "memories" with her friend, Sonia. The week before

Christmas Sonia surprised Lisa with a tray of freshly baked cookies. "We sat at my kitchen table drinking coffee and chatting about each cookie in turn when, suddenly," Lisa said to me through tears and laughter on the phone, "I tasted one cookie and started to cry. I couldn't stop. I had chills. My mother was standing in front of me again. I asked Sonia where she got that recipe. 'From a library book,' she replied. We put on our coats and went right to the library. We found the book, and would you believe, Susan, it was your *Christmas Cooking Around the World,* with Anna Olson's Spritz Cookies? My friend did not know Olson was my maiden name and she didn't know who you were, but she brought my mother back to me, through you. It is the best Christmas gift I can imagine."

Snapshots. Taste memories . . . they bind us to our past, and they comfort us. What is comfort food, after all, but the food of our childhoods, sweet nursery foods, cookies, puddings that we turn to no matter what our age? If you want to start a conversation with a stranger anywhere in the world, just ask about food, especially desserts, the icing on the cake, the moments to remember. You will find people as quick to share their recipes as their children's photographs. No mystery there, the impulse comes from the same place—the heart.

I hope this book will bring you back to the kitchen, to the joys of home baking. With never-let-you-down delicious treats to make with ease and share with pleasure, how can you resist?

Wouldn't you like to hear an appreciative "Wow, that looks good!" as you bring a hot-from-the-oven pie to the table? Wouldn't you like your child to be standing next to you on a stool helping you stir milk and eggs together instead of watching television? Nothing replaces the time spent together with your children, nieces and nephews, grandchildren, or friends . . . and a lot

more goes into the process than just making something to eat. More even than sharing time and love. One passes along family history and traditions, dreams, and values, sharing the very ingredients of life as well as of cookies.

As I travel around the country teaching baking, I meet so many people who love the subject, who are eager to describe, or share, a favorite recipe. They tell me they wish they had more time to bake or more skill or recipes quick and dependable enough to count on when they find a moment to spare.

This book is my response. The recipes do not require special baking skills, hard-to-find ingredients, or elaborate equipment. In fact, the Pan Volume and Serving Chart on page 206 and the yield in each recipe, indicating the amount of batter, will enable you use the pans you already have on hand instead of having to run out and buy the one called for. The advanced preparation and freezing tips will help save time. Whenever possible, I simplified procedures, aiming for delicious results rather than classical techniques. Most of the recipes are quick, easy, and elementary, others require a little more time and patience. If a recipe looks long, it is not because it is complex, but rather because I have added helpful hints to guarantee success.

The recipes are reliable and home-tested. After I developed them, I passed out copies to friends to test so I could be sure that they work in other people's kitchens. I listened to the comments of my friends and their kids. When a busy dad who visits with his kids for just a few hours each Saturday afternoon told me they spent their time together baking brownies that were quick, easy, and a great hit, I knew I had a keeper. When one tester said that her sons, ages five and eight, loved the bread pudding but not the pie, I saved one recipe and discarded the other.

I am often asked where the recipes come from.

The short answer is: my life. From my own experience, my family, my past work and teaching; many have been shared with me by my students and friends, my professional colleagues. Others come from traveling, or are generic variations on traditional themes, like my take on devil's food cake.

This is a personal collection of home-baked desserts—the way your mom made them or the way you wish your mom had made them—rather than professional-looking, pastry shop sweets. These are meant to look as homemade as they taste. I hope you will find your own favorites, treats that will become part of your life, your own specialties to make over and over and, by popular demand, to hand down to your own kids.

Today, in our highly technical lives, the family baker I remember from my childhood is an endangered species. Most moms are out there carrying briefcases, not showing the kids how to roll out dough. Standing here in my denim apron, I invite you back into the kitchen—even if for a brief stay—and be sure to bring the kids.

About the Recipes in This Book

- Before baking, read the sections on ingredients and equipment (pages 208 and 227), to familiarize yourself with information and techniques that will guarantee successful results.

- Before starting a recipe, read it through from start to finish, so you will know what ingredients and equipment to have on hand, and how to plan your time.

- To achieve success in baking, use the specified pan sizes; a pan that is too large will produce a cake that is too thin and does not bake properly. A too-small pan may cause the cake to overflow in the oven. If you don't have the pan size called for, see the Pan Volume and Serving Chart (page 206) to find another pan size. Most recipes can be baked in a variety of pans. See the total volume of batter in the yield for each recipe and use this figure to calculate a substitute pan size.

- All dry measurements are level.

- All eggs are U.S. Grade A Large (2 ounces). Eggs should be at room temperature when added to a recipe.

- I prefer to bake with butter (see page 208). If you choose to substitute margarine, the flavor will vary. Use only solid stick margarine, never soft spreads or tub margarines, which will almost always cause baking failures because they contain undisclosed amounts of water and additives.

- Lemon or orange zest refers to the brightest part of the peel, which contains all the flavor. Do not grate the white portion of the peel, which can be bitter.

- Orange and lemon juice are best when freshly squeezed. As a substitute for fresh lemon juice, use Minute Maid 100% fresh lemon juice from concentrate, available in the frozen food section of the supermarket; never use an artificial juice.

- Nutmeg has a more pungent flavor when freshly grated, but store-bought, grated nutmeg can be substituted.

- Room temperature means 68° to 72°F. All baking ingredients should be at room temperature before you begin so they will blend properly.

- Oven temperatures vary considerably and are the greatest cause of baking failures. To prevent problems, purchase a separate auxiliary oven thermometer in a cookware or hardware store and keep it on the middle shelf inside your oven. Adjust the external indicator as needed to keep the correct internal temperature.

- When instructed to double-wrap baked goods for freezing, the procedure is to completely cool the item, then wrap it tightly in plastic wrap or foil, and place it inside a heavy-duty plastic bag or a crush-proof plastic freezer container labeled with the date it was baked.

- When a range of times is given for doneness ("Bake for 30 to 40 minutes") always check the item at the first time, then watch closely until the second; your oven and mine may differ, and the only thing that really matters is how the baked product looks and tastes.

Observe the visual clues for doneness given in the recipe as much as the baking time.

- For reliable cake baking, use the type of flour specified. Cake flour and all-purpose differ in their protein content, acidity, and ability to absorb moisture. See pages 211–212 for flour specifics and information on sifting and measuring.

- When a recipe calls for ½ cup chopped nuts, the nuts are chopped before measuring. If it calls for ½ cup nuts, chopped, they are chopped after measuring.

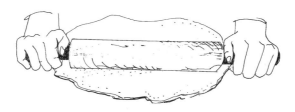

THESE ARE THE DELIGHTS OF THE TABLE, the extras that add a special touch to any meal, from breakfast to high tea or dinner.

ONE THING THEY ALL HAVE IN COMMON is their ease of preparation. They are in what I call the less-is-more category, so handle as little as possible to make them tender and flaky. Good news for the baker.

BISCUITS RANGE FROM BUTTERMILK, where the acidity of the milk guarantees tenderness, to Baking Powder Biscuits and six delightful variations, including Charley's Jam Snacks and Quick Sticky Breakfast Buns. Southern Sweet Potato Biscuits have a sunny golden color and are as at home at high tea as with baked ham and red-eye gravy.

Biscuits, muffins, AND scones

MUFFINS ARE MY PERSONAL FAVORITE—I could live on them alone, and frequently do—toasted or warm from the oven, there's nothing better, at any time of day. The recipes include Grandpa's Blueberry Muffins and several variations, two types of corn muffins, and the classics: fruit, whole wheat apple, pumpkin 'n' spice, raisin bran, and the famous Morning Glory Muffins, which remind me of carrot cake.

NOTE: When baking muffins, add several tablespoons of water to any unused cups in the pan so the heat will be evenly distributed.

SCONES ARE A SCOTTISH STAPLE that sound fancy but are amazingly easy to make and add a special touch to breakfast or brunch (served warm in a basket), high tea (served warm with sweet butter, crème fraîche, strawberry preserves), or any other time of day.

Baking Powder Biscuits

WANT TO TURN dinner into a special event? Serve a basket of these easy-to-make, tender biscuits piping hot from the oven. For breakfast or afternoon tea, serve them split and toasted, with butter and raspberry jam; for dessert, pile on berries and sweetened whipped cream. Be creative with add-ins, from herbs and spices to cheese and other flavorings, and let the children help mix and shape the dough. When my daughter, Cassandra, was ten years old, she penciled in her own notes on our original butter-stained recipe: "You can also stir 1 tablespoon vinegar or plain yogurt into the milk. And, P.S., a teaspoon of sugar doesn't hurt either." To make Charley's Jam Snacks or Quick Sticky Breakfast Buns, see the variations following.

for good measure

> When making biscuits: the less you handle dough, the more tender the result.

special equipment: Cookie sheet; baking parchment, optional; pastry blender, optional; 2- to 2½-inch round cookie cutters or similar-size juice glass or small can or tablespoon; pastry brush, optional

advance preparation: Biscuits are best hot from the oven, but can be made in advance, then reheated at 325°F about 10 minutes before serving warm. Or, completely cooled biscuits can be double-wrapped and frozen up to 1 month; thaw and warm before serving.

temperature and time: 425°F for 12 to 15 minutes

yield: 10 drop biscuits or 8 to 10 (2½-inch) or 14 to 16 (2-inch) cut round biscuits

biscuits

Butter or solid shortening for preparing pan
2 cups unsifted all-purpose flour
4 teaspoons baking powder
1 teaspoon salt
¼ cup (½ stick) cold unsalted butter, cut up
2 tablespoons chilled solid shortening (Crisco)
⅔ cup milk, or as needed

glaze and toppings, optional

2 tablespoons milk
Sesame or poppy seeds

1. Position a rack in the center of the oven and preheat it to 425°F. Butter the cookie sheet or cover it with baking parchment.

2. In a large mixing bowl, whisk together the flour, baking powder, and salt. Cut in the butter and shortening by pinching it into the flour with your fingertips or mixing it with a pastry blender or 2 cross-cutting table knives until the mixture has small lumps about the size of peas. Pinch and rub the dough a few more times until it resembles a coarse meal. Add the milk and toss it in only until the dough holds together. Add a drop or two more milk if the dough is too powdery.

3. To make drop biscuits, scoop 10 equal portions of the dough onto the baking sheet, placing them at least 1 inch apart.

To make cut biscuits, turn the dough out onto a lightly floured surface and pat it into a disk about ¾ inch thick. Cut out the biscuits using a floured 2- to 2½-inch round cutter. Arrange the biscuits about 1 inch apart on the prepared baking sheet. Gather the scraps, re-form, and repeat cutting. If desired, use a pastry brush to paint the biscuit tops with a little milk and sprinkle on the topping of your choice. Bake 12 to 15 minutes, until a light golden brown on top. Cool on a wire rack; serve warm.

Whole Wheat Biscuits: Replace 1 cup all-purpose flour with 1 cup whole wheat flour; these will rise slightly less than with all white flour.

Herb Biscuits: Add 1 tablespoon *each* of minced fresh (or ¾ teaspoon dried) dill, thyme, and parsley (or your favorite herb blend) plus 1 teaspoon minced fresh chives.

Cheese-Mustard Biscuits: Add with flour: ⅓ cup grated Parmesan or Romano cheese, 2 tablespoons dry mustard powder; add with milk: 1 tablespoon regular or coarse-grain Dijon mustard, optional. Top with grated cheese, optional.

Orange Brunch Biscuits: Add with flour: 3 tablespoons granulated sugar and a pinch of nutmeg; add with milk: 2 tablespoons grated orange zest and 1 teaspoon orange extract, optional.

Quick Sticky Breakfast Buns: Prepare biscuits as above, but add 1 tablespoon granulated sugar to the dry ingredients. Grease with butter or coat with vegetable spray twelve 2½-inch muffin cups. Put a generous ½ teaspoon unsalted butter and 1½ tablespoons of your favorite fruit preserves in the bottom of each cup. In a small pan or microwavable bowl, melt 2 tablespoons unsalted butter. In a cup, mix together 2 tablespoons granulated sugar and 1 teaspoon cinnamon. Set out ¼ cup fruit preserves or orange marmalade.

On a lightly floured surface, pat out the dough into a rough 9-inch square, ¼ inch thick. Brush the dough with melted butter, spread on ¼ cup of preserves or marmalade, and sprinkle evenly with half the cinnamon sugar. Roll up into a tight jelly roll and cut into 12 equal slices. Place each slice, cut side up, into a muffin cup and sprinkle the tops with the remaining cinnamon sugar. Bake as directed, until golden brown.

Cover a jelly roll pan or tray with aluminum foil. When the biscuits are baked, cover them with the foil tray. Using potholders, hold both together and invert. Lift off the muffin tin, leaving the jam-topped rolls on the tray. Use a spoon to scoop out any jam left in the pan and replace it on the buns. Serve warm.

CHARLEY'S JAM SNACKS

These two-layer biscuits filled with raspberry jam were made by my Parisian-American friend Charley as an American-style after-school snack for her daughters, who liked them almost as much as *pain au chocolat,* the traditional French after-school snack of croissant pastry filled with chocolate. Prepare basic biscuits above. Beat 1 egg with a teaspoon of water in a cup and set it aside for a glaze. Pat out the dough about ½ inch thick and cut half the dough into 2-inch rounds with a cookie cutter. Cut the remaining dough with a 2-inch donut cutter (or cut 2-inch rounds and use a 1-inch round cutter to remove the centers). With a pastry brush dipped in egg glaze, moisten a ring around the outer edge of each full-size round; add ½ teaspoon of jam in the center. Top these with the dough rings, pressing lightly on top to "glue" the layers together. The jam should show in the center. Bake as directed. Makes seven or eight 2-inch jam snacks.

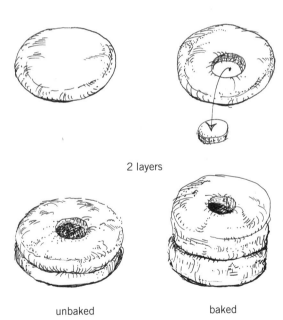

2 layers

unbaked   baked

Buttermilk Biscuits

BUTTERMILK GIVES THESE classic biscuits their extra-tender crumb. They are so quick to make you can whip them up just before mealtime and serve them warm from the oven, split open and topped with butter, jam, or gravy. Or, serve them for dessert topped with sweetened berries and whipped cream.

for good measure

If you don't have liquid buttermilk, substitute powdered buttermilk (available in the baking aisle in many markets and specialty food shops) and follow directions on the package, adding the powder with the dry ingredients and substituting water for milk.

special equipment: Cookie sheet; pastry blender, optional; baking parchment, optional; 2- to 2½-inch round cookie cutter or similar-size juice glass or small can; pastry brush, optional

advance preparation: Biscuits are best hot from the oven, but can be made in advance, kept covered with a tea towel, then reheated before serving. Completely cooled biscuits can be double-wrapped and frozen up to 1 month; thaw and warm before serving.

temperature and time: 425°F for about 15 minutes

yield: 8 to 10 (2½-inch round) or 12 rectangular or 10 drop biscuits

biscuits

Butter or solid shortening for preparing pan, optional

2 cups unsifted all-purpose flour

1 tablespoon baking powder

½ teaspoon baking soda

¾ teaspoon salt

⅓ cup (5⅓ tablespoons) cold unsalted butter, cut up

1 cup buttermilk

glaze

3 tablespoons buttermilk

1. Position a rack in the center of the oven and preheat it to 425°F. Butter the cookie sheet or cover it with baking parchment.

2. In a large mixing bowl, whisk together the flour, baking powder, baking soda, and salt. Cut in the butter by pinching it into the flour with your fingertips or mixing it with a pastry blender or 2 cross-cutting table knives until the mixture has small lumps about the size of peas. Or, pulse everything together rapidly in the food processor. Add the buttermilk and stir just until the dough begins to clump together with no large, dry pockets of flour; do not overbeat. If using the processor, remove the dough from the bowl as soon as it begins to form clumps; do not overwork. Turn the dough out onto a lightly floured surface and pat it together into a rough ball.

3. To make drop biscuits (which don't rise quite as high as cut biscuits), scoop 10 equal portions of the dough onto the baking sheet, placing them at least 1 inch apart.

To make round cut biscuits, pat the dough into a 7-inch disk about ¾ inch thick. Cut out the biscuits using a floured 2- to 2½-inch round cutter. Gather the dough scraps, re-form, and repeat cutting. Set the biscuits about 1 inch apart on the baking sheet.

To make square cut biscuits, pat the dough into a 6 × 8-inch rectangle about ¾ inch thick. Divide each side into 2-inch segments and use a long-bladed knife to cut into 12 pieces. Place them 1 inch apart on the baking sheet. Use a pastry brush to paint the biscuit tops with a little buttermilk. Bake about 15 minutes, or until the biscuits begin to look golden brown on top. Cool on a wire rack; serve warm.

Southern Sweet Potato Biscuits

A BASKET OF these bright golden "southern specials" served steaming hot alongside a baked ham and a bowl of coffee-flavored red-eye gravy has been known to make a strong southern gentleman weep—with nostalgia for his mom's baking.

The biscuits can be made either with freshly baked or canned (drained) sweet potatoes or with yams, which have a slightly more assertive taste. To shape the biscuits easily, you can either drop the dough from a spoon or cut it into squares.

for good measure

- For breakfast, split and toast biscuits and top them with sweet butter and cherry preserves.
- For dinner, serve warm biscuits with gravy or top with homemade sage butter: 1 stick softened unsalted butter mixed with 1 tablespoon fresh (or 1½ teaspoons dried) chopped sage; season to taste with salt, pepper, and a dash of cayenne.

special equipment: Cookie sheet; baking parchment, optional; pastry blender, optional; pastry brush, optional

advance preparation: Biscuits are best hot from the oven, but can be made in advance, kept covered with a tea towel, then reheated before serving warm.

temperature and time: 425°F for 15 to 17 minutes

yield: 12 (2-inch square) or 10 to 12 drop biscuits

biscuits

1½ cups sifted all-purpose flour

1 tablespoon baking powder

1 teaspoon salt

1 tablespoon granulated or packed light brown sugar

Pinch of ground nutmeg

¼ cup (½ stick) unsalted butter, cut up, or chilled solid shortening, plus extra for preparing pan, optional

1 cup cold mashed sweet potatoes or yams (9 ounces [2 medium] baked sweet potatoes or yams, peeled and mashed)

3 tablespoons milk, or as needed

glaze

2 tablespoons milk, optional

1. Position a rack in the center of the oven and preheat it to 425°F. Butter the cookie sheet or cover it with baking parchment.

2. If working by hand, in a large mixing bowl, whisk together the flour, baking powder, salt, sugar, and nutmeg. Cut in the butter or shortening by pinching it into the flour with your fingertips or mixing it with a pastry blender or 2 cross-cutting table knives until the mixture has small lumps about the size of peas. Stir in the sweet potatoes with just enough milk to make a soft dough, tossing the mixture only until the dough holds together.

If using a food processor, pulse the dry ingredients and fat until the mixture has lumps the size of peas, then add the sweet potato and 2 to 3 tablespoons of milk; pulse only until dough begins to clump.

Turn the dough out onto a lightly floured surface. Add a few drops more milk if the dough is still too dry, then pat it into a rough ball.

3. To make drop biscuits, scoop 10 to 12 equal portions of the dough onto the baking sheet, placing them at least 1 inch apart.

To make cut biscuits, pat the dough into a 6 × 8-inch rectangle about ¾ inch thick. Divide each side into 2-inch segments and use a long-bladed knife to cut the dough into 12 pieces. Place them about 1 inch apart on the baking sheet. If desired, use the pastry brush to paint the biscuit tops with a little milk. Bake about 15 minutes, until the biscuits rise and their golden color is somewhat darker around the top edges. Cool on a wire rack; serve warm.

Grandpa's Blueberry Muffins

THIS RECIPE IS a family heirloom handed down to me from my maternal grandfather, Harry Joslin, an inventor, artisan, and artist. He could do anything with his hands, from bending sheet metal to baking these muffins, which were always on the table for breakfast when we visited him in Florida. You can use this basic recipe as a foundation, adding your favorite fruit or berries, but don't forget Grandpa's finishing touch: a generous sprinkling of granulated sugar on top of each muffin before baking.

for good measure

> For a less rich muffin, reduce melted butter or oil to 3 tablespoons; for a less sweet muffin, reduce sugar to ½ cup.

special equipment: Twelve 2½-inch muffin cups; sifter

advance preparation: Muffins can be baked ahead, double-wrapped, and frozen up to 2 months. Defrost and warm before serving.

temperature and time: 400°F for 20 to 22 minutes; slightly longer with frozen fruit

yield: About 4 cups batter; 12 muffins (2½-inch diameter)

muffins

Butter-flavor no-stick vegetable spray or solid shortening for preparing pan

2 large eggs, at room temperature

½ cup plus 2 tablespoons milk

¼ cup (½ stick) unsalted butter, melted, or canola oil

2 cups unsifted all-purpose flour

1 tablespoon baking powder

½ teaspoon salt

⅔ cup granulated sugar

1½ cups fresh blueberries, picked over, rinsed, and blotted dry on paper towels (or whole frozen unthawed berries with all ice particles removed)

topping

Granulated sugar

1. Position a rack in the center of the oven and preheat it to 400°F. Coat the muffin cups with cooking spray or shortening.

2. In a large bowl, whisk together the eggs, milk, and melted butter. Place a sifter over the bowl and measure into it the flour, baking powder, salt, and sugar. Stir/sift the dry ingredients onto the wet. Stir just to blend; don't overbeat. Gently stir in the berries.

3. Divide the batter among the muffin cups, filling nearly full. Generously sprinkle granulated sugar on top. Bake 20 to 22 minutes, until the muffins rise and are golden brown on top; a cake tester inserted in the center should come out clean. Cool the muffins on a wire rack. Serve warm.

> **Blueberry-Orange Muffins:** Add 2 teaspoons grated orange zest and 1 teaspoon orange extract along with the berries in the basic recipe.
>
> **Cranberry-Orange Muffins:** Replace blueberries in the basic recipe with whole fresh or frozen (unthawed) cranberries; at the same time, add 2 teaspoons grated orange zest, 1 teaspoon orange extract, ½ cup chopped walnuts (optional), and ½ teaspoon cinnamon.
>
> **Plum-Good Muffins:** Reduce sugar in basic recipe to ½ cup. Replace blueberries with 1½ cups unpeeled, pitted, cut-up plums (¼- to ½-inch pieces) tossed with 1 tablespoon lemon juice, 4 tablespoons sugar, and ½ teaspoon nutmeg.

Double Corn Muffins

THESE ARE EXTRA-MOIST corn muffins with the added flavor and texture of chopped corn kernels. Serve the muffins toasted for breakfast or warm and buttered to accompany roasted meat or poultry.

for good measure

- To reduce the fat, you can cut out 2 tablespoons of the butter or oil and use 2% milk.
- To make plain corn muffins, use the recipe for corn bread on page 24.

special equipment: Twelve 2½-inch muffin cups; food processor or knife and cutting board

advance preparation: Muffins can be baked ahead, double-wrapped, and frozen up to 2 months. Defrost and warm before serving.

temperature and time: 400°F for 20 to 25 minutes

yield: 3⅓ cups batter; 12 muffins (2½-inch diameter)

Butter-flavor no-stick cooking spray or solid shortening for preparing pan

1 cup yellow cornmeal

1⅓ cups unsifted all-purpose flour

1 tablespoon baking powder

½ teaspoon salt

2 large eggs, at room temperature

¾ cup milk

¼ cup (½ stick) unsalted butter, melted, or canola oil

¼ cup granulated sugar

¾ cup frozen corn kernels (Niblets) chopped with a knife or pulsed in the food processor *with* ¼ cup milk or cream (or substitute ½ cup canned cream-style corn)

1. Position a rack in the center of the oven and preheat it to 400°F. Coat the muffin cups with cooking spray or shortening.

2. In a medium bowl, whisk together the cornmeal, flour, baking powder, and salt. In a large bowl, whisk together the eggs, milk, melted butter, sugar, and corn. Stir the dry ingredients all at once into the wet, mixing just to combine; do not overbeat.

3. Divide the batter among the muffin cups, filling nearly full. Bake 20 to 25 minutes, or until the muffins rise, begin to look golden brown on top, and a cake tester inserted in the center comes out clean. Cool the muffins about 10 minutes in the pan on a wire rack, then remove them from the pan and cool completely on the rack. Serve warm or split and toasted.

Roasted Cornmeal Blueberry Muffins

SEVERAL YEARS AGO when my daughter and I were traveling through Northampton, Massachusetts, we stopped for lunch at Paul and Elizabeth's, a natural foods restaurant on Main Street. I still remember the delectable dessert, a warm Indian pudding with maple syrup–whipped cream, but their muffins and rolls were even better. When we complimented the creative young baker, Michael McClellan, he explained that he liked to roast grains before baking with them in order to enhance their taste. Michael offered to share with us a muffin recipe he was then developing using roasted cornmeal; this is my adaptation. These special muffins have a complex corn flavor that is well balanced by the fresh sweet-tart berries.

for good measure

To pan-roast cornmeal, place cornmeal in an ungreased frying pan over medium heat and stir the cornmeal on and off for 7 to 10 minutes, until it begins to turn a light tan color and smells aromatic. Or, roast the meal in a metal pan at 350°F about 20 minutes, stirring often.

special equipment: Twelve 2½-inch muffin cups; medium-size heavy frying pan

advance preparation: Baked muffins can be double-wrapped and frozen up to 2 months; defrost and reheat by placing in the muffin tin and warming at 325°F about 10 minutes.

temperature and time: 400°F for 20 to 25 minutes

yield: 4 cups batter; 12 muffins (2½-inch diameter)

muffins

Butter-flavor no-stick vegetable spray or solid shortening for preparing pan

1 cup yellow cornmeal

1 large egg, at room temperature

½ cup pure maple syrup

¼ cup (½ stick) unsalted butter, melted and slightly cooled

¼ teaspoon vanilla extract

½ cup milk

¼ cup sour cream or plain yogurt

1 cup unsifted all-purpose flour

2½ teaspoons baking powder

½ teaspoon salt

1½ cups fresh blueberries, picked over, rinsed, and blotted dry on paper towels (or whole frozen unthawed blueberries with all ice particles removed)

topping

Granulated sugar

1. Position a rack in the center of the oven and preheat it to 400°F. Coat the muffin cups with cooking spray or shortening. Roast the cornmeal (see For Good Measure).

2. In a large bowl, whisk together the egg, maple syrup, melted butter, vanilla, milk, and sour cream. Directly on top of this wet mixture add—but don't stir in—the flour, baking powder, salt, and roasted cornmeal. Stir the dry ingredients all at once into the wet, mixing just to combine; do not overbeat. Add the berries and stir once or twice.

3. Divide the batter among the prepared muffin cups, filling them a generous three-quarters full. Sprinkle some sugar on top of each muffin. If you have any *unfilled* cups in your muffin pan, carefully ladle a little water into each empty cup.

4. Bake the muffins about 20 minutes, or until they rise, look golden brown on top, and a cake tester inserted in the center comes out clean. Cool the muffins in the pan on a wire rack about 5 minutes, then coax them out with a fork and serve warm.

Morning Glory Muffins

THESE DELIGHTFULLY MOIST, flavorful muffins will remind you a little of carrot cake. I always believed they were a regional New England classic, since they are so popular in country inns and neighborhood kitchens from Nantucket to Boston and as far south as Connecticut, with variations as profuse as Cape Cod morning glories climbing a picket fence. To my surprise, I recently I found them in San Francisco, called Good Morning Muffins; their origin may be unclear and their ingredients vary slightly, but there is no doubt they are a great way to start a day. My favorite version, which includes ½ cup chopped cranberries, comes from an Acton, Massachusetts, friend and excellent baker, Jacquie Colman Manley, who perfected this recipe with her fourteen-year-old son, Jesse.

special equipment: Eighteen 2½-inch muffin cups; sifter

advance preparation: Some bakers prefer to refrigerate the batter overnight before baking the muffins to let the flavors blend; not essential, but a good idea if you have time. Muffins can be baked ahead, double-wrapped, and frozen up to 2 months. Defrost and warm at 325°F about 10 minutes before serving.

temperature and time: 350°F for 30 to 35 minutes

yield: About 6 cups batter; 16 to 18 muffins (2½-inch diameter)

muffins

Butter-flavor no-stick vegetable spray or solid shortening for preparing pans

½ cup packed seedless raisins

½ cup fresh or whole frozen cranberries, chopped, optional

1 cup crushed fresh or canned pineapple, well-drained

1 tart apple, peeled, cored, finely chopped (¼-inch pieces)

½ cup (about 2 ounces) shredded coconut, sweetened or unsweetened

About 4 large carrots, peeled and grated (2 cups, grated)

½ cup (2 ounces) chopped walnuts or pecans, optional

3 large eggs, at room temperature

1 cup canola or other vegetable oil

1¼ cups granulated sugar

2 teaspoons vanilla extract

2 cups unsifted all-purpose flour

2 teaspoons baking soda

½ teaspoon salt

2 teaspoons ground cinnamon

topping

Packed dark brown or granulated sugar

1. Position a rack in the center of the oven and preheat it to 350°F. Coat the muffin cups with cooking spray or shortening.

2. In a large bowl, combine all the fruits, coconut, carrots, and nuts, if using. In another large bowl, whisk together the eggs, oil, sugar, and vanilla. Place the sifter over this bowl, measure into it the flour, baking soda, salt, and cinnamon, then all at once sift these ingredients directly onto the wet mixture. Stir everything together until just blended; do not overbeat. Stir in the fruit mixture.

3. Divide the batter among the muffin cups, filling almost to the top. Sprinkle brown or granulated sugar on top. Bake for 30 to 35 minutes, until the muffins rise, are golden brown on top, and a cake tester inserted in the center comes out clean. Cool the muffins in pans at least 10 minutes on a wire rack. Use the tip of a paring knife to help ease the heavy, moist muffins from the tins and place them on a wire rack to cool. Serve warm.

Whole Wheat Apple Muffins

APPLES AND CIDER add special flavor to these healthful, not-too-sweet muffins: a perfect brunch or lunch-box treat. If you don't have cider, substitute apple, cranberry, orange, or white grape juice.

for good measure

- For a richer muffin, melted butter can be substituted for oil and increased up to 6 tablespoons. Nuts are optional, but add crunch.

- To boost nutrition and texture, substitute ½ cup old-fashioned rolled oats (not instant) for ½ cup of all-purpose flour.

special equipment: Twelve 2½-inch muffin cups; sifter

advance preparation: Muffins can be kept at room temperature in a plastic bag for 2 to 3 days or double-wrapped and frozen up to 2 months. Defrost and warm before serving.

temperature and time: 400°F for 20 minutes

yield: 4 cups batter; 12 muffins (2½-inch diameter)

topping

Butter-flavor no-stick vegetable spray or solid shortening for preparing pan

1 tablespoon all-purpose flour

1 tablespoon packed brown sugar

½ teaspoon ground cinnamon

1 tablespoon unsalted butter, at room temperature, cut up

muffins

2 large eggs, at room temperature

½ cup plus 2 tablespoons apple juice or cider

¼ cup (½ stick) unsalted butter, melted, or ¼ cup canola oil

⅓ cup granulated or packed light brown sugar

1 cup unsifted all-purpose flour

1 cup unsifted whole wheat flour

2 teaspoons baking powder

½ teaspoon salt

1 teaspoon ground cinnamon

1 large apple (Golden Delicious or other eating apple), peeled, cored, and chopped into ¼- to ½-inch pieces

½ cup packed seedless raisins

½ cup (2 ounces) chopped walnuts, optional

1. Position a rack in the center of the oven and preheat it to 400°F. Coat the muffin cups with cooking spray or shortening. Prepare the topping: In a small bowl, combine all the topping ingredients and pinch them together to make crumbs.

2. In a large bowl, whisk together the eggs, apple juice, butter, and sugar. In another bowl, whisk together both flours, baking powder, salt, and cinnamon. Add the dry ingredients to the wet and stir just to blend; don't overbeat. Gently stir in the apple, raisins, and nuts, if using.

3. Divide the batter among the muffin cups, filling the cups to the top; the muffins will rise but not overflow because the batter is quite heavy. Sprinkle a scant teaspoon of topping crumbs on each muffin. Bake about 20 minutes, until the muffins rise, are golden brown on top, and a cake tester inserted in the center of a muffin comes out clean. Cool the muffins on a wire rack. Serve warm.

Raisin-Bran Muffins

THESE OLD-FASHIONED CLASSICS are bursting with plump raisins and lots of flavor, perfect for breakfast or brunch. The fact that they are good for you is completely beside the point.

for good measure

- For proper texture, be sure to soak the bran in milk until it absorbs the liquid and softens before mixing the batter.
- Classic bran muffins contain raisins but you can substitute or add chopped dried apricots or dried cranberries or cherries, or chopped walnuts.
- Granulated sugar can be substituted for brown sugar.

special equipment: Twelve 2½-inch muffin cups

advance preparation: Muffins can be kept at room temperature in a plastic bag for 2 or 3 days or double-wrapped and frozen up to 2 months. Defrost and warm at 325°F about 10 minutes or split and toast before serving.

temperature and time: 400°F for 15 to 17 minutes

yield: 3⅓ cups batter; 12 muffins (2½-inch diameter)

Butter-flavor no-stick vegetable spray or solid shortening for preparing pan

1⅓ cups 100% All-Bran cereal (not flakes)

1¼ cups milk

½ cup packed dark or light brown sugar

1 cup seedless raisins

1 cup unsifted all-purpose flour

2 teaspoons baking powder

½ teaspoon baking soda

½ teaspoon salt

1 teaspoon ground cinnamon

1 large egg, at room temperature, lightly beaten

¼ cup (½ stick) unsalted butter, melted, or ¼ cup canola oil

1 teaspoon vanilla extract

1. Position a rack in the center of the oven and preheat it to 400°F. Coat the muffin cups with cooking spray or solid shortening.

2. In a medium bowl, stir together the bran, milk, sugar, and raisins, then set them aside to soak for 10 minutes, until the bran is soft.

In another bowl, whisk together the flour, baking powder, baking soda, salt, and cinnamon.

3. When the bran is soft, beat into it the egg, melted butter, and vanilla. Add the flour mixture all at once and stir just until well blended; do not overbeat.

4. Divide the batter among the muffin cups, filling right to the top. Bake 15 to 17 minutes, or until they rise, look golden brown, and a cake tester inserted in the center of a muffin comes out clean. Cool the muffins in their pan on a wire rack about 5 minutes, then lift them out of the pan and transfer them to the wire rack to cool completely.

Pumpkin 'n' Spice Muffins

THESE LIGHTLY SPICED pumpkin muffins are an ideal lunch-box treat, especially on Halloween. They are also wonderful warmed for breakfast, served with hot soup on a cold autumn day, or piled high in a basket beside the Thanksgiving turkey.

for good measure

- For a nutritional boost, replace ¼ cup of all-purpose flour with ¼ cup raw or toasted wheat germ.
- For a "lighter" version, substitute 1% milk, use the canola oil, and use 1 whole egg plus 1 egg white in place of 2 eggs. Omit nuts in the batter, but put 3 tablespoons finely chopped nuts into the topping.

special equipment: Twelve 2½-inch muffin cups; sifter

advance preparation: Muffins can be kept at room temperature in a plastic bag for 2 or 3 days or double-wrapped and frozen up to 2 months. Defrost and warm at 325°F about 10 minutes before serving.

temperature and time: 400°F for 20 to 25 minutes

yield: 5¾ cups batter; 12 muffins (2½-inch diameter)

muffins

Butter-flavor no-stick vegetable spray or solid shortening for preparing pan

2 large eggs, at room temperature

½ cup milk

⅓ cup (5⅓ tablespoons) unsalted butter, melted, or ⅓ cup canola oil

1 cup plain pumpkin puree, canned

½ cup granulated or packed light brown sugar

2 cups unsifted all-purpose flour

1 tablespoon baking powder

½ teaspoon salt

½ teaspoon ground cinnamon

½ teaspoon ground nutmeg

¼ teaspoon ground ginger

¼ teaspoon ground cloves

½ cup (2 ounces) finely chopped walnuts

topping

1 tablespoon granulated sugar

½ teaspoon ground cinnamon

1 tablespoon wheat germ, optional

1. Position a rack in the center of the oven and preheat it to 400°F. Coat the muffin cups with cooking spray or solid shortening.

2. In a large bowl, whisk together the eggs, milk, melted butter, pumpkin, and sugar.

Place a sifter over this bowl and measure into it the flour, baking powder, salt, and all spices. Stir/sift the dry ingredients onto the wet mixture below, toss in the nuts, then mix everything together until just combined; do not overbeat.

3. Divide the batter among the muffin cups, filling them right to the top. Mix the topping ingredients in a cup, sprinkle on the muffins, and bake 20 to 25 minutes, or until the muffins rise, look golden brown, and a cake tester inserted in the center of a muffin comes out clean. Cool the muffins in their pan on a wire rack about 5 minutes, then lift them out of the pan and transfer them to the wire rack to cool completely.

Cranberry Walnut Muffins

THIS IS A basic, versatile recipe for a tender, moist cranberry muffin brightened with a tad of orange flavoring. I like to add lots of fruit and nuts, which add weight and prevent a very high rise. I go for taste and texture over altitude, but the choice is yours. Whole fresh cranberries mixed with dried cranberries and walnuts are my favorite, but you can also use all fresh berries or all dried cranberries or Craisins, and omit the nuts.

for good measure

- Be sure to select dried cranberries that are flexible and moist; if dry, they can be plumped by soaking in orange juice.

- If using chopped cranberries, toss them with half the measured sugar and the orange extract before adding them to the batter—they absorb more flavor. Chopped berries, especially if frozen, may tend to turn the batter slightly pink.

special equipment: Twelve 2½-inch muffin cups; sifter

advance preparation: Muffins can be kept at room temperature in a plastic bag for 2 or 3 days or double-wrapped and frozen up to 2 months. Defrost and warm at 325°F about 10 minutes before serving.

temperature and time: 400°F for 20 to 22 minutes

yield: 4 cups batter; 12 muffins (2½-inch diameter)

muffins

Butter-flavor no-stick vegetable spray or solid shortening for preparing pan

1 large egg, at room temperature

1 cup plain, vanilla, or orange yogurt, top liquid poured off

½ cup granulated sugar

¼ cup (½ stick) unsalted butter, melted

1 teaspoon orange extract, optional

2 teaspoons grated orange zest, optional

1½ cups unsifted all-purpose flour

2 teaspoons baking powder

½ teaspoon baking soda

½ teaspoon salt

½ teaspoon ground cinnamon

1 cup whole or coarsely chopped fresh or frozen (unthawed) cranberries

½ cup dried cranberries or Craisins (or substitute 1½ cups fresh or frozen cranberries)

½ cup (2 ounces) chopped walnuts

topping

2 tablespoons granulated or packed light brown sugar

1. Position a rack in the center of the oven and preheat it to 400°F. Coat the muffin cups with cooking spray or shortening.

2. In a large bowl, whisk together the egg, yogurt, sugar, melted butter, and orange extract and grated zest, if using.

Place a sifter over this bowl and measure into it the flour, baking powder, baking soda, salt, and cinnamon. Stir/sift the dry ingredients onto the wet mixture below. Stir just to blend; don't overbeat. Gently stir in the cranberries and nuts.

3. Divide all the batter among twelve muffin cups, mounding it in the cups. Sprinkle on the topping sugar and bake 20 to 22 minutes, or until the muffins look golden brown and a cake tester inserted in the center of a muffin comes out clean. Cool the muffins in their pan on a wire rack about 15 minutes, then lift them out and transfer them to the wire rack to cool. Serve warm.

Whole Wheat Cranberry Muffins: Prepare basic recipe but substitute 1 cup whole wheat flour for 1 cup all-purpose flour.

Cranberry-Apple-Nut Muffins: Instead of all cranberries, use a mixture of 1 tart apple, peeled, cored, cut into ½-inch chunks (about 1 cup) plus ¾ cup whole fresh, frozen, or dried cranberries or Craisins.

Blueberry Scones

THIS BASIC SCONE, with its characteristically tender but slightly chewy crumb, is the perfect foil for juicy, sweet/tart blueberries. In order to keep the berries whole, shape the dough into rustic "rolls" or mounds instead of cutting wedges. You can vary the recipe using whole cranberries or any other fresh berries, sliced peaches, or nectarines.

This recipe will forever remind me of my Vermont friend Amelia Robinson-Fritz. We spent one gloriously sunny summer afternoon together beside a lake tasting our way through five different variations. This recipe won, tan hands down.

for good measure

> For slightly less sweet scones, cut the sugar to ¼ cup.

special equipment: Baking sheet, baking parchment or wax paper; pastry brush

advance preparation: Scones are best when freshly baked, but can be kept at room temperature in a plastic bag 2 or 3 days or double-wrapped and frozen up to 1 month. Serve warm or toasted.

time and temperature: 425°F for 12 to 15 minutes

yield: 3 cups batter; 8 scones (about 3¼-inch diameter)

scones

2 cups unsifted all-purpose flour

2½ teaspoons baking powder

⅓ cup granulated sugar

1 teaspoon salt

½ teaspoon ground nutmeg

6 tablespoons (¾ stick) cold butter, cut up

1 large egg, at room temperature

½ cup milk

1 cup fresh blueberries, picked over, rinsed, and blotted dry on paper towels (or whole frozen unthawed berries with all ice particles removed)

glaze

2 tablespoons milk

2 teaspoons granulated or large-crystal sugar

1. Position a rack in the center of the oven and preheat it to 425°F. Cover a baking sheet with baking parchment or leave ungreased.

2. In a large bowl, whisk together the flour, baking powder, sugar, salt, and nutmeg. Cut in the butter by pinching it into the flour with your fingertips or mixing with a pastry blender or 2 cross-cutting table knives until the mixture has small lumps about the size of peas.

3. In a small bowl, whisk together the egg and milk, then use a fork to lightly stir this into the flour mixture. Add the blueberries and stir only to combine; don't overbeat. The batter will be thick and sticky.

4. With a big spoon, divide the batter into 8 scoops and place them about 1 inch apart on the baking sheet. To glaze, use a pastry brush to coat the top of each scone with a little milk, then add a generous sprinkle of sugar. Bake 12 to 15 minutes, or until the scones are golden brown. Transfer to a wire rack to cool. Serve warm, plain or with butter.

Cranberry-Orange Scones: Replace blueberries with whole fresh cranberries plus 2 teaspoons packed grated orange zest.

Blueberry-Lemon Scones: Add 1 tablespoon packed grated lemon zest.

Currant–Dried Cherry Buttermilk Scones

TRADITIONAL SCONES ARE often made with dried currants. For a change, as well as extra color and flavor, I like to add dried cherries as well. Buttermilk makes scones especially tender. These are quickly mixed in a food processor, but they can also be prepared by hand in a bowl like the Blueberry Scones (page 20).

for good measure

- If you don't have liquid buttermilk, you can substitute the powdered form sold in supermarkets and natural food shops (or see Mail-Order Sources and Suppliers, page 240); follow directions on the package, adding the powdered buttermilk with the dry ingredients and mixing the water with the eggs.

- For a less sweet scone, reduce sugar to ¼ cup. For a slightly darker color, substitute packed light or dark brown sugar.

- For greater richness, you can increase butter up to 8 tablespoons (1 stick).

special equipment: Baking sheet, baking parchment or wax paper; food processor; pastry brush

advance preparation: Scones are best when freshly baked, but will keep well several days stored or tightly double-wrapped and frozen up to 1 month. Serve warm.

time and temperature: 425°F for 10 to 12 minutes

yield: 3¼ cups batter; 8 scones (3½-inch diameter)

scones

2 cups sifted all-purpose flour

⅓ cup granulated sugar

2½ teaspoons baking powder

¼ teaspoon baking soda

1 teaspoon salt

6 tablespoons (¾ stick) cold unsalted butter, cut up

1 large egg, at room temperature

½ cup buttermilk

½ cup packed dried currants or raisins

½ cup dried tart or Bing cherries (or use all currants or seedless gold or black raisins)

glaze

2 tablespoons buttermilk

2 teaspoons granulated sugar

1. Position a rack in the center of the oven and preheat it to 425°F. Cover the baking sheet with parchment or wax paper.

2. In the workbowl of a food processor, combine the flour, sugar, baking powder, baking soda, and salt. Pulse twice just to combine. Add the butter and pulse 10 to 12 times, just until the butter forms pea-size pieces. In a cup, lightly beat together the egg and buttermilk, then pour it into the processor, add the fruit, and pulse 4 to 6 times, only to combine. Don't overwork the batter or the scones will be tough instead of tender.

3. Remove the workbowl. Use a flexible spatula to scoop out the thick, sticky batter, placing 8 irregular mounds on the prepared sheet. In a cup, stir together the glaze ingredients, then paint it on scones with a pastry brush. Bake 10 to 12 minutes, until golden brown. Cool the scones on a wire rack.

Walnut-Cherry Scones: Prepare basic recipe and add ½ cup chopped walnuts.

Pine Nut–Cherry Scones: Prepare basic recipe and sprinkle some pine nuts (pignoli) over the glazed scones before baking.

Orange Scones: Prepare basic recipe and add 1 tablespoon grated orange zest plus 1 teaspoon orange extract.

Whole Wheat Scones: Substitute 1 cup unsifted whole wheat flour for 1 cup all-purpose flour in basic recipe.

Bridgewater Apricot Scones

THESE SCONES TASTE like the essence of apricot. When I first tasted them, I was certain the batter contained apricot nectar and was surprised when pastry chef Robin von Reyn shared her recipe and its tricks; she uses soft, moist Turkish or Australian apricots, which she mixes with the sugar and passes through a commercial grinder before adding them to the batter.

At home, I can achieve a similar result by finely chopping the apricots and sugar in a food processor. To avoid overmixing, pulse the dough just a few times after adding the buttermilk and remove the dough from the workbowl as soon as it begins to look lumpy. Or, you can pinch the flour and butter together in a bowl, add the processor-chopped apricot/sugar mixture, then lightly mix in the liquid with a spoon.

for good measure

- Be sure to use plump, moist apricots, generally available in priceclubs, natural food stores, and most supermarkets.
- If you like almond flavoring, increase the almond extract to ¼ teaspoon.

special equipment: Food processor; baking sheet; baking parchment or wax paper or aluminum foil; pastry brush

advance preparation: Scones are best when freshly baked, but will keep well several days stored in an airtight container or double-wrapped and frozen up to 1 month.

time and temperature: 425 ° F for 20 to 22 minutes

yield: 9 scones (3-inch diameter)

scones

Solid shortening for preparing pan, optional

3 tablespoons granulated sugar

1 cup (6 to 7 ounces) soft, moist dried apricots

1½ cups sifted all-purpose flour

1 tablespoon baking powder

½ teaspoon salt

¼ teaspoon ground nutmeg

¼ cup (½ stick) chilled unsalted butter, cut up

1 large egg, at room temperature

¼ cup heavy cream

¼ cup buttermilk (or cream or milk stirred with 1 tablespoon fresh lemon juice or yogurt)

1 teaspoon vanilla extract

⅛ teaspoon almond extract

topping

2 tablespoons cream or buttermilk

2 teaspoons granulated sugar

1. Position a rack in the center of the oven and preheat it to 400°F. Cover a baking sheet with baking parchment or wax paper or coat foil with solid shortening.

2. In the workbowl of a food processor, combine the sugar and apricots and grind/pulse until the apricots are very finely chopped (⅛-inch bits). Add to the workbowl—but don't mix in—the flour, baking powder, salt, and nutmeg. When all the dry ingredients are added, pulse 2 or 3 times, then add the cut-up butter and pulse 5 or 6 times, to begin to cut the butter into the flour mixture; it should just begin to look lumpy.

3. In a medium-size bowl, whisk together the egg, cream, buttermilk, and extracts. Pour the liquid through the feed tube into the processor and pulse only 3 or 4 times, until the dough looks moistened and *just begins* to clump together; don't let the dough form a ball or it will be overworked.

4. Turn the dough out into a bowl and press it into a rough ball with your hands. With a large spoon, scoop out 9 dough mounds, placing them on the prepared baking sheet. Use a pastry brush to paint the mounds with a little cream, then sprinkle sugar on top. Bake 20 to 22 minutes, until the scones are golden brown. Cool the scones on a wire rack and serve warm.

QUICK BREADS ARE JUST WHAT YOU WOULD EXPECT—casual, easy to prepare, with quick-rising (non-yeast) batters. They are related in spirit and method to muffins, and share the basic less-is-more technique: Mix the dry ingredients, mix the wet ingredients, then lightly stir the two together. The less you do, the more tender the result (and the happier the baker and diner).

QUICK BREAD BATTERS can also be baked as cupcakes in muffin pans (see Poppy Seed–Lemon Loaf, page 29). Be sure to add several tablespoons of water to any unused cups in the muffin pan so the heat will be evenly distributed.

Quick breads

A SLICE OF QUICK BREAD is appropriate to serve with a cup of coffee or tea at any time of the day—or even with a glass of port at night. The recipes in this chapter include two delicious but different corn breads, each as good for breakfast as beside a suppertime bowl of chili, served warm in squares or split and toasted. The category of fruit/nut breads ranges from zucchini, pumpkin, and cranberry-orange to poppy seed–lemon and chocolate walnut. All are traditional highlights of fall holiday buffets, including Thanksgiving and Christmas, but are also welcome on a silver tray to be served year-round at high tea. In addition, these breads make delicious gifts from your kitchen when baked in small loaf pans and wrapped up with the recipe attached. If you plan to make Carol's Holiday Stollen for a gift, be sure to bake an extra one for yourself and serve it warm on Christmas morning—a holiday gift to your whole family.

New England Corn Bread

I OFTEN MAKE this classic recipe with stone-ground yellow cornmeal from a Rhode Island mill. While I love the quality of stone-ground meal sold in natural foods shops, any type sold in supermarkets works well, too. Quick and easy to prepare, corn bread is best served warm from the oven. For breakfast, it is great split and toasted, with butter.

You can vary the recipe depending upon what it will be served with: For a sweet brunch version, I often add ⅓ to ½ cup golden or seedless black raisins; for a savory dinner accompaniment, I cut the sugar to 3 tablespoons and occasionally add 4 slices of crisp-cooked, crumbled bacon.

special equipment: 8 or 9 × 1½-inch square baking pan

advance preparation: Corn bread can be kept covered at room temperature several days.

temperature and time: 425°F for 20 to 22 minutes

yield: 3 cups batter; 8 × 8-inch bread; 9 to 12 servings

¼ cup (½ stick) unsalted butter, melted and cooled (or corn or canola oil), plus extra for preparing pan

1 large egg, at room temperature

1 cup milk

¼ cup plain yogurt or sour cream

¼ cup granulated sugar

1 cup yellow cornmeal

1 cup unsifted all-purpose flour

1 tablespoon baking powder

⅛ teaspoon baking soda

½ teaspoon salt

1. Position a rack in the center of the oven and pre-heat it to 425°F. Butter the pan and set it aside.

2. In a large mixing bowl using a sturdy spoon or whisk or an electric mixer, beat together the melted butter, egg, milk, yogurt, and sugar. Add on top all the remaining ingredients in the order listed and stir together just to blend.

3. Turn the batter out into the prepared pan and bake for 20 to 22 minutes, until the top is just starting to turn a little brown and a cake tester inserted in the center comes out clean. Don't overbake or it will be dry. Cool on a wire rack. Cut in squares and serve directly from the pan.

Vermont Maple Corn Bread

MY FAMILY AND I spend a lot of time in the Northeast Kingdom of Vermont, a region proud of its maple syrup production. Local Grade B syrup is our favorite, and I developed this recipe to take advantage of its deep rich taste. We are fortunate to be able to buy it from friends who sell the lighter Fancy Grade to the public and usually keep this for their family use. Occasionally, Grade B is available in stores, but any "pure" maple syrup will give a sweet woodsy flavor to the corn bread. For a breakfast or brunch treat, I like to cut a piece of day-old corn bread in half horizontally and serve it toasted, with butter.

special equipment: 8 or 9 × 1½-inch square baking pan

advance preparation: Corn bread can be kept covered at room temperature several days.

temperature and time: 425°F for 20 to 22 minutes

yield: 3 cups batter; 8 × 8-inch bread; 9 to 12 servings

¼ **cup (½ stick) unsalted butter, melted and cooled (or corn or canola oil), plus extra for preparing pan**

1 **large egg, at room temperature**

½ **cup milk**

¾ **cup maple syrup**

¾ **cup yellow cornmeal**

1 **cup unsifted all-purpose flour**

½ **teaspoon salt**

2 **teaspoons baking powder**

1. Position a rack in the center of the oven and preheat it to 425°F. Butter the pan and set it aside.

2. In a large mixing bowl using a sturdy spoon or whisk or an electric mixer, beat together the butter, egg, milk, and syrup. Add on top all the remaining ingredients in the order listed and beat together just to blend.

3. Turn the batter out into the prepared pan and bake for 20 to 22 minutes, until the top is lightly golden and a cake tester inserted in the center comes out clean. Don't overbake or it will be dry. Cool on a wire rack. Cut in squares and serve directly from the pan.

Irra's Zucchini Loaf

BORN IN RIGA, Latvia, Irra is a family friend who lives near Long Island Sound on the Connecticut shore. When my mother-in-law, Lucille, who was her neighbor and fellow-beachwalker, brought a colorful bouquet of August garden flowers to Irra's porch one evening, Irra returned the next morning with a loaf of her favorite zucchini cake. I was lucky enough to arrive for tea that afternoon, just in time to taste the last slice and request a copy of the recipe.

This not-too-sweet tea cake is dotted with apricots, raisins, and walnuts and has a tender crumb. Irra has a special trick to prevent the zucchini from draining any moisture into the batter: She grates the zucchini just before adding it.

for good measure

You can substitute whole wheat flour for *half* the all-purpose flour.

special equipment: Medium-size loaf pan (4½ × 8 ½ × 2½ inches); box grater or food processor fitted with medium grating disk; sifter

advance preparation: Cake keeps about 1 week at room temperature or double-wrapped and frozen up to 2 months.

temperature and time: 350°F for 60 to 65 minutes

yield: 3⅓ cups batter; 1 medium loaf (14 to 16 slices) *Note:* You can double the recipe to make two loaves BUT use only 3 eggs and just 3 cups of flour; all other ingredients double evenly.

Butter-flavor no-stick vegetable spray or solid shortening for preparing pan

½ **cup (2 ounces) chopped walnuts or pecans**

¼ **cup packed cut-up dried apricots**

¼ **cup packed seedless or golden raisins**

2 **large eggs, at room temperature**

1 **cup granulated sugar**

½ **cup canola or other mild vegetable oil**

1 **teaspoon vanilla extract**

1½ **cups plus 2 tablespoons unsifted all-purpose flour**

¼ **teaspoon baking powder**

½ **teaspoon baking soda**

½ **teaspoon salt**

1 **teaspoon ground cinnamon**

1 **small zucchini, about 4 ounces, grated (1 cup)**

1. Position a rack in the center of the oven and preheat it to 350°F. Coat the loaf pan with vegetable spray or shortening and set it aside. Toss the nuts, apricots, and raisins together in a bowl.

2. In the large bowl of an electric mixer, beat together the eggs, sugar, oil, and vanilla. Place the sifter over the bowl and measure into it the flour, baking powder, baking soda, salt, and cinnamon. Stir/sift the dry ingredients onto the wet mixture below, then slowly blend everything together. The batter will be quite stiff.

3. Grate the zucchini onto a piece of absorbent paper toweling; blot the zucchini if it appears at all moist, then stir the zucchini and fruit mixture into the batter until thoroughly incorporated.

Turn the batter into the prepared pan, smooth the top, and bake 60 to 65 minutes, or longer if needed, until the loaf is risen, golden brown, and a cake tester inserted in the center comes out clean. (*Note:* If your grated zucchini stands too long before being added to the batter and baked, it will release moisture, causing the batter to be wet and need extra baking time.) Cool the baked loaf about 10 minutes on a wire rack, then run a knife between the side of the loaf and the pan. Invert, remove the pan, then turn the loaf right side up and cool it completely on the rack. Once it is cold, slice with a serrated knife.

Cranberry-Orange Loaf

CRANBERRY-ORANGE loaf is our family's Thanksgiving staple, but we do get more adventurous on other occasions and have been known to add or substitute chopped apricots or make the Cinnamon-Apple-Raisin variation. The recipe is quick, easy, and mixed entirely by hand, although a nut chopper or food processor speeds chopping the cranberries and nuts. For holiday gifts, double the recipe and bake it in baby loaf pans, wrapped with the recipe attached.

for good measure

- Bake the bread a day in advance so it will slice neatly.
- ½ cup dried cranberries or dried cherries, soaked in orange juice or sweet red vermouth, are a tasty addition.

special equipment: Grater; nut chopper or food processor; loaf pan 9 × 5 × 3 inches or 3 baby loaf pans 5¾ or 6 × 3½ × 2 inches

advance preparation: Cake keeps a week, wrapped, at room temperature, or double-wrapped and frozen up to 2 months.

temperature and time: 350°F for 55 to 60 minutes for large loaf; 35 to 40 minutes for baby loaves

yield: 4 cups batter; 1 large loaf (14 to 16 slices), or 3 baby loaves (8 to 10 slices each)

Butter-flavor no-stick vegetable spray or solid shortening for preparing pan(s)

2 cups whole fresh cranberries, picked over, rinsed, blotted dry, or frozen (unthawed) cranberries

½ cup (2 ounces) walnut pieces

2 cups unsifted all-purpose flour

1½ teaspoons baking powder

½ teaspoon baking soda

¾ teaspoon salt

1 cup granulated sugar

3 tablespoons wheat germ, toasted or plain

¼ cup (½ stick) unsalted butter or solid stick margarine, melted

Grated zest of 1 orange (1½ to 2 tablespoons)

¾ cup orange juice

1 large egg, at room temperature

1. Position a rack in the center of the oven and preheat it to 350°F. Coat the baking pan(s) with vegetable spray or shortening. With a nut chopper or food processor, combine and coarsely chop the cranberries and nuts.

2. In a medium bowl, whisk together the flour, baking powder, baking soda, salt, sugar, and wheat germ. In a large bowl, whisk together the melted butter, orange zest, orange juice, and egg. Slowly stir the dry mixture into the wet, then mix in the cranberries and nuts; blend just to combine but don't overbeat.

3. Spoon the batter into the pan(s). Smooth the tops, and bake a large loaf for 55 to 60 minutes, or baby loaves 35 to 40 minutes, or until the cake rises, looks golden, and a cake tester inserted in the center comes out clean. Cool the cake(s) in the pan(s) on a wire rack about 10 minutes, then tip the cake(s) out of the pan(s) and cool completely on the rack.

Cinnamon-Apple-Raisin Loaf: Omit orange zest, replace orange juice with apple juice or cider, add ½ teaspoon cinnamon, and replace cranberries with 2 large apples, peeled, cored, cut into ½-inch cubes, plus ½ cup raisins. Before baking, add topping: 2 tablespoons granulated sugar tossed with ½ teaspoon cinnamon.

Pumpkin Bread

THE SECRET OF this flavorful moist bread is the addition of a grated apple; you don't even have to peel the apple before grating, though I usually do. The flavor of the bread develops and is richer the day after it is baked. This is a good recipe to give as a holiday gift, baked in baby loaf pans, wrapped in a pretty napkin, with a wooden spoon and the recipe attached.

for good measure

- Nuts give texture, but are not essential; ½ to 1 cup golden raisins can be substituted or added along with nuts.
- Any leftover pumpkin puree can be frozen in a small plastic bag for later use.

special equipment: Loaf pan 9 × 5 × 3 inches, or 3 baby loaf pans 5¾ or 6 × 3½ × 2 inches; sifter

advance preparation: Bread keeps fresh, wrapped, at room temperature about 1 week, or double-wrapped and frozen up to 2 months. It will slice more easily once it is completely cold.

temperature and time: 350°F for 60 minutes for large loaf; 35 to 45 minutes for baby loaves

yield: 4 cups batter; 1 large loaf (14 to 16 slices) or 3 baby loaves (8 to 10 slices each)

batter

Butter-flavor no-stick vegetable spray or solid shortening for preparing pan(s)

1 large egg, at room temperature

½ cup canola or other mild vegetable oil (or ¼ cup oil plus ¼ cup [½ stick] unsalted butter, melted)

2 tablespoons water or apple juice

1 cup granulated sugar

1 cup plain pumpkin puree, canned

1 large apple (such as Golden Delicious), peeled or unpeeled and grated (about 1 cup)

2 cups unsifted all-purpose flour

½ teaspoon baking powder

1 teaspoon baking soda

½ teaspoon salt

½ teaspoon ground cinnamon

½ teaspoon ground nutmeg

½ teaspoon ground cloves

½ cup (2 ounces) chopped walnuts, optional

crumb topping

2 tablespoons unsalted butter, at room temperature

2 tablespoons granulated sugar

3 tablespoons all-purpose flour

½ teaspoon ground cinnamon

1. Position a rack in the center of the oven and preheat it to 350°F. Coat the baking pan(s) with vegetable spray or shortening.

2. In a large mixing bowl, whisk together the egg, oil, water, sugar, pumpkin, and grated apple.

Place a sifter over the pumpkin mixture and add to it the flour, baking powder, baking soda, salt, and all spices. Stir/sift the dry ingredients onto the wet, then blend the two together just until incorporated; do not overbeat. Stir in the nuts, if using.

3. Turn out the batter into the prepared baking pan(s). Mix the topping ingredients together and sprinkle on the batter. Bake a large loaf 60 minutes, small loaves 35 to 45 minutes, or until risen, golden brown on top, and beginning to pull away from the pan sides; a cake tester inserted in the center will come out dry. Cool the large bread on a wire rack about 30 minutes, then gently tip it out of the pan and set upright to cool completely on the rack. Baby loaves can be left to cool in their pans.

Poppy Seed–Lemon Loaf or Cupcakes

I FIRST TASTED this recipe at a bakery in Vienna, where dainty sugar-glazed slices were served with afternoon coffee. That is a ritual I heartily recommend, wherever you live and whatever you drink. You can bake the cake as a loaf or cupcakes; I have omitted the icing and streamlined the technique, making this as easy to prepare as it is to eat. Serve it as a special treat at holiday time.

special equipment: Loaf pan 9 × 5 × 3 inches, or muffin pan (2½-inch cups); sifter

advance preparation: Loaf keeps 2 or 3 days, covered at room temperature, or double-wrapped and frozen up to 2 months.

temperature and time: 350°F for 55 to 60 minutes for loaf; 20 to 25 minutes for cupcakes

yield: 4 cups batter; 1 large loaf (14 to 16 slices) or 12 cupcakes (2½-inch diameter)

Butter-flavor no-stick vegetable spray or solid shortening for preparing pan

½ cup (1 stick) unsalted butter, melted, or ½ cup canola oil

1 cup granulated sugar

2 large eggs, at room temperature

Grated zest of 1 lemon (2 to 3 teaspoons)

3 tablespoons fresh lemon juice

1 cup lemon-flavor or plain yogurt (top liquid poured off) or sour cream

2¼ cups unsifted all-purpose flour

2 teaspoons baking powder

½ teaspoon baking soda

½ teaspoon salt

¼ teaspoon ground nutmeg

¼ cup poppy seeds

1. Position a rack in the center of the oven and preheat it to 350°F. Coat the baking pan with vegetable spray or shortening and set it aside. Coat the muffin cups with vegetable spray for easiest removal.

2. In a large bowl, whisk together the butter, sugar, eggs, lemon zest, juice, and yogurt. Place a sifter over this mixture and measure into it the flour, baking powder, baking soda, salt, and nutmeg. Stir/sift the dry ingredients onto the wet mixture below, then blend the two together just until incorporated; don't overbeat. Stir in the poppy seeds.

3. Turn the batter out into the prepared loaf pan, or scoop about ⅓-cup portions into each muffin cup, filling nearly full. Bake 55 to 60 minutes for a large loaf, or 22 to 25 minutes for cupcakes, until lightly golden on top and a cake tester inserted in the center comes out clean. Cool the loaf or cupcakes on a wire rack about 10 minutes, then tip out and cool completely on the rack.

Carol's Holiday Stollen

YOU KNOW THE holidays are just around the corner when my friend Carol Fyfield and her daughter, Joy, bake this stollen to give to family and friends. It is the kind of recipe you want to share—even out of season—as I discovered late last spring while sitting in the garden of Carol's home near Portland, Oregon. Filled with rum-soaked raisins and cherries, the moist, dense texture of this quick-to-make (no yeast) stollen will remind you of a scone. There is so much dough that Carol divides it in half, shaping two medium-size loaves. A good holiday gift idea is to wrap the oval-shaped, sugar-coated stollen in clear plastic wrap and tie it with a big red ribbon. Carol's tip: Prepare the stollen a day or two before you need it; after it sits a few days, the flavors mellow and it tastes even better.

for good measure

- Stollen is traditionally flavored with vanilla; for variety, you can add 1 teaspoon orange or almond extract as well.

- For more texture, add ½ cup (2 ounces) chopped walnuts.

- Substitute orange or cranberry juice for the rum.

- The batter can also be baked in medium- or mini-loaf pans; adjust baking time accordingly.

special equipment: Strainer; cookie sheet; 12- to 14-inch square of aluminum foil; pastry blender, optional; rolling pin; dough scraper or pancake turner, optional; pastry brush; sifter

advance preparation: Plan ahead: Soak the raisins and cherries in rum a day in advance, or overnight, or speed the process by plumping them in the microwave for 4 minutes. The stollen can be baked 1 or 2 days ahead and kept covered at room temperature; serve warm or toasted, or double-wrap and freeze up to 1 month.

temperature and time: 350°F for 40 to 45 minutes

yield: 4 cups batter; 1 large stollen (about 16 slices, ½ to ¾ inch thick) or 2 medium-sized stollen

stollen

½ **cup packed seedless or golden raisins**

½ **cup dried sweet or tart cherries**

½ **cup light rum or orange juice**

2½ **cups unsifted all-purpose flour, plus extra for pan and countertop**

1 **tablespoon baking powder**

½ **teaspoon ground cardamom or nutmeg**

½ **teaspoon salt**

¾ **cup granulated sugar**

½ **cup (1 stick) cold unsalted butter, cut up in ½-inch pieces**

1 **cup cottage cheese (preferably creamy style), or ricotta**

1 **large egg, at room temperature**

1 **tablespoon vanilla extract**

Solid shortening or butter for preparing foil

3 **tablespoons unsalted butter, melted**

topping

1 **or 2 tablespoons confectioners' sugar**

1. In a medium bowl, soak the raisins and cherries in the rum at least 2 hours, or overnight. Or, put in a microwave-safe large glass measure, partially cover with plastic wrap (turn back one corner), and microwave on high for about 4 minutes, until the fruit is plump and juicy. Strain the soaked fruit into a small bowl and discard (or drink!) the juice.

2. Position a rack in the center of the oven and preheat it to 350°F.

3. In a large mixing bowl, whisk together the flour, baking powder, cardamom, salt, and sugar. Cut in the butter by pinching it into the flour with your fingertips or mixing it with a pastry blender or 2 cross-cutting table knives until the mixture has small lumps about the size of peas.

4. In a separate bowl, mix together the cottage cheese, egg, vanilla, and drained raisins and cherries. Stir this into the flour mixture, working lightly only until the dough begins to come together and form a shaggy, quite sticky ball.

Spread about ¼ cup flour on the counter and turn out the dough. Knead the dough about 10 times, working in the flour: Fold the dough in half and push it away from you, then give it a quarter turn and repeat. Use a dough scraper or pancake turner to gather dough scraps as you work. At first, the dough will be sticky, but it quickly smooths out.

5. Lightly coat a 12-inch square of foil with shortening or butter and place the dough in the center. Pat the dough into a circle about 9 inches in diameter and ¾ inch thick. Brush the top with 1 tablespoon of melted butter, then fold the dough *almost* in half, positioning the folded edge slightly off center, as shown. Slide the foil onto the cookie sheet and brush on the remaining 2 tablespoons of butter.

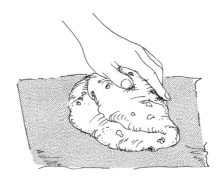

Bake about 40 minutes, or until the top is golden brown, firm to the touch, and a cake tester inserted in the center comes out clean. As it bakes, the dough spreads into a large, slightly flat oval shape (it will look prettier when covered with powdered sugar). Slide the foil holding the stollen onto a wire rack, then slip the foil out from under the stollen so it can cool directly on the rack. When it is cool, sift on a generous coating of confectioners' sugar. Cut the stollen into ½- to ¾-inch-thick slices with a serrated knife.

Chocolate Walnut Bread

CHOCOLATE LOVERS WILL APPRECIATE the rich flavor of this moist loaf packed with crunchy nuts. It is my easy-to-mix rendition of a classic walnut bread recipe developed years ago by the Diamond Walnut Company. For extra texture and flavor, I sometimes add chopped dates and/or chopped apricots, but purists can stick to chocolate and nuts. If you are a walnut purist, you can even hold the chocolate and make the classic California Nut Bread variation. Whatever the flavor, this is a good cake to make in small loaves for holiday gifts.

special equipment: Loaf pan 9 × 5 × 3 inches or 3 baby loaf pans 5¾ or 6 × 3½ × 2 inches

advance preparation: Bread keeps a week, wrapped, at room temperature, or double-wrapped and frozen up to 2 months.

temperature and time: 350°F for 55 to 60 minutes for regular loaf; 35 to 40 minutes for baby loaves

yield: 4 cups batter; 1 large loaf (14 to 16 slices) or 3 baby loaves (8 to 10 slices each)

batter

Butter-flavor no-stick vegetable spray or solid shortening for preparing pan(s)

¼ **cup unsifted unsweetened cocoa, preferably Dutch-processed, plus extra for preparing pan**

2 **cups sifted all-purpose flour**

2 **teaspoons baking powder**

¼ **teaspoon baking soda**

¾ **teaspoon salt**

¾ **cup packed dark brown sugar**

1 **large egg, at room temperature**

1 **cup milk**

⅓ **cup canola oil or unsalted butter, melted**

1 **teaspoon vanilla extract**

1 **cup (4 ounces) chopped walnuts**

¾ **cup (5 ounces) semisweet chocolate chips**

½ **cup (3 ounces) chopped pitted dates and/or dried apricots, optional**

topping

2 **tablespoons chopped walnuts**

2 **tablespoons semisweet chocolate chips**

1. Position a rack in the center of the oven and preheat it to 350°F. Lightly coat the pan(s) with vegetable spray or solid shortening, then dust with cocoa; tap out excess cocoa.

2. In a medium mixing bowl, whisk together the cocoa, flour, baking powder, baking soda, and salt. In a large bowl using a whisk or an electric mixer, blend together the sugar, egg, milk, oil, and vanilla. Slowly add in the dry ingredients, beating just until combined. Stir in the walnuts, chocolate chips, and dates.

3. Turn the batter out into the baking pan(s), sprinkle on a few topping nuts and chocolate chips, and bake 55 to 60 minutes for a large loaf or 35 to 40 minutes for baby loaves, or until risen and a cake tester inserted in the center comes out clean or with just a dab of melted chocolate showing. Cool on a wire rack about 10 minutes, then tip each loaf out of the pan and cool completely on the rack.

California Nut Bread: Prepare basic recipe but omit cocoa; use 2¼ teaspoons baking powder and omit baking soda; substitute granulated sugar for the brown sugar; omit chocolate chips and dates.

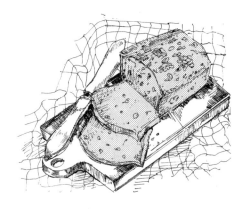

THIS IS THE PLACE TO TURN TO WHEN YOU ARE FEELING BLUE, need a friendly pat on the shoulder, or long for something soothing. Puddings are warm, cozy, comfort foods, the tastes of our childhood. When my sister and I were growing up, we could count on Mother to ease us through sad or serious moments with a big bowl of warm, fluffy tapioca, and, in fact, she still does. We have passed on this excellent home remedy to our own children and husbands, and now, whatever the ailment, they, too, get the tapioca treatment. Creamy Stove-Top Rice Pudding or warm bread pudding is almost as effective, though we aren't too scientific about keeping records. We know what works . . . anything called pudding.

Puddings bread AND puddings

THE "SCRATCH" CHOCOLATE PUDDING RECIPE IS one of my new best friends, developed for my literary agent, Liv Blumer, who was recently on a quest for the best chocolate pudding she could find. This recipe passed her taste test, and she is an impassioned cook and devoted baker.

WHILE IT IS NOT A COOKED PUDDING, Fresh Fruit Fool fits my definition of luxurious comfort food and, in any case, is an essential ingredient in a basic dessert repertoire. It is nothing more than a blend of whipped cream and sweetened mashed or cooked fruit—as easy and as good as any dessert I know.

Fluffy Tapioca Pudding

WARM, CREAMY TAPIOCA pudding with clouds of meringue and redolent of vanilla . . . this is IT for me, the first place to turn for comfort when life closes in. I have made versions with fruit, melted chocolate, and using whole (instead of separated) eggs, but I always come back to this one. My personal weakness is to eat it plain and very warm, though others may prefer it cold, topped by a dollop of raspberry or strawberry preserves.

for good measure

This recipe uses small-grained, quick-cooking tapioca rather than the large pearl type. It is important to shake the box well before measuring the tapioca in order that your portion will include both the fine granules, which sink to the box bottom, and the larger granules, which stay on the top; the combination of both ensures a well-set pudding.

special equipment: 2½- or 3-quart heavy-bottomed saucepan

advance preparation: Serve warm or chilled; can be made in the morning and served that evening; pudding may soften after standing overnight. Keep refrigerated.

temperature and time: Stove top: 10 to 12 minutes

yield: About 8 cups pudding; 8 (1-cup) servings

4 cups milk, divided (3½ cups and ½ cup)

2 large eggs, at room temperature

½ cup granulated sugar, divided (¼ cup and ¼ cup)

⅓ cup plus 2 tablespoons quick-cooking tapioca

¼ teaspoon salt

1 tablespoon vanilla extract

1. In the saucepan, heat 3½ cups of milk until just hot to the touch, but *not* boiling. Separate the eggs, putting the yolks in a medium bowl and the whites in a large absolutely grease-free bowl for the electric mixer.

2. Whisk the remaining ½ cup cold milk into the yolks, then add ¼ cup of the sugar, the tapioca, and salt. Blend well, then pour the mixture into the hot milk in the saucepan. Cook the tapioca on medium heat, whisking on and off, about 5 minutes; then whisk constantly for an additional 5 minutes or more until the tapioca comes to a full bubbling boil. Whisk constantly while at a full boil for one full minute longer (count slowly to 60), then remove the pan from the heat and stir in the vanilla. Set the pan aside.

3. With the electric mixer, whip the whites on medium speed until they look foamy. Gradually add the remaining ¼ cup sugar while beating continuously. When the whites look thick and foamy, increase speed to high and whip until you begin to see beater tracks on top and the whites look smooth and satiny. Beat a little longer until, when the mixer is turned off and the beater is lifted, the whites at the tip form a peak that droops very slightly.

4. Spoon a generous cup of hot tapioca onto the whipped whites and fold them in with a whisk or flexible spatula. Continue adding and folding in the tapioca until it is all incorporated. Set the pudding aside without stirring for at least 20 minutes to allow it to set. Serve warm, or cool completely, then refrigerate and serve cold.

Creamy Stove-Top Rice Pudding

WARM, CREAMY RICE pudding is comfort food at its most irresistible. Studded with plump raisins, scented with vanilla, cinnamon, and nutmeg—its very presence is reassuring. This pudding is made entirely on the stove top, rather than being baked in the oven. The foolproof method is to cook plain rice first, then cook the rice again, simmering it slowly in a double boiler, until it absorbs a sweetened egg custard.

You can use many different types of rice for this pudding, but each contributes a different amount of starch and takes a slightly different amount of time to cook until the grains are tender; long-grain, or extra-long-grain rice takes at least 5 minutes longer than medium-grain or Italian arborio rice; brown rice and "converted" rice can also be used.

for good measure

Instead of black raisins you can substitute golden raisins or dried cranberries or dried sweet cherries.

special equipment: 2- to 3-quart saucepan with lid

advance preparation: The plain rice cooked in water and milk can be made several hours or up to 1 day in advance and kept refrigerated. Bring to room temperature before adding and cooking the custard. Pudding is best served the day it is made, but can be refrigerated, then warmed before serving.

temperature and time: Stove top: first cooking for rice, about 30 minutes; cooking of rice with custard, about 45 minutes

yield: About 5 cups pudding; 8 (heaping ½-cup) servings

1 cup water

2½ cups milk, divided (1 cup and 1½ cups)

¼ teaspoon salt

1 cup medium- or long-grain white rice, or rice of preference

2 large eggs, at room temperature

⅓ cup granulated sugar

½ teaspoon ground nutmeg

¼ teaspoon ground cinnamon

1 tablespoon cornstarch dissolved in 2 tablespoons milk

½ cup packed seedless raisins

2 teaspoons vanilla

1. Don't rinse the rice, as its starch makes the pudding more creamy. In a large pot (uncovered so you can watch it), bring 1 cup of water and 1 cup of milk just to a boil. As soon as the liquid begins to bubble, stir in the salt and rice and cover the pot. Turn the heat down to its lowest setting and simmer the rice for about 30 minutes, or longer if necessary, until the liquid is absorbed and the grains, when bitten, are tender throughout. (If using extra-long-grain rice, you may need to add a tiny bit more water and cook a little longer than for other types of rice.) Remove the pan from the heat and set it aside. This step can be done several hours or a day in advance.

2. In a medium bowl, whisk together the eggs, sugar, spices, and dissolved cornstarch. Whisk in the remaining 1½ cups milk, then stir this mixture into the precooked rice and add the raisins.

3. Place the rice-custard in the top of a double boiler over gently simmering water (or set the rice pot over a larger pan containing simmering water). Cover the rice and cook at a gentle simmer for about 45 minutes, stirring frequently. Keep the heat very low so you don't get scrambled eggs. Cook and stir until most of the liquid custard is absorbed and the rice appears to be very creamy.

4. When cooking is completed, remove the pan from the heat and stir in the vanilla. Taste and add more sugar if desired. Cover the pot, and let the pudding stand at least 15 minutes. Serve warm. Refrigerate leftovers. If the pudding has thickened after chilling, add a tablespoon or two of cream or milk before warming in the microwave or in a pan, stirring, over the lowest heat. Serve warm.

Old-Fashioned Chocolate Pudding

IF YOU ARE feeling nostalgic for the chocolate pudding you loved when you were a kid (complete with a skin on top, which was my favorite part), this is for you. It is easy to make and infinitely better than "boxed" because it contains both cocoa and solid chocolate. You may think of chocolate pudding as homey comfort food, but this silken version is sinfully decadent and rich enough to serve to company in stemmed glasses. In fact, if you really like the company, treat them to a variation, dreamy Chocolate Cream Pie filled with this pudding.

for good measure

- For the richest flavor, use Dutch-processed cocoa, but if you don't have it, regular Hershey's cocoa works too.

- If you are using block chocolate instead of chips, be sure to chop it finely so it will melt fast. If you are making pudding for kids, they may prefer a slightly less rich and intense version prepared without the butter and using only 2 ounces of semisweet chocolate.

special equipment: 1½- to 2-quart saucepan

advance preparation: Pudding takes about 2 hours to cool and chill. It is also good served warm. It will keep, covered in the refrigerator, 2 or 3 days.

temperature and time: Stove top: 10 to 15 minutes; refrigerator: at least 2 hours

yield: 3 cups pudding; 6 (½-cup) servings

¼ **cup unsifted unsweetened Dutch-processed cocoa**

¼ **cup unsifted cornstarch**

½ **cup granulated sugar**

⅛ **teaspoon salt**

Scant pinch of ground nutmeg

1 **large egg, at room temperature**

2½ **cups milk**

2 **tablespoons unsalted butter, cut up**

4 **ounces semisweet chocolate, finely chopped, or ⅔ cup chips**

2 **teaspoons vanilla**

1. In a saucepan, whisk together the cocoa, cornstarch, sugar, salt, and nutmeg.

In a bowl, whisk the egg into the milk, then pour about ½ cup of this mixture into the dry cocoa mix and whisk until all the powders are blended in and look quite smooth. Whisk/stir in the remaining egg mixture, taking care to stir into the pan corners to pick up any powdery cocoa. Set the cut-up butter and chopped chocolate nearby.

2. Place the saucepan over medium heat and whisk the pudding on and off for about 5 minutes, until it heats to the point where you begin to see steam rising around the edges.

3. Add the butter and chocolate to the hot liquid and whisk *without stopping* (to avoid lumps) 4 to 5 minutes, until the mixture starts to thicken, looks smooth, and comes to a bubbling boil. As soon as you see fat bubbles bursting on the top, begin to count slowly to 60 (don't cheat) while whisking constantly to cook the cornstarch one full minute and thicken the pudding. The pudding should now be very thick and smooth, like a rich sour cream. Remove the pan from the heat, stir in the vanilla, and set the pudding aside to cool. If you want to prevent a skin from forming, press a piece of plastic wrap over the surface.

Chocolate Cream Pie: Prepare the Chocolate Crumb Crust on page 103, in a 9-inch pie plate. Do not bake the crust; rather, set it in the refrigerator to chill while you make the Chocolate Pudding, above. Pour the pudding into the pie shell and refrigerate at least 3 hours to set. Before serving, whip 1 cup of chilled heavy cream (36% butterfat) with 1 tablespoon sugar and ½ teaspoon vanilla extract until medium-stiff peaks form. Spread the cream on the cake and serve. For a gala garnish, top the cream with a few Chocolate Curls or Chocolate Shavings, page 196.

Persimmon Pudding

RIPE PERSIMMONS taste like an exotic cross between apricots and ripe cantaloupe. Delectably tart and sweet, the pulp is used for many types of desserts, including puddings and cake and cookie fillings. There is a variety of this fruit tree that grows wild in America, but the fruit most commonly sold in markets is native to China and Japan. Sometimes called "Apple of the Orient" or Asian or Japanese (kaki) persimmon, it is available on the East Coast in late fall. Look for very soft fruit that is slightly puckered, has some pale brown spots dotting the orange-gold skin, and gives easily to the pressure of your finger. Persimmons can fool you—when unripe, the color is a rich orange, the skin is smooth, and the fruit is impossibly sour; when they appear to be overripe, they are finally sweet enough to scoop from their skin and eat with a spoon.

This recipe is a specialty of my aunt, Phoebe Vernon, who lives near Philadelphia in a magically lovely home with a bountiful persimmon tree in her courtyard. Since the persimmons ripen in November, she always serves this dish at Thanksgiving.

for good measure

> If you have extra persimmons, the puree can be frozen for 3 months without loss of flavor.

special equipment: Baking pan 8 × 8 × 2 or 7½ × 11¾ × 1½ inches; food processor or blender

advance preparation: Pudding can be baked 1 day in advance and refrigerated.

temperature and time: 325°F for 50 to 60 minutes

yield: 9 servings (about 2½-inch squares)

¼ cup (½ stick) unsalted butter, melted

4 to 5 very ripe persimmons (1½ to 1¾ pounds)

1¾ cups milk

3 large eggs, at room temperature

1¼ to 1½ cups granulated sugar, depending upon sweetness of fruit

2 cups sifted all-purpose flour

½ teaspoon baking soda

½ teaspoon salt

½ teaspoon ground cinnamon

½ teaspoon ground nutmeg

1. Position a rack in the center of the oven and preheat it to 325°F. Pour about 1 tablespoon of the melted butter into the baking pan to coat it, then set it aside.

2. Cut the tops off the persimmons, scoop out the pulp with a teaspoon, and mash it well with a fork; or puree the pulp in a food processor or blender (you need 2 cups of puree). In a large mixing bowl with a sturdy spoon or whisk, beat together the remaining 3 tablespoons butter, persimmon pulp, milk, and eggs. Slowly beat in all remaining ingredients.

3. Spoon the batter into the buttered pan and smooth the top. Bake for 50 to 60 minutes, or until the edges are slightly browned and a knife inserted into the pudding slightly off center comes out clean. Cool on a wire rack; the pudding solidifies as it cools. Cut it into squares and serve it from the pan, slightly warm or at room temperature. If you feel indulgent, add a small dab of whipped cream on the side. Refrigerate leftovers.

Grandma's Apple-Raisin Bread Pudding with Warm Maple Sauce

CUSTARDY APPLE-RAISIN bread pudding is just what you need when things are less than perfect in your world . . . this is powerful medicine to ease broken hearts of any age. If you are grown up, you might speed the cure by adding a couple of tablespoons of brandy or bourbon to the maple sauce. Be sure to warm up both the pudding and the sauce before serving.

Rose Sinkins, my talented recipe tester from Marshfield, Massachusetts, suggests serving this for brunch. When she did, it was enjoyed as much by her children as by the adults in her family, who liked the balance of not-too-sweet pudding with the sweet maple sauce. I enjoy it for breakfast, dinner, and midnight snack.

for good measure

- If you don't have raisin bread, use any type, and add ½ to ¾ cup seedless black or golden raisins.
- Be sure to use McIntosh or other soft eating apples in the pudding instead of hard green apples, which take too long to bake.
- In the Maple Sauce, the addition of extract depends on the quality and flavor of your syrup; pure maple extract is sold in most supermarkets or see Mail-Order Sources and Suppliers, page 240.

special equipment: 2-quart ovenproof casserole or heat-proof baking dish

advance preparation: Note that the bread must soak in milk about 15 minutes before the other ingredients are added and the pudding is baked. Pudding is best served warm from the oven, but will keep 2 or 3 days, covered in the refrigerator. Rewarm individual servings, topped by a dash of milk, in the microwave.

temperature and time: 350°F for 55 to 65 minutes

yield: 6 cups pudding; 1 cup sauce; 8 (¾-cup) servings

pudding

3 cups milk, divided (2 cups and 1 cup)

¼ cup packed dark brown sugar

4 to 5 cups lightly packed, torn pieces stale raisin or cinnamon-raisin bread (8 or 9 slices)

2 McIntosh or other medium-soft eating apples, peeled, cored, and sliced ⅛ inch thick (2 cups slices)

3 large eggs, at room temperature

⅓ cup granulated sugar

Pinch of salt

½ teaspoon ground cinnamon

½ teaspoon ground nutmeg

1 teaspoon vanilla extract

⅓ cup toasted wheat germ, optional

2 to 4 tablespoons unsalted butter, melted, optional

maple sauce

½ cup medium or heavy cream, or water

½ cup pure maple syrup

Pinch of ground cinnamon

¼ teaspoon maple extract, optional

2 teaspoons cornstarch dissolved in ¼ cup cold water

1. Position a rack in the center of the oven and preheat it to 350°F.

2. In an unbuttered baking dish, whisk together 2 cups of the milk with the brown sugar. Submerge the bread in this mixture, press it down well, and set it aside to soak about 15 minutes, turning the bread pieces once or twice. During this time, prepare the apple slices.

3. Stir the apple slices into the soaked raisin bread, mixing them in well.

In another bowl, whisk together the remaining 1 cup of milk with the eggs, granulated sugar, salt, spices, and vanilla. Pour this over the apple-bread mixture and stir. To add a crunchy topping, sprinkle the wheat germ over the top and then the melted butter.

4. Bake 55 to 65 minutes, or until puffed up, browned on top, and a knife inserted in the center of the pudding comes out clean. The temperature on an instant-read thermometer placed in the pudding center will be 170°F. Serve warm.

5. To make the sauce, combine the cream, maple syrup, cinnamon, and extracts, if using, in a saucepan over medium heat and stir well. Stir in the dissolved cornstarch and bring to a hard boil for 1 minute, until the sauce thickens enough to coat the back of a spoon. Serve warm. Store refrigerated in a covered jar.

Clara's Noodle Pudding

MY GRANDMOTHER CLARA'S noodle *kugel* (pudding) is at the top of my family's list of favorite foods. Filled with cottage cheese, sour cream, apples, raisins, and dried apricots, it is rich and creamy. I usually serve it with roast poultry or meat; occasionally I spread apricot preserves on the top and serve it warm for dessert. If you are feeling adventurous, you can replace the apricots and raisins with other cut-up dried fruits: apples, pears, peaches, or cherries.

for good measure

If you wish to reduce the fat in this rich recipe, use 2 tablespoons canola oil instead of butter in the noodles, replace 1 of the eggs with 1 white, use 2% milk, replace sour cream with low-fat vanilla yogurt, and use 2% cottage cheese.

special equipment: Large pot with lid; colander; 9 × 13-inch baking dish

advance preparation: Pudding is best served on the day it is baked, but it can be kept refrigerated several days. Rewarm individual servings in the microwave (with a splash of milk) or top with foil and bake at 325°F 15 to 20 minutes until warm.

temperature and time: 350°F for 35 to 40 minutes

yield: 12 (1-cup) servings

1½ teaspoons salt, divided (1 teaspoon and ½ teaspoon)

12 ounces broad egg noodles (about 8 cups *before* cooking)

3 tablespoons butter or solid stick margarine, plus extra for preparing pan

4 large eggs, at room temperature

1½ cups milk

1 teaspoon vanilla extract

16 ounces (2 cups) sour cream

10 ounces (1¼ cups) cottage cheese

⅓ cup granulated sugar

½ teaspoon ground cinnamon

½ teaspoon ground nutmeg

3 small or 2 medium apples, preferably McIntosh or Golden Delicious, peeled, cored, and cut into ¼-inch-thick slices (about 1½ cups)

½ cup packed golden or seedless raisins

½ cup (3 ounces) dried apricot halves, cut into small pieces

½ cup toasted wheat germ or crushed cornflakes

1. Set a large, covered pot of water on high heat and bring it to a rolling boil. Position a rack in the center of the oven and preheat it to 350°F.

Add 1 teaspoon of salt to the boiling water and follow directions on the package to boil noodles, uncovered, until just tender. Drain the cooked noodles into a colander, then return them to the empty pot and stir in the butter. Butter the baking pan.

2. In a large bowl, whisk together the eggs, milk, vanilla, sour cream, cottage cheese, sugar, the remaining ½ teaspoon salt, cinnamon, and nutmeg. Stir this mixture into the buttered noodles in the pot, along with the apples, raisins, and apricots. Blend everything together well, spread it in the prepared pan, and sprinkle with the wheat germ. Bake the pudding 35 to 40 minutes, or until golden brown on top and a knife inserted in the center comes out clean. Set the pan on a heat-proof surface to cool. Cut the pudding into squares and serve warm from the pan or at room temperature. Refrigerate leftovers.

Harvest Pumpkin Bread Pudding

PUMPKIN BREAD PUDDING is a treat that has recently become restaurant fare. Boston's tony Grill 23 & Bar serves its steaming brioche pumpkin pudding with a mellow whiskey-custard sauce. Another sophisticated version, developed by Chef Greg Bonsignore at Max and Mary's Restaurant in New Milford, Connecticut, includes specially baked pumpkin bread as well as challah, soaked with a yolk-and-cream-rich custard; it is served warm and garnished with vanilla ice cream. For a home baker, making pumpkin bread just for a pudding seems too labor-intensive; using up stale bread is more my style, so I decided to combine a creamy pumpkin custard pie filling with my basic bread pudding. This recipe is the result. Serve it warm, topped with a splash of heavy cream or vanilla ice cream.

for good measure

- To create an Indian-Pudding–like variation, replace about 2 cups plain bread with stale corn bread and add 2 or 3 tablespoons unsulphured molasses to the custard.

- Mashed baked sweet potatoes or butternut squash can be substituted for the pumpkin puree.

special equipment: 2-quart ovenproof casserole or heat-proof baking dish

advance preparation: Pudding is best warm from the oven, but can be kept 1 or 2 days, covered in the refrigerator. Reheat individual portions before serving.

temperature and time: 350°F for 70 to 80 minutes

yield: 6 cups pudding; 6 to 8 (¾- to 1-cup) servings

bread mixture

2 cups milk

¼ cup packed dark brown sugar

1 teaspoon vanilla extract

1 teaspoon ground cinnamon

½ teaspoon ground ginger

½ teaspoon ground allspice

⅛ teaspoon ground cloves

1 cup golden raisins, packed, optional

6 cups packed, torn pieces of stale or lightly toasted challah, or French or Italian bread or brioche, or leftover pumpkin bread

pumpkin custard

3 large eggs, at room temperature

½ cup granulated sugar

2 tablespoons melted butter, optional

½ teaspoon salt

1½ teaspoons ground cinnamon

1 teaspoon ground nutmeg, plus extra for topping

1 teaspoon ground ginger

¼ teaspoon ground cloves

2 cups plain pumpkin puree, canned

1 cup heavy cream plus ½ cup milk (or use all cream or milk)

1. In an unbuttered baking dish, prepare the bread mixture first. Whisk together 2 cups of milk with the brown sugar, vanilla, and spices. Add the raisins, if using. Submerge the bread pieces in this mixture, press them down well, and set the mixture aside to soak about 15 minutes, turning the bread pieces several times. Cover the bread with a plate if it won't stay submerged.

2. Position a rack in the center of the oven and preheat it to 350°F.

Prepare the pumpkin custard while the bread soaks. In a large bowl, whisk together the eggs, sugar, melted butter, salt, and spices until well blended, then mix in the pumpkin, cream, and milk.

3. Stir the soaking bread. Once it has absorbed all the soaking liquid, pour on the pumpkin custard and stir to combine. Sprinkle a little nutmeg over the top and bake 70 to 80 minutes, or longer, until puffed up slightly, golden brown on top, and a knife inserted in the pudding about 1 inch from the edge comes out nearly clean, showing only a slight streak of pudding (180°F on an instant-read thermometer); in the center, the pudding will be a little creamier and the knife less clean (155°F). Cool slightly and serve warm.

Chocolate Bread Pudding with White Chocolate Cream

THIS IS THE stuff dreams are made of—wonderfully cozy chocolate dreams, the kind you can count on. Use any type of leftover bread, challah, plain yeast rolls, or a little leftover chocolate cake; I like to keep leftover baked goods in the freezer until I accumulate enough for bread pudding. This is best served warm, when the texture is soft and creamy. Add a generous splash of White Chocolate Cream or vanilla yogurt or ice cream.

for good measure

- For even more chocolate, coarsely chop 2 to 3 ounces of bittersweet (not unsweetened) or semisweet chocolate and stir it into the pudding just before baking.
- The White Chocolate Cream is divine but very sweet; to cut sweetness and boost flavor, add 2 drops of orange extract or pure orange oil.

special equipment: 2-quart ovenproof casserole or heat-proof baking dish; double boiler

advance preparation: Pudding is best warm from the oven, but can be kept 1 or 2 days, covered in the refrigerator. Reheat individual portions before serving.

temperature and time: 350°F for 55 to 65 minutes

yield: 6 cups pudding; 1¼ cups cream; 6 to 8 (¾- to 1-cup) servings

pudding

2 tablespoons unsalted butter, plus extra for preparing baking dish

4 ounces semisweet chocolate, chopped

3 cups milk, divided (1 cup and 2 cups)

6 cups packed, torn pieces of stale French or Italian bread or challah, toasted lightly if very soft (8 to 10 slices)

3 tablespoons unsweetened cocoa (any type)

¼ cup packed dark brown sugar

3 large eggs, at room temperature

½ cup granulated sugar

Pinch of salt

1 teaspoon ground nutmeg

1 teaspoon vanilla extract

white chocolate cream

1 cup heavy cream

5 ounces white chocolate, finely chopped (for the smoothest melt, use best quality available, such as Lindt, Callebaut, or Ghirardelli)

1 or 2 *drops* orange extract, optional

1. Position a rack in the center of the oven and preheat it to 350°F. Butter the baking dish.

2. In the top of a double boiler set over medium heat, combine the butter, chopped chocolate, and 1 cup of milk. Stir on and off until the chocolate melts. Remove the double boiler from the heat, lift off the top pan, and set it aside to cool.

3. Put the bread pieces into the prepared baking dish. In a small bowl, whisk the cocoa and brown sugar into ½ cup milk until most of the cocoa is blended in, then whisk in the remaining 1½ cups milk. Pour the milk over the bread; stir to coat, then let it soak 15 to 30 minutes, stirring occasionally to be sure all the bread is submerged.

4. In a medium bowl, whisk together the eggs, granulated sugar, salt, nutmeg, and vanilla. Whisk in the melted and cooled chocolate mixture (work quickly in case the chocolate is still warm; if too hot, it will cook the eggs).

5. Pour the chocolate mixture over the soaked bread and stir gently to blend. Bake 55 to 65 minutes, or until puffed up, and a knife inserted in the center comes out showing a few sticky crumbs but not a creamy film of unbaked custard. Cool slightly and serve warm.

6. Prepare the sauce while the pudding bakes. In a small saucepan, heat the cream until hot to the touch (about 120°F on an instant-read thermometer), but *not* boiling. Remove from the heat. Add the finely chopped chocolate and orange extract, if using, and gently stir until completely smooth. Serve the warm or room-temperature cream in a pitcher, pouring some over each serving of pudding. Refrigerate any leftover cream.

Pennsylvania Dutch Baked Apple Pudding with Warm Nutmeg Cream

SWEET SCALLOPED APPLES are an old–fashioned treat served right from the oven with warm nutmeg cream poured on top. This is definitely family comfort food, but your guests, and children, will love it, too.

for good measure

- Be sure to use McIntosh or another soft-eating apple instead of hard green apples, which take too long to bake.
- Adjust the quantity of sugar depending upon the sweetness of your apples.
- You can cut out half the butter if you wish.

special equipment: 1½- to 2-quart ovenproof casserole or heat-proof baking dish

advance preparation: Pudding is best served warm from the oven but can be kept 1 or 2 days, covered in the refrigerator. Reheat individual portions before serving.

temperature and time: 350°F for 70 to 80 minutes. *Note:* If baked in a larger pan, baking time will be shorter; test after 45 minutes.

yield: About 4 cups pudding; 1½ cups cream; 4 to 6 (generous ¾-cup) servings

pudding

¼ cup (½ stick) unsalted butter, melted, plus extra for preparing baking dish

5 medium or 4 large apples, peeled, cored, thinly sliced (preferably McIntosh; about 5 cups slices)

¾ cup granulated sugar, divided (¼ cup and ½ cup)

1 teaspoon ground cinnamon

3 large eggs, at room temperature

1 teaspoon vanilla

⅔ cup milk or apple cider

¼ cup unsifted all-purpose or whole wheat flour

1 teaspoon baking powder

½ teaspoon salt

¼ cup toasted wheat germ

¼ cup (1 ounce) chopped walnuts, optional

nutmeg cream

1½ cups medium or heavy cream

1¼ teaspoons ground nutmeg

½ teaspoon vanilla extract

1 or 2 tablespoons granulated sugar, to taste

1. Position a rack in the lower third of the oven and preheat it to 350°F. Butter the baking dish.

2. Slice the apples into the prepared baking dish, and toss with ¼ cup of the sugar and cinnamon. In a bowl, whisk together the eggs with the melted butter, remaining ½ cup sugar, vanilla, and milk, then beat in the flour, baking powder, and salt. Pour the batter over the apples and stir once or twice. Sprinkle the wheat germ and nuts on top, if using.

3. Bake 70 to 80 minutes, or until the top is golden brown and a knife inserted in the center goes in smoothly, with no resistance, and comes out clean. Serve the pudding warm from the oven. If made in advance and refrigerated, cover it with foil and reheat it 15 to 20 minutes at 325°F. Or, reheat individual portions in the microwave.

4. While the pudding bakes, prepare the Nutmeg Cream: Stir all the ingredients together in a small pan; do not boil. Serve warm, pouring a little over the warm pudding.

Fresh Fruit Fool

DON'T MAKE FUN of this fool, just make it for fun. Like its name, it is quirky, frothy, serendipitous (use whatever combination of berries or fruits you have on hand), and utterly divine. Resist the temptation to say any fool can do it, but you can almost make the recipe up as you go along. Simply cook together some cut-up sweetened fruit—the more colorful and juicy the better—(plums, rhubarb, cherries, berries), then chill it and fold it into whipped cream. Children love to put this together, enjoying the taste as well as the name. Although this is a homey pudding-style dessert, you can dress it up for company by serving it in long-stemmed goblets with a few whole berries or an Oatmeal Lace Cookie (page 50) perched on top.

for good measure

To reduce the fat: drain 2 cups vanilla yogurt through a strainer or coffee filter for at least 1 hour. Discard (or drink) the liquid. Stir the yogurt into the chilled fruit mixture, then fold in ½ cup heavy cream, whipped stiff.

special equipment: 3-quart saucepan; strainer set over bowl; chilled bowl and beater for whipping cream

advance preparation: Cooked fruit mixture can be prepared several days in advance. Fold the fruit into the whipped cream about 2 hours before serving, and chill so the flavors can blend.

temperature and time: Stove top: 8 to 12 minutes; refrigerator: 2 hours to 2 days

yield: About 8 cups; 8 (1-cup) servings

8 cups mixed fruit: For example, 4 cups cut-up, unpeeled, pitted purple plums (any type) or rhubarb (cut in 1-inch pieces) plus 1 quart (4 cups) whole fresh raspberries or strawberries, picked over, hulled, rinsed. Or blend 4 cups fresh or whole frozen raspberries or cranberries with 4 cups blueberries or pitted sweet cherries.

¼ cup orange juice (or other fruit juice)

½ to 1 cup granulated or packed light brown sugar

One 2- or 3-inch cinnamon stick

Two 2-inch strips lemon peel

1 cup heavy cream (36% butterfat), chilled

¼ teaspoon ground nutmeg

¼ teaspoon ground ginger, optional

1. In a large saucepan, combine the fruit, juice, sugar (to taste depending on sweetness of fruit), cinnamon stick, and lemon peel. Set over medium-high heat, bring to a boil, then quickly lower the heat, cover the pan, and simmer the fruit, stirring occasionally, for 8 to 10 minutes, until the fruit is soft. Uncover the pan, raise the heat, and stir on and off a few minutes longer to thicken the mixture slightly. You should have about 1 quart of fruit. Turn the mixture out into a bowl, pick out and discard the cinnamon stick and lemon strips, and adjust the sugar to your taste if necessary. Chill up to a day or two until ready to mix into the whipped cream.

2. About 2 hours before serving, assemble the fool. With a chilled bowl and chilled beater, whip the heavy cream until stiff peaks form. Fold the cream into the chilled fruit mixture, or, if you prefer, make separate layers of the fruit and cream in a glass bowl. Top with a little cream, a dash of nutmeg, and ginger, if you wish.

SWEET. CRUNCHY. CHEWY. SATISFYING. We love cookies for many reasons, not the least is that we don't have to share. We get to savor every little crumb all by ourselves, and can, in fact, stash them to be devoured in private. On the other hand, they are the most-shared of all desserts, and holiday cookie exchange parties are more popular than ever. The invitation to an exchange should read: "Bring a batch of your cookies with the recipe and its history, along with an empty box to take home your bounty of samples." Then share and compare.

Cookies

THERE ARE MANY DIFFERENT TYPES OF COOKIES in this collection: Some are dropped from a spoon; others are rolled and cut out, pressed, or hand-molded. Refrigerator cookies are among the easiest and most convenient, especially if you have children coming to visit, because they are designed to be rolled into cylinders, stored in the refrigerator, then sliced and baked whenever you want, or need, a freshly baked treat. Children will enjoy making the two easiest recipes in my cookie world, each with just three ingredients: Elmira and Mary's Walnut Date Balls and Impossible Peanut Butter Cookies.

YOU WILL FIND COOKIES to hang on the Christmas tree or use as gift tags or place cards, cookies to bake into bars and squares for easy transportation to picnics, plain and fancy brownies, elegant-but-easy biscotti, and just for fun Write-Your-Own Fortune Cookies, which will be the hit of any party. If the list seems bewildering and you are looking for just one basic recipe to satisfy all your cookie needs, you will fall in love with my Old-Fashioned Sugar Cookies. No matter how you vary their flavor or shape, they are prize-winners.

WHEN STORING COOKIES, it is important to remember that flavors as well as moisture can be transferred from one type to another. Pack strong-flavored spice cookies alone; separate soft or moist cookies from those that should remain crisp and dry.

Cookie Jar Oatmeal–Raisin Cookies

THIS IS MY rendition of the famous back-of-the-box Quaker Oats cookies. They are slightly chewy and very flavorful; if you bake them the minimum time, they will be slightly softer, while baking longer makes them browner, crisper, and toasts the oats for a nuttier flavor—your choice. You can personalize the recipe by substituting some of the suggested add-ins below.

for good measure

- Add-ins: Instead of, or in addition to, 1 cup raisins, add ½ to 1 cup dried cranberries or dried cherries, cut-up dried apricots, chopped walnuts or pecans, semisweet chocolate morsels, or chocolate-coated raisins (see Mail-Order Sources and Suppliers, page 240).

- For a slightly thicker and more chewy cookie, replace half the butter with solid shortening (Crisco).

- For a butterscotch flavor, use all light brown sugar (1½ cups, packed) instead of granulated plus brown sugar.

special equipment: Cookie sheets; baking parchment or wax paper, optional; flat paddle attachment for electric mixer, if available

advance preparation: Cookies can be kept in an airtight container at room temperature up to a week or double-wrapped and frozen up to 2 months.

temperature and time: 350°F for 12 to 16 minutes

yield: 50 to 55 cookies (2½- to 3-inch diameter)

1½ cups sifted all-purpose flour

1 teaspoon salt

½ teaspoon baking soda

½ teaspoon ground cinnamon

1 cup (2 sticks) unsalted butter, slightly softened

1 cup granulated sugar

½ cup packed dark or light brown sugar

2 large eggs, at room temperature

1 teaspoon vanilla extract

3 cups uncooked old-fashioned or quick-cooking oats (not instant)

1 cup packed seedless raisins

1. Position the racks to divide the oven into thirds and preheat it to 350°F. Leave the cookie sheets ungreased or cover them with baking parchment or wax paper.

In a medium bowl, whisk together the flour, salt, baking soda, and cinnamon.

2. In a large bowl using a sturdy spoon or an electric mixer with paddle attachment if available, beat together the butter and sugars until smooth and well blended. Beat in the eggs and vanilla. Stirring slowly or with the beater on the slowest speed, work in the flour mixture completely, then the oats and raisins. The batter will be very stiff. You can make the batter several hours ahead, cover, and refrigerate it at this point.

3. Drop the batter onto the cookie sheets by heaping tablespoons about 2 inches apart and bake 12 to 16 minutes, or until the cookies are golden brown (15 minutes is usually perfect for my taste; the longer they bake, the crisper they will be). Cool the cookie sheets on a wire rack for 2 or 3 minutes, then use a spatula to transfer the cookies to the rack to cool; or slide the baking parchment onto the wire rack to cool the cookies. Store in an airtight container.

Tracy's Extra-Chewy Oatmeal Raisin Cookies: These cookies are the specialty of my friend Tracy Glaves Spalding, a young Colorado mother whose two children, Emma and Preston (ages five and three), taste-tested the results.

Before beginning the recipe, whisk together in a medium bowl 2 eggs and the vanilla. Stir in the raisins, cover, and set aside for 1 hour so the raisins can plump and absorb flavor. Prepare the basic recipe above but use half butter, half solid shortening (Crisco). In step 2, beat the raisin mixture into the creamed butter and sugar before adding the flour and oats. Bake the cookies for 15 minutes.

Danish Oat Cookies

IN DENMARK, CHRISTMAS tradition holds that visitors to your home must taste your homemade cookies. If they do not, it is believed they will carry off the spirit of Christmas when they leave. To protect your home, make these crisp buttery *Havresmaakager* (oat cookies) that no one can resist. These are quick and easy to prepare, and so good that I usually make a double batch, giving some as gifts and freezing the rest.

special equipment: Cookie sheets; baking parchment, optional

advance preparation: Cookies can be kept in an airtight container at room temperature up to a week or double-wrapped and frozen up to 2 months.

temperature and time: 350°F for 10 to 15 minutes

yield: 55 to 60 cookies (2-inch diameter)

½ **cup toasted wheat germ (if raw, see step 1)**

1 **cup (2 sticks) unsalted butter, melted and cooled slightly, plus extra for preparing pans, optional**

¾ **cup granulated sugar**

1 **large egg, at room temperature**

1 **teaspoon vanilla extract**

2 **cups old-fashioned rolled oats (not instant)**

½ **cup unsifted all-purpose flour**

½ **teaspoon salt**

1. If using raw (untoasted) wheat germ, place it in a small frying pan set over medium heat and toast it until golden and aromatic. Set it aside to cool.

Position racks to divide the oven into thirds and preheat it to 350°F. Cover the cookie sheets with baking parchment or coat with butter.

2. In a large mixing bowl combine the melted butter with the sugar and beat with a sturdy spoon or an electric mixer. Beat in the egg and vanilla, then the oats, flour, salt, and wheat germ. The batter will be quite soft.

3. Drop the batter by the teaspoon about 1½ inches apart on prepared cookie sheets. Bake the cookies for 10 to 15 minutes, or until the tops turn a golden color and the edges darken to a rich golden brown. The longer the baking time, the crunchier the cookie, but beware of burning.

Slide the baking parchment onto a wire rack, or place the cookie sheet on a rack to cool for 3 or 4 minutes, then use a spatula to transfer the cookies to the rack to cool. Store in an airtight container.

Danish Chocolate Oat Cookies: Add 4 tablespoons cocoa for the entire batch of dough. If you want to make only half a batch chocolate, add only 2 tablespoons of cocoa to half the dough.

Oatmeal Lace Cookies

BUTTERY AND BEAUTIFUL, easy and elegant! These cookies would be perfect if they weren't so fragile; if they break, sprinkle the crumbs over ice cream and say you made them that way on purpose. The batter is easily mixed in a saucepan on the stove, then baked and shaped while warm into flat disks, rounded curves, or rolled-up "cigars."

for good measure

> Dough spreads as it bakes, so keep cookies well-separated on the baking sheet. Bake these on a dry day; humidity can soften the cookies.

special equipment: 2-quart heavy-bottomed saucepan; cookie sheets; pancake turner or wide spatula; for curved cookies, rolling pin

advance preparation: In dry weather, cookies can be kept in an airtight container at room temperature about 3 days.

temperature and time: 350°F for 6 to 7 minutes

yield: About 36 cookies (3-inch diameter)

Butter-flavor no-stick vegetable spray

½ **cup (1 stick) unsalted butter, cut up, plus extra for preparing pan, optional**

½ **cup packed light brown sugar**

1 **tablespoon light corn syrup**

¾ **cup uncooked old-fashioned rolled oats (not instant)**

¼ **cup unsifted all-purpose flour**

2 **tablespoons milk or fruit juice**

½ **teaspoon salt**

1 **teaspoon vanilla extract**

1. Position the racks to divide the oven into thirds and preheat it to 350°F. Lightly coat the cookie sheet with vegetable spray or butter.

2. In a saucepan, combine the butter, sugar, and corn syrup. Place the pan over medium-low heat and stir the mixture with a wooden spoon until the sugar is melted. Add the oats, flour, milk, salt, and vanilla. Cook over medium-low heat, stirring constantly, about 2 minutes longer. Remove the pan from the heat and let the batter cool about 5 minutes.

3. Drop the batter by the teaspoon about 3 inches apart on the prepared cookie sheets and bake about 6 minutes, or until the cookies are golden on top with slightly darker edges.

4. Set the cookie sheets on a rack to cool 1 minute; if the cookies are too hot, you won't be able to lift them; cool them a few seconds longer. While the cookies are still very warm and pliable, slide a spatula under them and immediately transfer them to a cooling surface to take shape: either a wire rack (with close-woven mesh) or a plate (for flat cookies) or draped over a rolling pin (for curves), or wrapped around the handle of a wooden spoon (for rolled-up cigars). *Note:* If you plan to shape curved or rolled-up cookies, bake them a pan at a time, since you have to work quickly while the cookies are warm. If the cookies are too cold to be pliable, return the cookie sheet to the oven for 10 to 15 seconds to warm them before shaping.

> **Orange Lace Cookies:** Add ½ to 1 teaspoon pure orange extract or orange oil and 2 teaspoons grated orange zest to batter.
>
> **Ginger Lace Cookies:** Add 1 or 2 tablespoons finely chopped crystalized ginger plus ¼ teaspoon ground ginger to batter.
>
> **Almond Lace Cookies:** Add ½ teaspoon almond extract and ½ cup finely chopped almonds to batter.

Old-Fashioned Sugar Cookies

WITHOUT THESE COOKIES, it just wouldn't be Christmas or Chanukah. My daughter and I begin baking them the week before the holidays and try to stash them in airtight boxes, or in the freezer, to have plenty on hand for gifts and guests. This is the only recipe you will ever need for all your decorative cookies: The dough is easy to mix, roll out, and cut, and the cookies taste great. You can add or change flavoring, paint the cut-outs with sugar icing or egg glazes, and hand-shape them into every design imaginable, from two-tone candy canes to vanilla-chocolate pinwheels. *Note:* The recipe isn't really long, it just has a lot of shaping ideas.

for good measure

- **Vary the flavor of sugar cookies by changing the extract and adding grated citrus zest; for example, instead of vanilla or almond, use 1 teaspoon lemon extract plus 2 teaspoons grated lemon zest.**

- **To make your own tinted sugar, put some granulated sugar in a plastic bag with a drop or two of vegetable food coloring; seal the bag and shake until the sugar is colored.**

special equipment: Cookie sheets; baking parchment, optional; flat paddle attachment for electric mixer, if available; sifter; rolling pin; wax paper, optional; cookie cutters; for icing: Small cups or bowls, pint-size self-sealing plastic bag and scissors or #5 or #6 plain round (or fancy) decorating tips

advance preparation: Dough can be prepared several days before use, covered, and refrigerated or frozen. Baked cookies can be kept in an airtight container at room temperature for at least a week or double-wrapped and frozen up to 3 months.

temperature and time: 350°F for 8 to 12 minutes

yield: About 60 cookies (2-inch diameter); ¾ cup icing; recipe can be doubled

dough

¾ cup (1½ sticks) unsalted butter, at room temperature, plus extra for preparing pan

1 cup granulated sugar

2 large eggs, at room temperature, lightly beaten

1 teaspoon vanilla or almond extract

2¾ cups unsifted all-purpose flour, plus extra if needed

1 teaspoon baking powder

1 teaspoon salt

egg white glaze, optional

1 egg white beaten with 1 teaspoon water

decorations, optional

Chopped nuts, raisins, granulated or coarse sugar (plain or tinted), silver dragées

decorative icing

2 tablespoons unsalted butter or margarine, melted

2 cups sifted confectioners' sugar

1 teaspoon vanilla extract or lemon juice

2 to 3 tablespoons milk or water

Vegetable food coloring (or seedless raspberry jam for pink color; frozen orange juice concentrate for yellow)

1. Position racks to divide the oven into thirds and preheat it to 350°F. Lightly butter the cookie sheets or cover them with baking parchment.

2. In the large bowl of an electric mixer fitted with a paddle attachment if available, beat the butter with the sugar until smooth and well blended. Beat in the eggs and vanilla. Scrape down the sides of the bowl and the beater. Remove the bowl from the mixer stand.

continued

Place a sifter over the egg-mixture bowl, and measure into it the flour, baking powder, and salt. Stir/sift the dry ingredients onto the egg mixture below, then beat with a spoon or the electric mixer on lowest speed until thoroughly incorporated. Form the dough into a ball; if it feels too sticky, add more flour 1 tablespoon at a time until easier to handle. (Excess flour makes cookies tough, so don't be too generous.) Work with one-third to one-half of the dough at a time, refrigerating the rest until needed.

3. On a lightly floured surface or between 2 sheets of lightly floured wax paper, roll the dough out about ⅛ inch thick. Cut shapes with cookie cutters dipped in flour. Use a spatula to transfer the cookies onto the baking sheet, placing them about 1 inch apart. If desired, brush the cookies with egg white glaze, then sprinkle the tops with finely chopped nuts or sugar. Or, decorate with icing after baking.

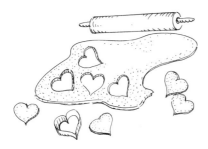

4. Bake the cookies 8 to 12 minutes, or until they are lightly golden around the edges. If baking appears to be uneven, rotate the pans in the oven halfway through baking. Let the cookies cool on the pans 2 to 3 minutes, then use a spatula to transfer them to a wire rack to cool completely.

5. To make decorative icing, combine the butter, sugar, and vanilla and beat until smooth. Add the milk one drop at a time if too stiff. To tint, place 2 or 3 tablespoons of icing in each of several cups; stir in about 1 drop of coloring (pale colors are more appealing to eat than the bright ones). When the cookies are completely cold, spread icing on them with a butter knife or draw on designs by squeezing colored icing out of a pint-size plastic bag with a tiny hole cut in one corner.

For fancier or more controlled lines, drop a metal decorating tip into a corner of the bag and cut a small hole so the tip pokes through; then add the icing and seal the bag. Place the decorated cookies on wire rack and let stand at room temperature until the icing is dry and hard (about 1 hour). Store the cookies in an airtight container, separated by layers of wax paper to protect the icing.

> **Vanilla-Chocolate Pinwheels:** Prepare Sugar Cookies through step 2. Divide dough in half, leaving half in bowl and placing half on a piece of wax paper. Add 2 tablespoons unsweetened cocoa to dough in bowl and use your hands or a spoon to blend it in completely. Shape each portion of dough into a cylinder 6 or 7 inches by 1½ inches. Then, on a lightly floured surface or between 2 lightly floured pieces of wax paper, with a rolling pin roll each cylinder into a long rectangle about 7 x 14 x ⅛ inch (the rectangles should be the same size). Place the chocolate dough on top of the plain dough, lining up the edges. Roll the 2 layers together like a jelly roll, wrap it in wax paper or plastic wrap, and chill until firm, or freeze. To bake, cut scant ¼-inch slices off the roll, place on greased cookie sheets, and bake as above.

Pinwheel

Wreaths, Pretzels, Hearts, Chanukah Stars, and Candy Canes: Prepare Sugar Cookies through step 2. Divide dough in half, or in smaller portions. Leave part of the dough white and color another portion by kneading in several drops of vegetable food coloring; to make chocolate dough, knead in a tablespoon or two of cocoa. After working with colors or cocoa, wash your hands, then lightly flour them. Between your palms, roll 1-inch balls of each color dough; roll each ball into a rope about ½ × 7 inches.

To shape wreaths: Set 2 different colored ropes together, pinch them at one end, and twist them over each other as you form a ring. Pinch ends to hold.

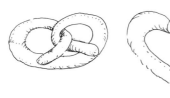

Wreath

To shape pretzels, or hearts: Bend single ropes into loose knots or heart shapes.

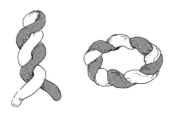

Pretzel   Heart

To shape stars: Make 2 triangle shapes, each from a separate rope; cross the triangles as shown, forming the 6-pointed star. Place the shapes on the prepared cookie sheets, brush with the egg white glaze, sprinkle with the finely chopped nuts or sugar if desired, and bake as directed.

Star

To shape candy canes: Roll ¾-inch-diameter balls of different colored dough and form them into ropes about ⅜ × 6 inches. Place 2 different colored ropes (red and white) together, pinch together at one end, then twist ropes over and over each other; pinch other end to hold, and bend top into cane shape. Place the canes on the prepared cookie sheets and bake as directed.

Candy Cane

Favorite Chocolate Chip Cookies

YES, THIS IS the recipe on the package of Nestlé's Semisweet Morsels; very few others really measure up. I'm pretty certain I have tasted every variation . . . I have been seriously working at it all my life. The results of this scientific study: Many are creative but very few are wonderful. My favorite, developed for a children's cooking class, is Cowboy Crunch (recipe below), which includes oatmeal and wheat germ.

for good measure

- To make a flat, very crisp, buttery tasting cookie, use all butter. To make a thicker, slightly chewy cookie, use half butter and half solid shortening (Crisco) for the fat.

- To personalize the classic, add in up to 1 cup of the following: coarsely chopped solid bittersweet chocolate; white chocolate—chopped or chips; raisins or chocolate-coated raisins (see Mail-Order Sources and Suppliers, page 240); chopped dates; butterscotch chips; dried sweet cherries; macadamia nuts; granola cereal.

special equipment: Cookie sheets; baking parchment, optional

advance preparation: Dough can be prepared a day in advance, covered, and refrigerated or frozen. Baked cookies keep airtight at room temperature at least a week or double-wrapped and frozen up to 3 months.

temperature and time: 375°F for 10 to 11 minutes

yield: About 60 cookies (2½- to 3-inch diameter)

Butter for preparing cookie sheets, optional
2¼ cups unsifted all-purpose flour
1 teaspoon baking soda
1 teaspoon salt
1 cup (2 sticks) unsalted butter, at room temperature
¾ cup granulated sugar
¾ cup packed dark brown sugar
2 large eggs, at room temperature
1 teaspoon vanilla extract
2 cups (12 ounces) semisweet chocolate chips or coarsely chopped chocolate
1 cup (4 ounces) chopped walnuts or pecans, optional

1. Position racks to divide the oven into thirds and preheat it to 375°F. Lightly butter the cookie sheets or cover them with baking parchment.

2. In a medium mixing bowl, whisk together the flour, baking soda, and salt. In a large mixing bowl, with a sturdy spoon or an electric mixer, beat together the butter and both sugars until smooth and well blended. Beat in the eggs and vanilla. Gradually beat in the flour mixture, then stir in the chocolate and nuts, if using.

3. Drop the batter by the rounded tablespoon about 2 inches apart on the cookie sheet. Bake for 10 to 11 minutes, or until golden brown. Slide the baking parchment onto a wire rack to cool, or place the cookie sheet on a wire rack to cool for 3 to 4 minutes, then use a spatula to transfer the cookies to the rack to cool. Store in an airtight container.

Cowboy Crunch Chocolate Chip Cookies: Prepare basic recipe but reduce the flour to 2 cups and add (along with the flour) ¼ cup toasted wheat germ and 1 cup old-fashioned rolled oats (not instant). Bake as directed above. Makes about 7 dozen cookies.

Shape Variations: You can shape the cookies as small as one bite or as big as a dinner plate, but when you change the cookie size, watch the baking time carefully and remove cookies from the oven when golden brown.

Chip Bars: Prepare basic recipe and spread it into a greased 9 × 13-inch pan; bake at 350°F for 30 to 35 minutes. Cool on a wire rack and cut into bars.

Chip Cakes: You can bake *half* the basic recipe in one buttered and wax paper–lined (and buttered) 9-inch round, square, or heart-shaped cake pan, or my favorite, a removable-bottom heart-shaped tart pan; bake at 350°F for 25 to 30 minutes. This will be chewier and more moist than a cookie baked on a cookie sheet. To frost the cake, coat the top with melted chocolate chips (put some chips in a plastic bag, seal the end well, and drop it into very hot water until melted).

Chip Ice Cream Cake: Bake 2 chip cake layers and sandwich softened ice cream between them. Wrap in foil and freeze at least 3 hours or overnight. Leave the frozen cake at room temperature about 15 to 20 minutes to soften before slicing.

Chip Ice Cream Pie: Make *half* the basic recipe and press it into a lightly greased 9-inch pie plate; bake at 350°F for 25 to 30 minutes. Cool completely. Spread with a thick layer of your favorite ice cream (about 1 quart) and freeze. Leave at room temperature 15 to 20 minutes to soften before slicing. Serve topped with All-American Hot Fudge Sauce, page 180.

Classic Peanut Butter Cookies

I TESTED SEVERAL variations of this recipe, passing them out to friends with young children. This final version was the unchallenged favorite of the eight-to eleven-year-old cookie-eaters. Because these cookies are so popular and keep well, I like to make a big batch; the recipe can be cut in half if you wish.

for good measure

> For best flavor, make this recipe with butter—not margarine—and use chunky peanut butter.

special equipment: Cookie sheets; baking parchment, optional; flat paddle attachment for electric mixer, if available; sifter

advance preparation: Cookies can be kept in an airtight container at room temperature about a week or double-wrapped and frozen up to 3 months.

temperature and time: 350°F for 12 to 15 minutes

yield: About 120 cookies (2-inch diameter); recipe can be cut in half (use just ¾ cup granulated sugar)

dough

1 cup (2 sticks) unsalted butter, at room temperature, plus extra for preparing pans, optional

¾ cup packed dark brown sugar

¾ cup granulated sugar

2 large eggs, at room temperature

2 teaspoons vanilla extract

2 cups peanut butter (preferably chunky)

2½ cups sifted all-purpose flour

½ teaspoon baking soda

1 teaspoon salt

topping

¼ cup granulated sugar

1. Position racks to divide the oven into thirds and preheat it to 350°F. Line the cookie sheets with baking parchment or lightly coat with butter.

2. In a large bowl with a sturdy spoon or an electric mixer fitted with a paddle attachment if available, beat together the butter and both sugars until smooth and well blended. Beat in the eggs, vanilla, and peanut butter. Place a sifter over this bowl and measure into it the flour, baking soda, and salt. Stir/sift these dry ingredients onto the peanut butter mixture then slowly beat everything together until thoroughly incorporated.

3. Place the topping sugar in a small bowl. To make each cookie, scoop up a heaping teaspoon of dough, dip the top of the dough ball in the sugar, then push the dough ball off the spoon onto the sheet. Place the balls, sugar up, about 1 inch apart. With the tines of a table fork pressed in a crosshatch pattern, flatten each dough ball to a scant ¼ inch thick.

4. Bake the cookies for 12 to 15 minutes, or until they begin to color very slightly on top and turn golden brown around the edges. Watch carefully because they can quickly over-brown on the bottom. Slide the piece of parchment onto a wire rack, or place the cookie sheet on a wire rack to cool for 3 or 4 minutes, then use a spatula to transfer the warm cookies to the rack to cool. Store in an airtight container.

Impossible Peanut Butter Cookies

IMPOSSIBLE, BUT TRUE! These *flourless* cookies contain just three ingredients and are so unbelievably quick and easy to make that even the youngest baker can help. They taste good, too, though a little sweet. Since there are so few ingredients, the amount of sugar and the peanut flavor vary depending upon the brand of peanut butter used.

I have no idea where this recipe originated (perhaps a peanut butter manufacturer), but it has been around a very long time. I once found a copy dating from the 1950s at a Vermont auction, carefully penciled into a child's scrapbook.

for good measure

> To add extra crunch, set out small bowls of chopped peanuts, walnuts, pecans, and/or toasted wheat germ. After scooping up each tablespoon of dough, press it into the chopped ingredients before flattening it on the baking sheet. Bake as directed.

special equipment: Cookie sheets; baking parchment, optional; flat paddle attachment for electric mixer, if available

advance preparation: Cookies can be kept airtight at room temperature a week or double-wrapped and frozen up to 3 months.

temperature and time: 350°F for 12 to 14 minutes

yield: About 36 cookies (2-inch diameter)

Butter or solid shortening for preparing pans, optional

1 large egg, at room temperature

1 cup granulated sugar

1 cup peanut butter, plain or chunky

1. Position racks to divide the oven into thirds and preheat it to 350°F. Line the cookie sheets with baking parchment or lightly coat with butter.

2. In a mixing bowl with a sturdy spoon or in an electric mixer fitted with a paddle attachment if available, beat all the ingredients together until completely blended.

Scoop up the batter by the level tablespoon and use another spoon or your fingertip to push the dough onto the prepared baking sheet, placing the cookies about 1 inch apart. Flatten the top of each cookie by dipping the tines of a fork into water to dampen, then pressing lightly on top of each cookie in a cross-hatch pattern. Or, use a damp finger to flatten each cookie until it is about ¼ inch thick.

3. Bake the cookies 12 to 14 minutes, or until they begin to color very sightly on top and turn golden brown around the edges. Slide the piece of parchment onto a wire rack, or place the cookie sheet on a rack to cool for 3 or 4 minutes, then use a spatula to transfer the cookies to the rack to cool. Store in an airtight container.

Anna Olson's Spritz Cookies

BUTTERY *SPRITSAR* ARE traditional Swedish Christmas cookies usually shaped with a special cylindrical cookie press, or *spritz-spruta*. You can also roll out the dough and cut it with cookie cutters or shape it by hand.

When my sister and I were children, a delightful woman named Anna Olson taught us how to bake spritz cookies and they have been favorites ever since. (See page 1.)

for good measure

> Spritz cookies are traditionally almond-flavored; if you prefer, you can substitute vanilla, orange or lemon extract.

special equipment: Cookie press (sold in cookware shops or by mail order; see Mail-Order Sources and Suppliers, page 240); sifter; wax paper or plastic wrap; cookie sheets; baking parchment, optional; pastry brush

advance preparation: Dough can be prepared, wrapped, and refrigerated several days; baked cookies can be kept in an airtight container at room temperature 3 or 4 days or double-wrapped and frozen up to 2 months.

temperature and time: 350°F for 8 to 12 minutes

yield: About 60 cookies (1½-inch diameter)

dough

1 cup (2 sticks) unsalted butter, at room temperature, cut up

½ cup granulated sugar

1 large egg yolk, at room temperature

1 teaspoon almond extract

2¼ to 2½ cups unsifted all-purpose flour

glaze

1 large egg white, at room temperature

decorations

Granulated white or tinted sugar

Finely chopped almonds

1. Position a rack in the center of the oven and preheat it to 350°F.

2. In a large bowl using a sturdy spoon or an electric mixer, beat together the butter and sugar until smooth and well blended. Beat in the egg yolk and extract. Scrape down the bowl and beater. Place a sifter over the bowl, add 2¼ cups of the flour, and sift it onto the butter mixture below. Slowly mix in the flour. Form the dough into a ball; if it feels too sticky to handle, knead in 1 or 2 additional tablespoons of flour. Wrap the dough in wax paper and refrigerate it about 30 minutes, or overnight.

3. To shape the cookies: Use the press following the manufacturer's directions. Add the dough to the tube and press out the cookies onto *ungreased* baking sheets (they may be lined with baking parchment if you wish), leaving about 1 inch between them. Wait a few seconds for the dough to adhere to the sheet before you twist the press slightly and lift it straight up. The cookie should stay flat on the tray. If the cookies do not press out easily, chill the baking sheet a few minutes in the refrigerator or add another egg yolk to the dough if it feels too stiff to press out.

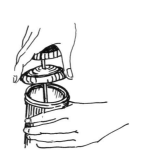

4. To mold the cookies by hand, you may need to add just a little more flour, so the dough doesn't stick to your fingers. Break off small bits of the dough and shape them with lightly floured fingers. Make walnut-size balls flattened with tines of a fork dipped in flour or confectioners' sugar, or roll pencil-thin ropes of dough and form small pretzels or wreaths. Or, roll out the dough on a lightly floured surface and cut shapes with cookie cutters.

5. To make the glaze: Lightly beat the egg white with a teaspoon of water. With a pastry brush, paint the glaze over the cookies, then sprinkle on the sugar, nuts, or other decorations. Bake 8 to 12 minutes, or until the cookies are slightly golden around the edges but still pale on top. Transfer the cookies to a wire rack to cool; if baked on parchment, simply slide the parchment onto the wire rack and let them cool. Store the cookies layered with wax paper in an airtight container.

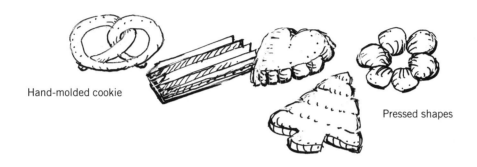

Hand-molded cookie

Pressed shapes

Gingerbread Cut-Outs

CHILDREN LOVE TO make these traditional holiday spice cookies. You can cut them with cookie cutters or design your own shapes by drawing around handmade stencils. This recipe for *pepparkakor* comes from Sweden, where cut-outs of pigs, horses, and roosters decorated with white sugar icing are popular Christmas motifs. Try angels, trees, teddy bears, and of course, gingerbread men and women. For Chanukah, cut out dreidel (top) shapes or six-pointed stars.

for good measure

- **To make Cookie Tree Ornaments,** use a drinking straw or a toothpick to poke ⅛-inch holes in the top of cut-out cookies before baking, then widen holes as soon as cookies come out of the oven. Decorate cookies, then tie thin red ribbons through the holes to make hanging loops.

- **To make Party Placecards,** cut out and bake 2 × 3-inch dough rectangles and write guests' names in icing.

- **To make Cookie Gift Tags,** cut out cookie cutter shapes and poke a hanging hole in one end; bake, write name in icing, and tie the tag onto a gift.

- **To measure molasses easily,** use an oiled measuring cup.

- **To avoid possible risk from salmonella bacteria** arising from use of uncooked egg whites, you can make icing with meringue powder sold in gourmet shops, or see Mail-Order Sources and Suppliers, page 240. As a general rule of thumb, 1 tablespoon dried egg white powder + 2 tablespoons warm water = 1 fresh egg white. If you prefer to use fresh egg whites, see recipe below for classic royal icing.

special equipment: Cookie sheets; baking parchment, optional; sifter; rolling pin; cookie cutters or stiff paper and scissors; paring knife; drinking straw or toothpick (to make hanging holes); plastic wrap; decorating tube fitted with #5 or #6 plain round tip, or a self-sealing freezer-style pint-size plastic bag with tiny hole cut in one corner; red ribbon, optional, for hanging shapes

advance preparation: Dough can be prepared 1 or 2 days before rolling out and kept covered in the refrigerator. Baked cookies can be double-wrapped and frozen up to 2 months.

temperature and time: 350°F for 8 to 10 minutes

yield: About 50 cookies (3-inch diameter) or about 30 figures (5 inches tall)

dough

Butter-flavor no-stick vegetable spray or solid shortening for preparing pans

½ cup (1 stick) unsalted butter or solid stick margarine, softened

½ cup packed dark brown sugar

½ cup molasses

1 large egg, at room temperature

3 to 3⅓ cups unsifted all-purpose flour, plus extra as needed for rolling out

½ teaspoon salt

½ teaspoon baking soda

1 teaspoon ground cloves

1 teaspoon ground cinnamon

½ teaspoon ground nutmeg

½ teaspoon ground allspice or cardamom

2½ teaspoons ground ginger

decorations

Raisins, chopped nuts, cherries, silver dragées, cinnamon hot candies, vegetable food coloring (liquid, powder, or paste type)

(choose one) meringue powder royal icing

3 tablespoons meringue powder

6 tablespoons warm water, or as needed

4 cups (1 pound) sifted confectioners' sugar

or classic royal icing

2 large egg whites, at room temperature

⅛ teaspoon cream of tartar

⅛ teaspoon salt

3½ cups sifted confectioners' sugar, or as needed

2 tablespoons fresh lemon juice, or as needed

1. Position racks to divide the oven into thirds and preheat it to 350°F. Lightly coat the cookie sheets with vegetable spray or solid shortening or cover them with baking parchment.

2. In a large bowl using a sturdy spoon or an electric mixer, beat together the butter and brown sugar until very soft, well blended, and without lumps. Beat in the molasses and egg. Scrape down the bowl and beater.

3. Sift directly onto the butter mixture 3 cups of the flour, plus the salt, baking soda, and all spices. Slowly mix all the ingredients together until thoroughly incorporated. If the dough feels sticky to the touch, add more flour 1 tablespoon at a time, up to ⅓ cup, until the dough is soft and pliable but not sticky.

4. To shape cookies: Use about one-third of the dough at a time; wrap and refrigerate the remainder until needed. Roll out the dough on a lightly floured surface to about ⅛ inch thick (a little thicker if the cookies will be hung on a tree). Cut shapes with the floured cookie cutters or use a sharp paring knife to cut around your own handmade paper stencils (rub flour on paper stencil before placing it on the dough so it will not stick). Peel away the dough from between the cut shapes and use a wide floured spatula to transfer the cookies to a baking sheet, placing them about 1 inch apart. Reroll the scraps and cut more shapes. Press on the raisins, nuts, or candies for eyes, nose, and buttons. Use a drinking straw or toothpick to poke a ⅛-inch-wide hole in the top of the cookies that will be hung up by a ribbon loop or tied onto a gift package.

5. Bake the cookies for 8 to 10 minutes, or until firm to the touch and a slightly darker color around the edges. Cool the cookies on the pan set on a wire rack for 3 or 4 minutes; use a straw or tooth-pick to widen precut hanging holes. With a spatula, slide the cookies onto a wire rack to cool completely. You should not have to regrease the pans before baking additional batches of cookies.

6. Select *one* of the icing recipes. If using the meringue powder royal icing, whisk together the powder and warm water, then let it sit about 3 minutes so the powder can absorb some liquid. Add the sifted sugar and beat with an electric mixer on lowest speed until the icing is smooth and about the consistency of softly whipped cream, forming soft peaks. Add a teaspoon or two more warm water if the icing is too stiff to spread.

If using the classic royal icing, combine all the ingredients and beat with an electric mixer on lowest speed until the icing is smooth and thick. Adjust the consistency by adding sugar or liquid until spreadable.

Note: Both types of royal icing air-harden quickly; keep the bowl covered at all times with plastic wrap or a damp towel. You may need to add a few drops more water after the icing stands for a period of time.

7. To decorate completely cooled cookies: Place the icing in a decorating tube or a small plastic bag with a very tiny hole cut in a corner, and draw designs on the cookies. To add colors, place a small amount of icing in cups and tint it by stirring in a drop or two of food coloring. To paint on the icing, thin it with a little water. When the icing is dry and hard to the touch, tie ribbons through the cookies that will hang on a tree. Store the cookies layered with wax paper in an airtight container.

Thumbalinas

I NAMED THESE old-fashioned thumb print cookies for the thumb-sized heroine of Hans Christian Andersen's story. Thumbalinas or thumb prints are especially fun to make with children, who love to stick their thumbs—or fingertips—into the dough balls to shape the well so it can be filled with fruit preserves. For the most attractive presentation, vary the color and type of preserves used: apricot, blueberry, strawberry, or gooseberry.

for good measure

> Instead of jam, the cookies can be filled with halved candied cherries or other dried fruits, dates, pudding, chocolate chips, or halved nuts.

special equipment: Cookie sheets; sifter

advance preparation: Dough can be made a day ahead, covered, and refrigerated. Baked cookies can be kept about 2 weeks, stored between layers of wax paper in an airtight container, or double-wrapped and frozen up to 1 month.

temperature and time: 350°F for about 15 minutes

yield: 26 to 28 cookies (1¼-inch diameter)

½ **cup sifted confectioners' sugar**

1 **cup (2 sticks) unsalted butter, at room temperature, cut up**

½ **teaspoon salt**

2 **teaspoons vanilla extract**

2 **cups unsifted all-purpose flour**

¾ **cup (3 ounces) finely chopped walnuts, optional**

¾ **cup fruit preserves, total (¼ cup each of several types and colors)**

1. Position racks to divide the oven into thirds and preheat it to 350°F.

2. In the large bowl of an electric mixer, beat together the confectioners' sugar, butter, salt, and vanilla until smooth and creamy. With the mixer on its lowest speed, gradually add in the flour. The dough can be used right away, or it can be covered and chilled several hours or overnight.

3. To shape the cookies: Pinch off walnut-size lumps of dough and roll them between the palms of your hands. If you want to coat the cookies with chopped nuts, roll the dough ball in the chopped nuts in a small bowl. Place the dough balls on an *ungreased* cookie sheet. Repeat, placing the cookies about 1 inch apart. With your thumb or fingertip, press a small well in the top of each cookie and fill with about ¼ teaspoon of fruit preserves. Bake the cookies 15 minutes, or until lightly golden. Transfer the cookies to a wire rack to cool, then store them layered with wax paper in an airtight container.

> **Walnut Thumbalinas:** Add ½ cup (2 ounces) finely chopped walnuts to the batter along with the flour.

Glazed Lemon Thins

THESE CRISP, LEMON-GLAZED slices are old-fashioned refrigerator cookies cut from a chilled roll of dough. Like others of this type, they are easy to prepare in advance, then slice and bake fresh when needed.

for good measure

- Brush on the lemon glaze while the cookies are still very warm so the glaze will melt into a shiny, hard coating.

- If you don't have lemon extract, add one extra tablespoon lemon juice to the batter (3 tablespoons total).

special equipment: Cookie sheets; grater; sifter; wax paper or plastic wrap; baking parchment, optional; pastry brush

advance preparation: For dough plus glaze you will need a total of 1 tablespoon of grated lemon zest and 3½ tablespoons of lemon juice, prepared in advance from 1 large or 3 small lemons. Prepare dough well before cookies are to be baked because it must be chilled until firm enough to slice. This takes 1 hour minimum in the freezer (dough can be kept frozen up to 2 months), or 2 hours in the refrigerator (or up to 1 week). Cookies can be kept in an airtight container at room temperature about 1 week or double-wrapped and frozen up to 2 months.

temperature and time: 350°F for 10 to 12 minutes

yield: 65 to 70 cookies (⅛ inch thick, 2-inch diameter); yield depends upon thickness of slices

dough

½ cup (1 stick) unsalted butter, at room temperature

1 cup granulated sugar

1 large egg, at room temperature

2 teaspoons grated lemon zest

2 tablespoons fresh lemon juice

1 teaspoon lemon extract

2 cups unsifted all-purpose flour

3 tablespoons unsifted confectioners' sugar

2 tablespoons cornstarch

½ teaspoon baking soda

Butter or solid shortening for preparing pans

glaze

¾ cup sifted confectioners' sugar

1 teaspoon grated lemon zest

1½ tablespoons fresh lemon juice

1. In a large bowl using a sturdy spoon or an electric mixer, beat together the butter and sugar until smooth and well blended. Beat in the egg and all the lemon flavoring. Scrape down the bowl and beater. Place a sifter over this bowl and measure into it the flour, confectioners' sugar, cornstarch, and baking soda. Stir/sift the dry ingredients onto the wet mixture below, then slowly beat everything together until thoroughly incorporated.

2. Divide the dough in thirds. Turn each portion out onto a piece of lightly floured wax paper or plastic wrap, and roll into a log 3½ inches long and 2 inches in diameter. When slicing chilled dough, work with one portion at a time and keep the rest cold. Set the dough logs in the freezer for at least 1 hour or refrigerate at least 2 hours, or overnight. If the logs are too hard to slice once frozen, let them sit at room temperature a minute or two.

3. Position a rack in the center of the oven and preheat it to 350°F. Butter the cookie sheets or cover them with baking parchment.

With a sharp knife, cut the hard-chilled dough into thin slices (about ⅛ inch) and place them on the prepared baking sheets about 1½ inches apart. Bake 10 to 12 minutes, or until the cookies are light golden brown around the edges. While the cookies bake, prepare the glaze: In a small bowl, mix together all the glaze ingredients until thick and creamy.

4. Once baked, use a spatula to transfer the hot cookies onto a wire rack set over a protective sheet of wax paper. Working with each batch as soon as it comes from the oven, use a pastry brush or the back of a spoon to paint the still-hot cookies with the glaze, which will melt, then become shiny and hard as it air-dries. Store the cookies layered with wax paper in an airtight container.

Quick Walnut Slices

WHENEVER YOU NEED a snack, you can slice-and-bake these tender-crisp nut cookies from a log of chilled dough. The ideal refrigerator cookie, they are quick to make, always on hand, and great for holiday entertaining. The dough is assembled most quickly in a food processor, but it can also be combined in an electric mixer or by hand.

for good measure

- To vary the flavor, substitute pecans, peanuts, almonds, or macadamias.
- The thinner the slice, the crisper the cookie.

special equipment: Food processor or nut chopper; cookie sheets, baking parchment, optional; ruler; wax paper or plastic wrap

advance preparation: Prepare dough well before cookies are to be baked because it must be chilled until firm enough to slice. This takes 1 hour minimum in the freezer (dough can be frozen up to 2 months), or 2 hours in the refrigerator (or up to 1 week). Cookies can be kept in an airtight container at room temperature about 1 week or double-wrapped and frozen up to 2 months.

temperature and time: 375°F for 8 to 10 minutes

yield: 30 to 40 cookies (¼ inch thick, 2-inch diameter); yield depends upon thickness of slices

dough

¾ **cup (3 ounces) walnut pieces**

½ **cup granulated sugar, divided (¼ cup and ¼ cup)**

1 **cup unsifted all-purpose flour**

½ **teaspoon salt**

⅓ **cup (5⅓ tablespoons) unsalted butter, at room temperature, cut up**

topping

3 **tablespoons granulated sugar, or as needed**

1. In the workbowl of a food processor, combine the nuts and ¼ cup of the sugar and pulse until nuts are chopped medium-fine.

2. Add the remaining ¼ cup sugar along with the flour, salt, and butter and pulse until the dough forms large crumbs and looks lumpy; don't overwork it or try to make a ball. Dump the dough out onto a piece of wax paper on the counter. Use your hands to squeeze it together into a ball; the warmth of your hands softens the butter so it can be molded. If the dough remains too crumbly, work in about 1 teaspoon of water.

3. Divide the ball in half and roll each piece into a log about 1½ inches in diameter and 7 or 8 inches long. Roll the logs in wax paper or plastic wrap, compressing the dough tightly, then put them in an airtight plastic bag and refrigerate or freeze until firm, about 2 hours or overnight.

4. Position a rack in the center of the oven and preheat it to 375°F.

Once the dough is firm, use a sharp knife to cut the logs into scant ¼-inch-thin slices and place them about 1 inch apart on an *ungreased* cookie a sheet or on a sheet covered with baking parchment. Sprinkle a pinch of granulated sugar on top of each cookie and bake for 8 to 10 minutes, or just until the edges begin to look golden brown. Cool the cookies on a wire rack. Store in an airtight container.

Peek-a-Boo Walnut Sandwich Slices: To make sandwich cookies, spread your favorite jam between two baked and cooled walnut slices. Or, before baking, cut a hole in each of the top cookies; when they are sandwiched you can peek at the jam in the middle.

Cornmeal Crisps

THESE THIN BUTTERY crisps, crunchy with cornmeal, are easy-to-prepare refrigerator cookies. Simply mix the dough in advance, chill it until firm, then slice and bake when you are ready. The recipe was shared with me by John George, pastry chef at 647 Tremont Street Restaurant in Boston, Massachusetts. John likes to sandwich the cookies with raspberry preserves, but their flavor is so delicate, I prefer them plain; try them both ways and decide for yourself.

special equipment: Cookie sheets; sifter; baking parchment, optional; plastic wrap or wax paper

advance preparation: Allow at least 2 hours for dough to chill before slicing and baking, or prepare it a day in advance. Or, wrap dough and freeze it up to 1 month. Slice while partially frozen, so dough is still firm.

temperature and time: 350°F for 8 to 9 minutes

yield: About 36 cookies, (⅛ inch thick, 2½-inch diameter); yield depends on thickness of slices

dough

1¼ cups sifted all-purpose flour

1 teaspoon baking powder

¼ teaspoon salt

1 cup (2 sticks) unsalted butter, at room temperature

1 cup granulated sugar

1 large egg, at room temperature

1 teaspoon vanilla extract

1 cup yellow cornmeal

Butter or solid shortening for preparing pans, optional

topping, optional

Confectioners' sugar

1. In a medium bowl, whisk together the flour, baking powder, and salt. Set it aside.

In the large bowl of an electric mixer, beat together the butter and sugar until smooth and well blended. Beat in the egg and vanilla. Scrape down the bowl and beater. Beat in the cornmeal, then with the mixer on lowest speed, blend in the flour mixture.

2. Turn the dough out onto a lightly floured surface and form it into a ball. Divide the ball in half and shape each portion into a roll about 7 inches long and 1½ inches in diameter. Wrap the rolls in plastic wrap or wax paper and refrigerate about 2 hours (or overnight), until hard-chilled.

3. Position racks to divide the oven into thirds and preheat it to 350°F. Lightly coat the cookie sheets with butter or shortening or cover them with baking parchment. With a sharp knife, cut the hard-chilled dough into slices ⅛ inch thick and place them about 2 inches apart on the prepared baking sheets. Bake 8 to 9 minutes, or until the edges just begin to turn golden brown. Cool the sheets on a wire rack for 3 to 4 minutes, then use a spatula to transfer the cookies to the rack to cool completely. Store in an airtight container. Before serving, lightly sift a little confectioners' sugar on top of the cookies.

Raspberry Sandwich Cookies: Spread about ¾ teaspoon seedless raspberry (or apricot) preserves between pairs of baked and cooled cookies. Yield: 18 sandwiches

Rosemary-Honey Cookies

I FIRST TASTED these unusual cookies in San Diego, California, where rosemary grows into tall, fragrant bushes, luxurious flowers and ubiquitous herbs know no bounds, and honeys are made from absolutely everything in sight. These buttery cookies have a chewy/crisp texture and a unique flavor that depends upon the strength and quality of both the rosemary and the honey. The dried herb can be substituted if aromatic and flavorful.

for good measure

If using dried rosemary, measure it into a small self-sealing plastic bag or mortar and pestle and crush the leaves very finely before adding them to the batter.

special equipment: Cookie sheets; small plastic bag and rolling pin (to crush dry rosemary if used)

advance preparation: Cookies stay fresh at least a week when kept in an airtight container.

temperature and time: 325°F for 12 to 14 minutes

yield: 30 to 34 cookies (3-inch diameter)

½ **cup solid shortening, plus extra for preparing pans**

¼ **cup (½ stick) unsalted butter, softened but not melted**

¾ **cup granulated sugar**

1 **large egg, at room temperature**

¼ **cup honey**

1 **tablespoon fresh lemon juice**

1 **teaspoon grated lemon or orange zest**

2 **cups sifted all-purpose flour**

1 **teaspoon baking soda**

½ **teaspoon salt**

½ **teaspoon ground cinnamon**

¼ **teaspoon ground nutmeg**

1 **tablespoon fresh rosemary, very finely chopped, or 2 teaspoons dried, finely crushed**

1. Position the racks to divide the oven into thirds and preheat it to 325°F. Coat the cookie sheets with solid shortening and set them aside.

2. In a large mixing bowl with a sturdy spoon or an electric mixer, beat together the shortening, butter, and sugar until smooth and well blended. Beat in the egg, honey, juice, and grated zest. On top of this mixture, add all the dry ingredients and the rosemary, then slowly stir or beat everything together until just incorporated.

3. Drop heaping teaspoons of batter on the cookie sheet, placing them 2 inches apart so the cookies can spread. Bake 12 to 14 minutes, or until golden brown with a slightly darker edge. Allow the cookies to cool on the baking sheet about 5 minutes, then use a spatula to transfer them to a wire rack. The cookies get crisper as they cool. Store in an airtight container.

Mocha Kisses

MERINGUE COOKIES, ALSO called angel kisses, are quick, easy-to-make, melt-in-your-mouth delights. This mocha variation was tested by Rachel Fagiano, ten-year-old daughter of New Jersey food writer Marge Perry.

for good measure

> To make Vanilla Angel Kisses, omit the coffee and cocoa.

special equipment: Cookie sheets; baking parchment or aluminum foil; sifter

advance preparation: Kisses can be kept in an airtight container at room temperature about 2 weeks, or double-wrapped and frozen up to 1 month.

temperature and time: 250°F for 40 to 45 minutes

yield: About 48 cookies (1¼-inch diameter at base)

Butter-flavor no-stick cooking spray or solid shortening for preparing pans

Flour for preparing pans

1½ teaspoons powdered instant coffee

1½ teaspoons vanilla extract

3 large egg whites, at room temperature

⅛ teaspoon cream of tartar

⅛ teaspoon salt

¾ cup superfine or granulated sugar

2 tablespoons unsweetened cocoa, preferably Dutch-processed

1. Position racks to divide the oven into thirds and preheat it to 250°F. Line the cookie sheets with baking parchment or foil placed shiny side down; "glue" the parchment or foil to the pans with a few dabs of butter or shortening. Coat the parchment or foil lightly with cooking spray or shortening and dust with flour; shake off excess flour.

2. In a cup, stir the coffee powder into the vanilla extract until dissolved. Set it aside.

3. In the large bowl of an electric mixer, combine the egg whites, cream of tartar, and salt and beat on medium speed until foamy. Gradually add the sugar and continue beating until you see the beater tracks on the whites and they form medium-stiff peaks. Add the coffee liquid and beat until the whites are satiny smooth and hold stiff peaks. Remove the bowl from the mixer stand and use a spatula to fold in the cocoa; the meringue may look slightly streaked.

4. To form the kisses, scoop out a teaspoon of meringue and use a second teaspoon to push it off onto the prepared cookie sheet, forming a peaked cone with a base about 1 inch in diameter. (Alternatively, you can pipe the kisses from a pastry bag fitted with a ½-inch star tip.) Place the kisses about 1 inch apart on the sheets.

5. Bake 40 to 45 minutes, or until the kisses are dry to the touch. After about 20 minutes, switch the positions of the baking sheets in the oven. Slide the parchment or foil off the baking sheets onto wire racks and leave the cookies on the sheets to cool 10 to 15 minutes or until completely crisp and cold. Peel the cookie bottoms off the sheets and store them in an airtight container.

Write-Your-Own Fortune Cookies

FORTUNE COOKIES ARE easy and fun to make at home—especially if you are having a party. Everyone enjoys writing the paper fortunes. For a children's party, let the kids write riddles or jokes on colored paper strips to read aloud to each other when the cookies are broken up. Adults enjoy giving fortune cookies as gifts packaged in Chinese food take-out cartons.

Before making the cookies, prepare twenty-two slips of white or colored paper (¼ × 2 or 3 inches) with a fortune (written with nontoxic ink) on each. If you want to wrap individual cookies, you can purchase small cellophane bags in some stationery or party supply stores, or you can wrap cookies in squares of plastic wrap.

For the authentic Chinese fortune cookie flavor, you need sesame oil, available in many supermarkets and Asian markets; regular vegetable oil can be substituted. *Note:* Children can prepare the paper strips, but adults should shape the cookies because they must be handled while still very hot.

for good measure

- If you are working alone, bake the cookies no more than 2 or 3 at a time so that you can shape them while they are still warm and flexible; they cool and harden very quickly.

- In very humid weather, the shaped cookies may soften; to recrisp, leave them in the muffin cups to hold their shape and place them in a preheated 300°F oven for about 10 minutes to dry out, then cool in pans on a wire rack.

special equipment: Paper fortunes; 2 cookie sheets (not nonstick); glass or jar with 3-inch diameter top (to mark cookie size on baking sheet); pottery bowl or large measuring cup with a thick rim (for shaping cookies); muffin pans with 2- to 2½-inch-diameter cups; sifter

advance preparation: Cookies will keep crisp at least a week if stored in an airtight container or double-wrapped and frozen in a crush-proof box up to 1 month.

temperature and time: 400°F for 3½ to 4½ minutes

yield: 22 to 30 cookies; yield depends upon thickness of cookies

Butter or solid shortening for preparing pans
½ cup sifted all-purpose flour
½ cup granulated sugar
¼ teaspoon salt
2 large egg whites, at room temperature
½ teaspoon sesame oil
½ teaspoon vanilla extract

1. Position a rack in the center of the oven and preheat it to 400°F. Butter the cookie sheets. Turn a 3-inch-diameter glass or jar upside down and press the top onto the greased cookie sheets, marking 2 or 3 rings several inches apart on each sheet.

2. In the large bowl of an electric mixer, combine all the ingredients and beat on medium speed until the batter looks smooth and creamy.

3. Drop 1 teaspoon of the batter into the center of each marked circle, then use the back of a teaspoon dipped into cold water to spread the batter into an even thin layer neatly filling the 3-inch circle. Repeat. If you are working by yourself, bake and shape 2 or 3 cookies before making more. Each batch must go on a clean, cooled and re-buttered cookie sheet. Bake the cookies 3½ to 4½ minutes; watch carefully—they bake so fast you can almost stand and watch. Peek at them often and remove them from the oven as soon as the edges *begin* to turn golden brown; the center will still be pale. Over-baked cookies will be too crisp to fold. As soon as the cookies are done, set the baking sheet on a wire rack and shape the cookies *immediately.* Work with one cookie at a time. Use a broad spatula or pancake turner to slide the cookie off the baking sheet, turn the cookie *upside down,* and place a paper fortune in the center. Fold the cookie in half over the paper (see sketches). Grasp both ends of the cookie, place the middle of the folded edge on the rim of a bowl or measuring cup, and gently but firmly pull down on the ends to curve the cookie. At the same time, run your thumb over the top edge to make it fold if it doesn't happen automatically while bending. Hold the curve for a few seconds, then set the cookie, tips down, into a muffin cup to cool and crisp completely. Repeat, using up all the batter. Store in an airtight container.

Mexican Wedding Cookies

KNOWN IN SPANISH as *Pastelitos de Boda,* or Bride's Little Cakes, these butter-rich, melt-in-your-mouth treats are served at Mexican weddings as well as on Christmas Eve. Packed with very finely chopped nuts, the just-baked cookies are rolled in powdered sugar while hot to create a meltingly sweet coating on the outside surface. There are closely related cookies in many other countries, including *kourabiedes* in Greece and *butterhornchen* in Austria. This version is my favorite. For a popular holiday gift, layer the cookies in powdered sugar and pack them in a decorative glass container with the recipe attached.

for good measure

- To change the flavor, change the nuts— try pecans, hazelnuts, or macadamia nuts.
- You can replace the almond extract with more vanilla (1½ teaspoons, total) or add 1 teaspoon lemon or orange or hazelnut extract along with 1 teaspoon vanilla.
- Cake flour makes a slightly more tender cookie but 2¼ cups sifted all-purpose flour can be substituted.

special equipment: Cookie sheets; baking parchment, optional; wax paper; sifter

advance preparation: Cookies can be kept in an airtight container at room temperature up to a week or double-wrapped and frozen up to 2 months.

temperature and time: 350°F for 15 to 20 minutes

yield: About 45 cookies (1¼-inch diameter)

1 cup (2 sticks) butter, at room temperature, cut up

2½ cups sifted cake flour

½ cup sifted confectioners' sugar

½ teaspoon salt

1 cup finely chopped walnuts or almonds

1 teaspoon vanilla extract

¼ teaspoon almond extract

2 cups sifted confectioners' sugar, for rolling and storing cookies

1. Position racks to divide the oven into thirds and preheat it to 350°F. Leave the cookie sheets ungreased or cover them with baking parchment.

2. In a large bowl using a sturdy spoon or an electric mixer on lowest speed, beat the butter until smooth and creamy, then work in the flour, ½ cup of sugar, salt, nuts, and extracts.

3. With lightly floured fingers, pinch off small lumps of dough, roll them between your palms into walnut-size balls, and set them on the cookie sheet about 1 inch apart. Bake for 15 to 20 minutes, or until a pale golden color.

4. While the cookies bake, sift about 2 cups of confectioners' sugar into a medium-size bowl and place a sheet of wax paper or baking parchment on a tray nearby. After baking, let the cookie sheet sit on a wire rack to cool about 4 to 5 minutes, then pick up each still-warm-but-not-hot cookie, roll it in the powdered sugar to coat well, then set it on wax paper to cool completely. Store the cookies in an airtight container layered with additional sifted confectioners' sugar.

Black and White Chocolate Crackles

FOR SERIOUS CHOCOLATE lovers. These black and white chocolate cookies have a shiny crackled finish and a chewy texture somewhere between a cookie and a brownie. The flavor is controlled by the quality of the chocolate used, so select the best semisweet or bittersweet and white chocolate available, in chips or solid bars, chopped.

for good measure

> For stronger coffee flavor, use 1 tablespoon instant espresso coffee powder.

special equipment: Double boiler or metal bowl set over a larger pan; parchment paper, optional

advance preparation: Cookies can be kept airtight at room temperature up to a week or double-wrapped and frozen up to 2 months.

temperature and time: 350°F for 12 minutes

yield: About 36 cookies (2½-inch diameter)

1¾ cups (11 ounces) bittersweet (not unsweetened) or semisweet chocolate chips or coarsely chopped chocolate, divided (1¼ cups and ½ cup)

½ cup (1 stick) unsalted butter, cut up, plus extra for preparing pans (optional)

¾ cup unsifted all-purpose flour

¼ teaspoon baking powder

¼ teaspoon salt

¼ teaspoon ground nutmeg

2 large eggs, at room temperature

¾ cup granulated sugar

2 teaspoons instant espresso powder

1 tablespoon vanilla extract

1 cup (4 ounces) coarsely chopped pecans

1 cup (6 ounces) best quality white chocolate chips (use largest size available), or solid white chocolate, very coarsely chopped (½-inch chunks)

1. Position racks to divide the oven into thirds. Coat the cookie sheets with butter or cover them with baking parchment.

2. In the top of a double boiler set over simmering water, melt 1¼ cups (about 8 ounces) of the bittersweet chocolate with the butter. Stir until smooth, remove the pan from the heat, and set it aside to cool.

3. Preheat the oven to 350°F. In a medium bowl, whisk together the flour, baking powder, salt, and nutmeg. Set it aside.

In a large bowl using a sturdy spoon or an electric mixer, beat together the eggs, sugar, espresso powder, and vanilla, then add the cooled chocolate mixture. Very slowly beat in the flour mixture, then stir in the chopped nuts, white chocolate, and the remaining ½ cup chopped dark chocolate. *Note: The batter is quite soft and fudgy when warm; this is correct and cookies are best baked now while the batter is soft. (It stiffens on chilling and if baked cold the cookies will taste fine but lack the shiny outer surface.)*

4. Drop the batter by rounded tablespoons on the prepared cookie sheets, placing them at least 2 inches apart. Bake about 12 minutes, until the cookies are dry, shiny, and crackled on top. Don't overbake, or the cookies get too hard. They are very soft inside when first baked; let the cookies sit on the sheets on a wire rack to cool 4 or 5 minutes, then use a broad spatula or pancake turner to transfer them to a wire rack to cool completely. Store in an airtight container.

Shortbread

SHORTBREAD IS A crisp/tender, melt-in-your mouth butter cookie made with very few ingredients and even less effort. Nothing is easier or more delicious.

In Scotland, there is a New Year's tradition known as First Footing, whereby a family's luck in the new year is determined by whoever is the first guest to set foot (first foot) in the door after the New Year strikes. For good luck, the first footer should lead with his right foot, have dark hair, and be carrying shortbread. According to tradition, Scottish shortbread is round (before being cut into wedges) because that is the shape of the sun, a reminder of pagan sun worship connected with the celebration of the new year; you can also shape shortbread into a rectangle and cut it into finger-size bars. For flavor variations, try Brown Sugar, Hazelnut, Ginger, Lemon or Orange, or Chocolate.

for good measure

In damp weather, you can recrisp shortbread by warming it in a 300°F oven for about 10 minutes.

special equipment: Sifter; cookie sheet; rolling pin; ruler

advance preparation: Shortbread can be kept airtight at room temperature for a week or double-wrapped and frozen up to 2 months.

temperature and time: 325°F for 25 to 35 minutes

yield: 8 large or 16 small wedges or 27 bars (1 × 3 inches)

1 cup (2 sticks) unsalted butter, at room
  temperature, cut up

½ cup sifted confectioners' sugar

2 cups unsifted all-purpose flour

½ teaspoon salt

1. Position a rack in the center of the oven and pre-heat it to 325°F.

2. In a large mixing bowl with a sturdy spoon or an electric mixer, beat together the butter and confectioners' sugar until smooth and well blended. Sift on the flour and salt and blend all together just until the dough forms large clumps. Turn the dough out onto a counter (not floured) and use your lightly floured hands to gather the dough into a ball. To keep the shortbread tender, it is important not to overhandle it.

3. Place the dough ball in the middle of an *ungreased* cookie sheet. Shape as follows.

To form a round shortbread divided into wedges: With lightly floured hands, pat the dough into a disk about ¾ inch thick and 8 inches in diameter. With a table fork dipped in flour, prick lines dividing the disk into quarters, then divide each quarter in half, making 8 wedges; do not separate the pieces. Or, to make smaller wedges, divide each quarter of the disk into 4 sections, making a total of 16 narrow wedges.

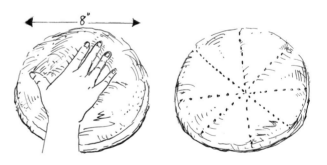

To shape bars: First pat the dough into a rough square. With a lightly floured rolling pin, roll the dough into a 9-inch square, ¼ inch thick. With a long-bladed sharp knife, divide the square crosswise

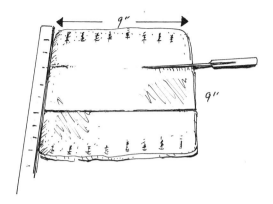

into three 3-inch sections and lengthwise into nine 1-inch sections; cut along the marked lines to make 27 bars but do not separate the pieces.

4. Bake a ¾-inch-thick disk for 25 to 35 minutes, or until dry to the touch and a pale golden color on top with barely darker edges. Use a wide spatula to slide the disk onto a wire rack to cool. When cold, carefully slide the shortbread disk onto a cutting board and cut into wedges using a sharp knife following the fork-marked lines. If you have made a square ¼-inch-thick shortbread, bake it 22 to 30 minutes, until dry to the touch, pale on top but with faintly darker edges. Remove from the oven but leave the shortbread on the baking sheet. Cool 2 or 3 minutes, then use a long-bladed sharp knife to neatly trim the edges square, cutting off a scant ⅛ inch all around; then neatly recut along the previously cut bar lines. Cool about 5 more minutes, then use a wide spatula to transfer the bars to a wire rack to cool completely. Store in an airtight container.

> **Brown Sugar Shortbread:** Prepare basic Shortbread but substitute ½ cup packed light or dark brown sugar for confectioners' sugar. Before baking, sprinkle on 2 or 3 tablespoons granulated sugar or finely chopped nuts. Cut and bake as directed above.

Hazelnut Shortbread with Chocolate Tips: Toast 1 cup (5 ounces) hazelnuts in a shallow pan at 350°F for about 8 minutes, then wrap them in a towel for a few minutes before rubbing to remove most of the skins. Finely chop the nuts. Prepare basic Shortbread but add, along with the flour, ¾ cup of the chopped hazelnuts (reserve the rest for a garnish) and ¼ teaspoon nutmeg. Shape the dough into 16 narrow wedges. To decorate, melt about ¾ cup (4½ ounces) semisweet chocolate chips in a double boiler set over simmering water. Dip the pointed tip of each baked and cooled wedge into the chocolate, then sprinkle it with reserved nuts and set it on wax paper to harden. Store shortbread wedges layered with wax paper in an airtight container.

Ginger Shortbread: Prepare basic Shortbread but add, along with flour, ½ teaspoon ground ginger and ¼ to ⅓ cup finely diced candied ginger. These are quite spicy—for ginger lovers. Shape the dough into 27 bars as directed above and bake 25 to 30 minutes.

Lemon or Orange Shortbread: Prepare basic Shortbread but add, along with the butter, 1½ teaspoons lemon or orange extract and 3 tablespoons grated lemon or orange zest.

Chocolate Shortbread: Prepare basic Shortbread but add an extra ½ cup sifted confectioners' sugar (1 cup total) and 1 teaspoon vanilla extract, beaten in with the butter. Reduce salt to ¼ teaspoon. Along with the flour and salt, sift in ½ cup unsweetened Dutch-process cocoa and a pinch of nutmeg. If the dough feels too powdery when you shape it into a ball, work in one or two drops of water. Pat the dough into a disk or a square and cut as directed above, but sprinkle with a little granulated sugar or cocoa if needed to prevent sticking as you shape the dough. Before baking, sprinkle over the dough a topping of 2 tablespoons granulated sugar mixed with ¼ teaspoon nutmeg. Bake about 30 minutes (for bars) to 35 minutes (for wedges).

Triple Chocolate–Nut Biscotti

BISCOTTI ARE CLASSIC Italian twice-baked cookies, easily prepared by making a dough log, then cutting it into slices, which are crisped with a second baking. They are the ultimate dunking cookie to serve with hot coffee, tea, or cocoa; perhaps the best known are the Tuscan biscotti di Prato, traditionally dipped into vin santo, a sweet dessert wine. This recipe is a triple treat for chocolate lovers because it contains both cocoa and chopped chocolate in the dough and has melted dark chocolate drizzled on top; if you want a color contrast, you can use white chocolate for the topping glaze. For extra flavor, I toast the nuts before using them; you can use hazelnuts, walnuts, pecans, or almonds.

for good measure

- To toast hazelnuts, place them in a shallow pan in a 350°F oven for about 8 minutes. Wrap them in a towel to steam a few minutes, then rub them to remove most of the skins. Chop and add them to the recipe as directed. Toast other nuts for 10 to 12 minutes.

- Quick Chocolate Melting Tip: For topping, put chips or chopped chocolate into a plastic bag, seal it tightly, and submerge it in a bowl of water that is very hot to the touch (135–140°F on an instant-read thermometer) until the chocolate melts. To use chocolate, cut a tiny hole in one corner of the bag and squeeze out the chocolate.

special equipment: Cookie sheet; baking parchment, optional; sifter; long spatula or pancake turner; double boiler or metal bowl set over a larger pan; wax paper

advance preparation: Biscotti can be stored at least 2 weeks in an airtight container at room temperature or double-wrapped and frozen up to 2 months.

temperature and time: First baking: 325°F for 30 minutes; second baking: 275°F for 15 to 20 minutes

yield: 36 to 42 cookies (about ½ inch thick)

dough

Butter-flavor no-stick cooking spray for preparing pan, optional

2½ cups unsifted all-purpose flour, or as needed

1½ teaspoons baking powder

½ teaspoon salt

¼ cup unsifted unsweetened cocoa, preferably Dutch-processed

3 tablespoons unsalted butter, softened

1 cup granulated sugar

3 large eggs, at room temperature

1 teaspoon vanilla extract

1½ teaspoons almond or hazelnut extract

¾ cup (about 4¼ ounces) coarsely chopped toasted hazelnuts (or combine nuts; for example, use ¼ cup chopped almonds or walnuts and ½ cup chopped hazelnuts)

½ cup (3 ounces) semisweet chocolate chips

topping

1 cup (6 ounces) semisweet chocolate chips or chopped bittersweet chocolate (or good-quality chopped white chocolate such as Baker's Premium or Lindt Swiss White)

1. Position a rack in the center of the oven and preheat it to 325°F. Lightly coat the cookie sheet with spray or cover it with baking parchment.

2. In a bowl, sift together the flour, baking powder, salt, and cocoa. In the large bowl of an electric mixer, beat together the butter and sugar until well blended into a paste, then beat in the eggs and both extracts. With the mixer on the lowest speed, add the flour mixture, chopped nuts, and chocolate chips all at once and beat just to combine. Scrape down the bowl and beater. Gather the dough into a ball and turn it out onto a lightly floured surface. Work in a tiny bit more flour if the dough feels too sticky to handle.

3. With floured fingers, divide the dough ball in half, then roll each half into a log approximately 13 inches long, 1½ inches wide, and 1 inch high. Place the logs about 2 inches apart on the cookie sheet. Gently flatten the tops of the logs, making them about 13½ × 1¾ × ¾ inches.

4. Bake the dough logs about 30 minutes, until they are dry on top and fairly firm to the touch; a cake tester inserted in the center should come out nearly clean, with just a trace of chocolate showing. Remove the pan from the oven and reduce the heat to 275°F.

Let the logs cool on their pan about 10 minutes, then use a long spatula to transfer them to a cutting board.

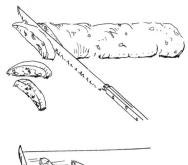

5. With a serrated knife and a sawing motion, cut the warm logs on the diagonal into ½-inch-thick slices. Place the slices cut side down on the same baking pan (don't regrease it). If necessary, use a second pan to hold the slices. Bake the slices 15 to 20 minutes this time, until dry and crisp; the longer they bake, the harder they will be—your choice. Note that they will get still harder when cold. Cool the biscotti on a wire rack set over a piece of wax paper (to catch drippings from the topping chocolate).

6. Prepare the topping while the biscotti bake. See the Quick Chocolate Melting Tip (For Good Measure) or measure chocolate chips into a small double boiler set over barely simmering water. Stir the chocolate until creamy and smooth. Place the baked biscotti close together on the cooling rack. Dip a fork into the melted chocolate and drizzle thin chocolate lines over the cookies. Cool the biscotti completely, then store them between layers of wax paper in an airtight container.

Raspberry Crumb Bars

BASED ON A classic shortbread recipe, this tender buttery cookie balances perfectly with its filling of sweet-tart raspberry preserves. The generous crumb topping is made with a portion of the dough mixed with oats and nuts. Easy to make and everyone's favorite, the recipe was developed by my daughter, Cassandra, who considers it a staple of her restaurant dessert repertoire.

for good measure

- Try other preserves for filling, such as apricot, cherry, or strawberry.

- Before serving, you can sift a tiny bit of confectioners' sugar over the top of the bars.

- To speed preparation, you can mix dough in the food processor but pulse for minimum length of time so dough will remain tender.

special equipment: 9 × 9 × 1½-inch baking pan; sifter; wax paper

advance preparation: Shortbread dough can be prepared a day in advance and stored refrigerated in a heavy-duty plastic bag. Cookies can be kept covered at room temperature several days or double-wrapped and frozen up to 1 month.

temperature and time: 375°F. First baking: 15 to 18 minutes; second baking: 20 to 24 minutes

yield: 16 bars approximately 2¼-inch square; recipe can be doubled and baked in a 9 × 13-inch pan

1 cup (2 sticks) unsalted butter, at room temperature, cut up, plus extra for preparing pan

½ cup sifted confectioners' sugar

2 cups unsifted all-purpose flour

½ teaspoon salt

½ cup old-fashioned rolled or quick-cooking oats (not instant)

½ cup (2 ounces) chopped walnuts

¾ cup seedless raspberry preserves

1. Position a rack in the center of the oven and preheat it to 375°F. Butter the baking pan.

2. In a large mixing bowl using a sturdy spoon or an electric mixer, beat together the butter and confectioners' sugar until completely smooth and well blended. Sift on the flour and salt and blend all together just until the dough forms crumbs or large clumps. Turn the dough out onto a piece of wax paper. With lightly floured hands, squeeze the dough into a rough ball. The warmth of your hands softens the butter and brings the dough together.

3. Divide the dough ball into thirds. Crumble one portion into a bowl and press the remaining portions in an even layer on the bottom of the prepared pan. Bake 15 to 18 minutes, or until golden brown around the edges and pale gold on top. Remove the pan to a heat-proof surface and let it cool.

4. Add the oats and nuts to the dough in the bowl and pinch it all together to form crumbs. Spread the preserves over the baked dough in the pan, then top evenly with the crumbs.

Return the pan to the oven to bake an additional 20 to 24 minutes, or until the crumbs are golden brown on top. Cool the pan on a wire rack, then divide each side into quarters and cut into 16 bars (2¼ × 2¼ inches). When the bars are cold, use a spatula to lift them onto a rack or plate, or serve them directly from the pan. The bars are extremely fragile while warm.

Lemon Squares

THIS CLASSIC RECIPE for a tender shortbread topped with tart lemon custard is such an essential part of my life that I have to include it here so I will always know where to find it. The original version was shared with me by my friend Susan "Charley" Kanas.

special equipment: 8 × 8 or 9 × 9 × 2-inch baking pan; grater; lemon squeezer; sifter

advance preparation: Squares can be baked a day in advance and refrigerated. They are best when fresh but will keep 3 or 4 days, covered and refrigerated.

temperature and time: 350°F for 20 minutes for dough alone, then 25 minutes longer with custard added

yield: 16 squares (2 × 2 inches)

dough

1 cup sifted all-purpose flour

½ cup (1 stick) unsalted butter, softened

¼ cup sifted confectioners' sugar

¼ teaspoon salt

custard filling

2 large eggs, at room temperature

1 cup granulated sugar

½ teaspoon baking powder

¼ teaspoon salt

2 teaspoons grated lemon zest

2 tablespoons fresh lemon juice

topping

1 tablespoon confectioners' sugar

1. Position a rack in the lower third of the oven and preheat it to 350°F.

In a mixing bowl using a sturdy spoon or an electric mixer, beat together the flour, butter, confectioners' sugar and ¼ teaspoon of salt until thoroughly blended. Press this dough into an even layer in the *ungreased* baking pan. The dough will look quite thin. Bake the dough for 20 minutes, then set the pan on a wire rack.

2. While the dough bakes, prepare the filling: In the large bowl of an electric mixer, beat together the eggs, granulated sugar, baking powder, lemon zest, and juice. Continue beating 3 to 4 minutes, until the mixture is pale in color and very foamy.

3. Pour the lemon mixture over the baked dough in the pan and return it to the oven to bake 25 minutes longer, or until no imprint of your finger remains on the top when lightly touched. Cool the pan on a wire rack. When cold, sift on the confectioners' sugar topping, then cut into 2-inch squares.

Picnic Raisin Squares

THIS FRUIT-FILLED bar cookie from my friend Carol Fyfield is similar to, but much better than, the store-bought raisin squares I loved when I was growing up. When made with dried cranberries and topped with icing glaze, these bars become a special treat for a holiday party; grown-ups enjoy them as much as kids. At taste-testing parties, these were always among the first cookies to disappear.

The recipe is not difficult to make, but takes a little more time to prepare than most regular cookies. Your reward is a tasty and unusual treat that you can make ahead and freeze for easy entertaining.

for good measure

- The pastry can be made like a pie crust in a bowl with a fork or a pastry blender or pinched together with your fingertips; however, I prefer to use a food processor, as it does the task so quickly and easily. If your processor bowl is not extra-large, you may want to do it in two batches.

- You can vary the filling by adding 1 cup finely chopped fresh or frozen cranberries or replacing the raisins altogether with Craisins or dried cranberries.

- Lemon zest and juice can be substituted for the orange.

special equipment: 2-quart saucepan; 10 × 15 × 1-inch jelly roll pan; wax paper; food processor or flat paddle attachment for electric mixer, if available; rolling pin

advance preparation: Both the raisin filling and the dough, separately, can be made a day or two in advance and refrigerated. If you have time, chill the dough about 30 minutes before baking to prevent it from shrinking. Cookies can be kept in an airtight container at room temperature for a week, or they can be layered with wax paper, double-wrapped, and frozen up to 2 months.

temperature and time: 350°F for 30 minutes

yield: 24 squares (2½ inches) or 30 bars (2 × 2½ inches)

raisin filling

3 cups lightly packed seedless raisins

About 2 cups water

½ cup granulated sugar

Grated zest of 1 large or 2 small oranges (2 to 3 tablespoons)

1 teaspoon ground cinnamon

½ teaspoon ground nutmeg

3 tablespoons all-purpose flour

pastry

Butter-flavor no-stick vegetable spray or solid shortening for preparing the pan

4½ cups sifted all-purpose flour, plus extra for preparing pan

1 teaspoon salt

¼ cup granulated sugar

1 cup (2 sticks) cold unsalted butter, cut up

½ cup chilled solid shortening (Crisco) or solid stick margarine

2 large egg yolks, at room temperature

2 tablespoons orange juice

½ cup milk

2 egg whites, at room temperature, plus 1 tablespoon water

½ cup apricot or plum preserves or orange marmalade

icing glaze

1 cup sifted confectioners' sugar

1 tablespoon unsalted butter, melted

½ teaspoon vanilla extract

2 tablespoons milk or water, or as needed

1. Prepare the filling: Put the raisins in the saucepan and add 2 cups of water, or enough to cover them. Cover the pot, set over high heat and bring to a boil, then uncover, lower heat, and simmer about 5 minutes until the raisins are plump and soft. Drain the raisins, discard the liquid (or save it to drink), and let the raisins cool for a few minutes. Stir in the sugar, orange zest, spices, and flour and mix thoroughly. Set the mixture aside to cool. You can do this up to 1 day in advance and refrigerate.

2. Coat the bottom and sides of the jelly roll pan with spray or shortening, dust with flour, and tap out the excess.

3. Prepare the pastry: Whisk or pulse together the flour, salt, and sugar in the workbowl of a food processor or the large bowl of an electric mixer, fitted with a paddle attachment, if available. Slowly mix in the butter and shortening until large crumbs form. Add yolks, orange juice, and milk and mix or pulse just until the dough begins to clump; don't form a dough ball or it will overwork and become tough. Turn out the crumbly, slightly powdery dough onto wax paper. Gather small bits of dough and slide the heel of your hand over them to press them together. Repeat, gathering together all the dough into a ball; divide it in half. Wrap and refrigerate the dough if time permits. You can make the dough up to this point and refrigerate it up to 1 day in advance, or you can use it right away.

4. Leave half the dough in the refrigerator. Roll the rest out between 2 lightly floured sheets of wax paper, making a rectangle about ½ inch larger all around than the jelly roll pan (test size by placing the pan over the dough). Peel off the top paper, invert the dough over the prepared pan, and peel off the backing paper. With lightly floured fingers, press the dough flat on the pan bottom and up the sides all around; trim away any dough overhang.

5. In a cup, make an egg white glaze by lightly beating together the egg whites and water. With a pastry brush, paint this all over the pastry and reserve the unused portion. Spread on the preserves, then the raisin filling, patting it into an even layer covering the bottom. Roll out the second piece of dough as above, position it over the filling, and peel off the paper. Press the dough into place, then use the tines

of a floured table fork to crimp or press the top and bottom pastry edges together all around to seal in the filling. Refrigerate the pan about 20 minutes to relax the dough and prevent it from shrinking.

6. Arrange a rack in the center of the oven and preheat it to 350°F. After the dough has chilled, brush some of the egg white glaze over the top of the pastry, then with the tip of a paring knife cut about 8 evenly-spaced steam vents in the top. Bake 30 minutes, or until the top pastry is golden brown, slightly darker around the edges, and a cake tester in the center comes out dry. Leave the pastry in its pan and set on a wire rack to cool.

7. While the pastry is baking, prepare the icing glaze: Whisk together all the ingredients in a medium-size bowl until the glaze is smooth, thick, and drips from the edge of a spoon in a wide ribbon. Adjust the sugar or liquid if needed. Cover the glaze with plastic wrap or a damp towel until ready to use or it will dry out quickly. *As soon as* the pastry comes out of the oven, spread the glaze evenly over the top. When the pastry is cold, use a sharp knife to mark, then slice, twenty-four 2½-inch squares (4 bars on the short end, 6 on the long end) or thirty 2 × 2½-inch bars (5 bars on the short end, 6 on the long end).

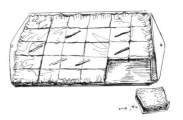

Elmira and Mary's Walnut Date Balls

WITH JUST THREE ingredients, this is the quickest and easiest treat in the world. Date balls are hard to categorize: They contain neither flour nor granulated sugar; they are sweet and chewy; and they taste like a cross between moist muffins and soft cookies. Call them whatever you like, but let the kids prepare the batter and enjoy the baked results.

The recipe was shared with me by Elmira Ingersoll and Mary Muhlhausen, two remarkable New England women who nourish a wide circle of fortunate individuals with their spiritual wisdom, loving friendship, and imaginative food. They have introduced me to many extraordinary things, including my favorite pie pastry, and now this little gem has happily entered my life. Mary and Elmira recommended their date balls as perfect, energizing snacks to carry when traveling, which they do often. Mary trekked in the Himalayas not long ago, and a recent card from Elmira noted that she was en route from Prague to northern Maine. I suspect that their special magic comes from more than a date ball, but it's a good place to start.

for good measure

- You can buy prechopped, pitted dates or whole, pitted dates that you chop yourself; the latter are softer and stickier than the prechopped but either one will work. If using the sticky dates, you may wish to coat the pans with Bakers' Joy (vegetable spray containing flour) or sift a little flour into the greased muffin cups to ensure easy release of the baked balls.

- Chopped dried apricots can be substituted for dates; pecans can be substituted for the walnuts.

- If you don't have enough muffin cups, bake the batter in several batches.

special equipment: 18 "baby" muffin cups (1¾ × ⅞ inches; 2- to 2½-tablespoon *capacity*) or 12 mini-muffin cups (2 × 1⅛ inches; ¼-cup *capacity*)

advance preparation: Date balls keep at least a week, wrapped, at room temperature.

temperature and time: 350°F for 10 to 12 minutes for baby date balls (about 1 tablespoon batter) or 14 to 15 minutes for mini-muffin date balls (about 2 tablespoons batter)

yield: 18 to 20 baby date balls (about 1¾-inch diameter) or 12 mini-muffin date balls (about 2-inch diameter)

Butter-flavor no-stick vegetable spray for preparing pan

3 large eggs, at room temperature

1 cup chopped, packed pitted dates

1 cup (4 ounces) walnuts, chopped

1. Position a rack in the center of the oven and preheat it to 350°F. Generously coat the muffin cups with vegetable spray.

2. In a mixing bowl, whisk the eggs well, then stir in the chopped dates and nuts. The batter will be quite runny.

3. Fill the prepared muffin cups with 1 to 2 tablespoons batter, depending upon the capacity of the cups. Be sure to scoop up some dates and nuts along with the eggs. Bake the baby date balls 10 to 12 minutes and the mini-muffin date balls 14 to 15 minutes, or until the balls are no longer sticky on top when touched and a cake tester inserted in the center of a ball comes out clean. Cool the date balls in their pans on a rack 4 to 5 minutes. Slide a knife blade between each ball and the pan to loosen it, then coax the balls from the pans with the tip of the knife; cool the date balls on a wire rack.

Double Fudge Brownies

FOR CHOCOLATE LOVERS these dark, moist brownies are doubly delicious, with melted chocolate *and* chocolate chips in the batter. They are as easy to make as they are to eat—no beaters to wash, just stir the batter together with a spoon. This is a big batch, good for parties and picnics. The recipe is my adaptation of one published by my friend Lora Brody in her book *Growing Up on the Chocolate Diet*.

special equipment: 9 × 13-inch pan (or two 8-inch square pans); double boiler or metal bowl set over a large pan

advance preparation: Brownies can be kept in an airtight container at room temperature about 1 week or double-wrapped and frozen up to 2 months.

temperature and time: 350°F for 22 to 25 minutes

yield: 24 to 28 brownies (2-inch squares); recipe can be doubled

8 ounces (8 squares) unsweetened chocolate, coarsely chopped

1 cup (2 sticks) unsalted butter, cut up, plus extra for preparing pan

4 large eggs, at room temperature

1¼ cups granulated sugar

¼ teaspoon salt

1 teaspoon vanilla extract

1 cup sifted all-purpose flour

2 tablespoons unsweetened Dutch-processed cocoa

1 cup (6 ounces) semisweet chocolate chips or chopped solid chocolate

½ to 1 cup (2 to 4 ounces) chopped walnuts or pecans, optional

1. Position a rack in the center of the oven and preheat it to 350°F. Lightly butter the pan.

2. In the top of a double boiler set over simmering water, melt the unsweetened chocolate together with the butter. Stir until smooth, remove the pan from the heat, and set it aside to cool.

3. In a large mixing bowl, with a sturdy spoon, beat together the eggs, sugar, salt, and vanilla, then add the melted chocolate mixture. Slowly stir in the flour, cocoa, and chocolate chips and beat until no streaks of flour or cocoa are visible. The batter will be quite thick.

4. Spread the batter into the prepared pan and sprinkle on the nuts, if using. Bake 22 to 25 minutes, or until a toothpick inserted in the center comes out with just a few moist crumbs attached; don't overbake or the brownies will be dry. Cool the brownies in the pan on a wire rack, then cut into 2-inch squares.

Walnut Brownies: Stir walnuts into the batter instead of adding them on top.

Peanut Butter Brownies: At the end of step 3, dot the batter with 2 to 4 tablespoons of chunky peanut butter; pull a table knife through the batter to create streaks of peanut butter.

Black and White Brownies: Replace semisweet chocolate with white chocolate chips or solid white chocolate, coarsely chopped.

Butterscotch Brownies: Replace chocolate chips with butterscotch chips.

Brownie Sundae: Top a brownie with a scoop of vanilla ice cream and ladle on All-American Hot Fudge Sauce, page 180.

Steve's Brownies

MY FRIEND STEVE Keneipp is the charming and knowledgeable chef/proprietor of one of Indiana's greatest treasures, the Classic Kitchen Restaurant in Noblesville. Steve's decadent brownie recipe, previously published in the *Chicago Tribune,* more than lives up to his modest claim that the taste is "better than boxed" in every way. These are quick to put together, fudgy and dense; you can use any type of nuts you have, or omit them if you prefer.

for good measure

Don't overbake brownies or they will dry out.

special equipment: 8 × 8 × 1½-inch pan

advance preparation: Brownies can be double-wrapped and frozen up to 2 months.

temperature and time: 325°F for 30 to 35 minutes

yield: 16 brownies (2-inch squares); recipe can be doubled or tripled

Solid shortening or butter-flavor no-stick vegetable spray for preparing pan

6 tablespoons (¾ stick) unsalted butter

½ cup unsifted unsweetened Dutch-processed cocoa

1 cup granulated sugar

2 large eggs, at room temperature

1 teaspoon vanilla extract

½ cup unsifted all-purpose flour

⅛ teaspoon salt

1 cup (6 ounces) semisweet chocolate chips or solid chocolate, coarsely chopped

½ cup (2 ounces) chopped walnuts, optional

1. Position a rack in the center of the oven and preheat it to 325°F. Coat the baking pan with shortening or spray and set it aside.

2. Melt the butter in a small pan over low heat or microwave it in a heat-proof glass bowl on high power about 1 minute.

In a large mixing bowl using a sturdy spoon or an electric mixer, combine all the ingredients and beat until well blended. The batter will be very thick.

3. Spread the batter in the prepared pan and bake 30 to 35 minutes, or until the brownies look dry on top and just begin to pull away from the pan sides. A cake tester inserted in the center should come out with just a few moist crumbs attached. Cool the brownies in the pan on a wire rack, then cut into squares.

IN MY ESTIMATION, pies are the perfect dessert—they are beautiful to look at, heavenly to eat, neither intimidating nor difficult to prepare. Pie pastries *can* be a snap. You will be surprised how easy it is to make my Press-in-Place Pastry. It is in the less-is-more category: The less you handle the ingredients, the more tender and flaky the result—a baker's bonus. Many of these pies have crumb crusts, which ask nothing more than a firm rolling pin to crush them and a light touch to press them into place.

YOU WILL FIND YOUR FAVORITES HERE, from good old Mom's Apple Pie (with four variations) to classic Blue Ribbon Cherry Pie (with a secret: the world's easiest lattice crust you bake separately) and fool-proof Lemon Meringue. For the holidays, you will enjoy two variations on Pecan Pie, a Pumpkin Chiffon, a rich Peanut Butter Pie with Chocolate Icing, and three crumb-topped fruit pies—down-home delicious.

Pies, pizzas, AND tarts

MY FAVORITE PIE OF ALL IS NOT. Call it a *crostata* (as they do in Italy), a *galette* (in France), or simply a fruit pizza; it is just a free-form piece of dough topped with sugared fruit. Setting a new trend, this rusti-cated cousin of the pie has recently appeared on television, in food magazines, and even gained entry to the most elegant American restaurants. Like biscotti and tiramisù, other recent darlings of the food glit-terati, the crostata is home-style fare that got invited to the party. Deservedly so.

HEAVENLY STRAWBERRY ANGEL PIE is another surprise: a pie plate heaped with crisp melt-on-your-tongue meringue topped by sweetened berries and whipped cream—the very opposite of a traditional angel pie, which is a meringue crust filled with a custard.

FOR A DINNER PARTY, try the sophisticated flavor of Mocha Walnut Tart or my Favorite Fresh Fruit Tart— a winner in the Baking for Bluffers Department (maximum applause, minimum effort): It is nothing more than flavored cream cheese topped by fruit slices.

Mom's Apple Pie

THIS IS MY mom's classic, the all–American favorite, hands–down blue-ribbon winner of "favorite pie" contests across the country. Under the golden, sugar-glazed butter crust, a generous dome of cinnamon-scented juicy apples wafts its perfume throughout your home. Don't even try to resist. If you can only master one recipe in this book, this should be it.

Apple pie is an American icon, a fact hilariously depicted in a 1992 *New Yorker* cartoon by Mischa Richter that hangs over my desk: The Statue of Liberty (dressed in her gown and spiked crown) and Uncle Sam (in his star-spangled top hat and striped trousers) are sitting around a coffee table, cups in hand, like a long-married couple. He is reading the paper. He glances over absently at the table, notices that she has served dessert, and barks "Not apple pie *again!*"

for good measure

- I prefer to use a heat-proof glass pie plate because it bakes slightly quicker than metal and you can see the color of the bottom crust to know when it is sufficiently browned.

- This butter pastry contains an egg yolk that guarantees it will be easy to handle. The pastry recipe is large so you will have extra dough to roll out and cut cookie cutter leaf or heart shapes to decorate the top of the glazed pie.

- Egg glaze and sugar give the baked pie a rich golden color and a sparkle; you can substitute plain milk for a less shiny finish.

special equipment: 9-inch pie plate, preferably heat-proof glass; wax paper; rolling pin; pastry brush; aluminum foil for frame (see page 231)

advance preparation: Pastry can be prepared 1 or 2 days in advance, wrapped, and refrigerated, or it can be double-wrapped and frozen 2 to 3 months. The completely filled but unbaked (and unglazed) pie can also be double-wrapped

and frozen 3 months. Cut steam vents, add glaze, and bake the frozen pie without thawing, following general instructions, but extend the baking time by 15 minutes if necessary (cover top pastry with foil if over-browning).

temperature and time: 425°F for 15 minutes, then 350°F for 40 to 45 minutes

yield: 9-inch pie; 8 to 10 servings

flaky pastry

- **3 cups unsifted all-purpose flour**
- **2 tablespoons granulated sugar**
- **¾ teaspoon salt**
- **¾ cup (1½ sticks) unsalted butter, chilled or frozen, cut up**
- **6 tablespoons chilled solid shortening (Crisco) or solid stick margarine, cut up**
- **1 large egg yolk**
- **2 tablespoons fresh lemon juice or white vinegar**
- **5 to 8 tablespoons ice water, or as needed**

egg glaze

- **1 large egg beaten with 1 teaspoon water**

filling

- **7 or 8 large Granny Smith apples (or a blend of Jonathan, Golden Delicious, Rome, or other flavorful cooking apples), peeled, cored, sliced ⅛ inch thick (8 cups slices)**
- **⅓ to ½ cup packed dark brown sugar (amount depends upon tartness of apples)**
- **Juice of 1 lemon**
- **3½ tablespoons all-purpose flour**
- **1 teaspoon ground cinnamon**
- **½ to 1 teaspoon ground nutmeg**
- **2 tablespoons unsalted butter, cut up, optional**
- **½ cup graham cracker or plain cracker crumbs or crushed cornflake cereal**

topping

- **1 tablespoon granulated sugar, optional**

1. Prepare the pastry. In a food processor or bowl of an electric mixer, pulse or mix the flour, sugar, and salt to blend, then add the butter and shortening. Pulse or beat just until the mixture is cut into pieces the size of small peas. Add the yolk and lemon juice along with about 2 tablespoons of ice water. Pulse or beat a few seconds, then add more ice water, 1 tablespoon at a time, until the dough just begins to look clumpy. The amount of water needed will vary; it is best to add more by hand after the dough is out of the bowl. Do not allow a dough ball to form in the machine. Turn the clumpy dough out onto a piece of wax paper, gather it into a ball, and wrap and refrigerate it about 30 minutes, or longer, if time permits.

Divide the dough ball in half; leave one portion refrigerated while rolling the first. On a lightly floured surface, with a floured rolling pin, roll out the dough until it measures about 1 inch larger around than the pie plate (invert the plate on the dough to measure it).

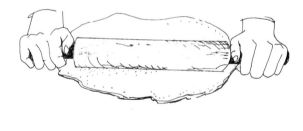

Fold the dough into quarters and fit it into the pie plate, positioning the folded point at the center. Unfold and gently drape the pastry over the pan; do not stretch it. Allow the dough to extend about 1 inch beyond the plate rim, then cut off excess. Set aside the pastry-lined pan, or refrigerate it, while preparing the filling. Position a rack in the lower third of the oven and preheat it to 425°F.

2. In a large bowl, toss the sliced apples with the sugar, lemon juice, flour, and spices. With the pastry brush, paint a coating of egg glaze over the entire layer of pastry in the pie plate. Sprinkle on the crumbs or crushed cereal (to absorb excess juices). Pile on the fruit, add the butter if using it, and press the filling with your palms into a firmly packed dome.

3. Roll out the remaining dough about 2 inches larger than the pie plate (you will have some extra dough). Use the tip of a knife or a ½-inch round cutter to make a small vent hole right in the middle of the rolled pastry. Fold the pastry into quarters as before, and fit it over the fruit; unfold and drape it evenly over the apples. Trim a ¾-inch overhang. Fold the edge under the edge of the bottom

continued

crust and pinch them together to seal. Pinch up a raised pastry rim all around, then pinch it into points or flutes with your fingers, or press it down with a fork. With a knife tip, cut 5 slits in the crust for steam vents.

Brush the pie top with egg glaze. If you wish to add decorations, roll out leftover dough, cut out shapes, and set them on the glazed pie top. Brush the shapes with the glaze. Sprinkle topping sugar over the whole pie top.

4. If you are not pressed for time, refrigerate the pie for about 30 minutes, so the dough will relax; it will be a little more tender and shrink less. You can also bake it right away.

Bake the pie in the lower third of the oven for 15 minutes, then reduce the heat to 350°F and continue baking an additional 40 to 45 minutes, until the pastry is a rich golden brown and the fruit is tender when pierced with the tip of a knife through a vent. *Note:* Look at the pie after about 25 minutes and, if the crust edges are browning too quickly, add a foil edging. To make a foil frame, see page 231. Cool the baked pie on a wire rack. Serve warm, topped with slices of cheddar cheese or vanilla ice cream.

Apple-Cranberry Pie: Add ¼ cup more sugar plus 1 cup fresh or frozen whole cranberries and ½ cup (2 ounces) chopped walnuts.

Kentucky Bourbon Apple Pie: Sprinkle 3 tablespoons bourbon over the basic filling.

Apple-Raisin Pie: Add 1 cup golden raisins to the basic apple filling.

Apple-Dried Cherry Pie: Add 1 cup dried sweet or tart cherries plumped 1 hour in orange juice or sweet red vermouth.

Blue Ribbon Cherry Pie with Quick Lattice Topping

IN 1991, THIS delicious cherry pie won a first prize silver rolling pin for its creator, Diane Cordial of Powell, Ohio, at the Crisco American Pie Celebration National Bake-Off in New Orleans. To reach that exalted position, Diane had previously won a blue ribbon with this recipe at her native Ohio State Fair. I was fortunate enough to be one of the judges at the New Orleans Bake-Off, when Diane's entry competed with the winners from the other forty-nine state fairs. I have never forgotten how Diane's pie stood out because of its simplicity, clarity of flavor (highlighted by a touch of vanilla and almond), and beautiful presentation. The top crust of Diane's pie was whimsically decorated with small cherry cut-outs made with a cookie cutter (the holes doubled as steam vents). One of her winners sported a map of the state of Ohio, another the word "Ohio" carefully cut out of the pastry top.

You will find my adaptation of her recipe a winner at your house, too. It is easy to prepare and has a simple but fancy "mock" lattice topping that is baked separately and slipped onto the pie before serving.

for good measure

Diane's pie uses tart cherries; you can substitute sweet cherries (fresh or frozen) but must reduce sugar in the filling to 1 cup, or slightly less, depending upon the taste of the fruit.

special equipment: 9-inch pie plate, preferably heat-proof glass; rolling pin; pastry brush; aluminum foil; sharp paring knife; ruler; cookie sheet

advance preparation: The cherry filling can be made in advance, as it needs at least 1 hour to cool. The pastry can be prepared 1 or 2 days in advance, wrapped, and refrigerated, or it can be double-wrapped and frozen 2 to 3 months. The lattice topping, which is baked by itself, can be shaped and baked no more than 1 day in advance; keep the remaining pastry refrigerated until ready to roll and fill it.

temperature and time: Pie: 425°F for 15 minutes, then 350°F for 25 to 30 minutes; lattice top: 350°F for 14 to 15 minutes

yield: 9-inch pie; 8 to 10 servings

filling

1¼ cups granulated sugar

¼ cup cornstarch

4 cups fresh tart red cherries, pitted, or 1 bag (20 ounces) frozen dry-pack pitted sweet or tart cherries, or two (16-ounce) cans pitted tart cherries in water, drained

2 tablespoons unsalted butter

¾ teaspoon vanilla extract

½ teaspoon almond extract

1 or 2 drops red vegetable food color, optional

crisco pastry

3 cups unsifted all-purpose flour

1½ tablespoons granulated sugar

1 teaspoon salt

1 cup plus 2 tablespoons chilled solid shortening (Crisco)

1 large egg, lightly beaten

1 tablespoon fresh lemon juice or white vinegar

4 to 8 tablespoons ice water, or as needed

egg glaze

1 large egg, at room temperature, beaten with 1 teaspoon water

topping

2 to 3 teaspoons granulated sugar

continued

1. Prepare the filling: In a medium saucepan, stir together the sugar and cornstarch, then add the cherries. Set over medium-high heat and stir about 10 minutes, or until the mixture comes to a rolling boil for at least one minute and is thickened and clear. Remove the pan from the heat and stir in the butter, both extracts, and coloring if using. Set aside to cool.

2. Prepare the pastry: In a large mixing bowl, combine the flour, granulated sugar, and salt. Cut in the Crisco using a pastry blender or 2 cross-cutting table knives or your fingertips until the mixture is in pieces the size of small peas.

In a small bowl, beat together the egg and lemon juice. Sprinkle it over the flour mixture, and add about 4 tablespoons of the ice water. Toss the mixture lightly, adding more water 1 tablespoon at a time just until the dough clumps together and begins to form a ball; you may *not* need all the liquid. Divide the dough in half, press each piece into a flat disk, and wrap it in plastic wrap or foil. Refrigerate the pastry until ready to roll it out.

3. Prepare the lattice topping: Overlapped pastry strips are easy to bake by themselves on the dull side of a 14-inch-square piece of aluminum foil spread with Crisco or butter. (If you don't have heavy-duty foil, use a double layer of regular foil.) Invert the pie plate onto the buttered foil and use a toothpick or your fingernail to draw around the rim, clearly marking its size. Set the marked foil aside.

4. To roll out the bottom crust, remove one portion of the refrigerated dough. On a lightly floured surface, with a floured rolling pin, roll out the dough until it measures about 1 inch larger around than the pie plate (invert the plate on the dough to measure it).

Fold the dough into quarters and fit it into the pie plate, positioning the folded point at the center (see sketches, page 85). Unfold and gently drape the pastry over the pan; do not stretch it. Allow the dough to extend about ½ inch beyond the plate rim, then cut off excess. Fold under the ½-inch overhang and press it flat onto the rim of the pie plate with your fingers or a fork.

5. Position racks to divide the oven into thirds and preheat it to 425°F. Place a piece of foil, shiny side up, on the oven floor to catch potential drips. With a pastry brush, paint a coating of egg glaze on the pastry in the pie plate. Spoon in the cherry filling and bake the pie in the lower third of the oven for 15 minutes. Then, reduce the heat to 350°F and bake it an additional 25 to 30 minutes, until the filling is bubbly and the pastry crust is golden brown. The filling thickens as it cools. While the pie bakes, prepare the lattice.

6. Roll out the remaining dough on a lightly floured surface, making a circle about 12 inches in diameter and ⅛ inch thick. With a sharp knife held against a ruler, or by eye, cut the dough into 10 strips, each approximately ¾ to 1 inch wide; start measuring in the center of the rolled circle in order to cut long strips from the widest portion of the dough.

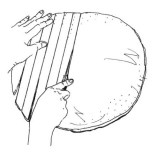

7. To form the lattice, follow the sketches and use as a base the buttered foil marked in step 3. First lift off one of the longest cut dough strips and place it in the center of the buttered foil circle. Then evenly space 2 strips to each side of the center. Brush the tops of each strip with egg glaze. Now lift off 5 more strips and place them at right angles to the first layer but at similar intervals. Use your fingertip to press gently on the top strips to seal them to the layer below.

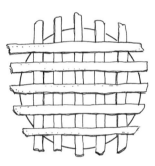

8. With a paring knife, cut around the edge of the marked foil circle, removing excess dough strips. Brush the top strips with egg glaze.

9. To make an edging border around the lattice, cut the leftover dough scraps into strips about ½ inch wide. Reroll the dough scraps if necessary for this. Press the strips onto the ends of the lattice following the marked circle. Overlap the ends of each border strip. Press gently on this border to seal it to the strips below. Brush the border with egg glaze and sprinkle a little sugar over the entire lattice.

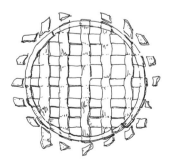

10. Slide the foil containing the lattice onto a cookie sheet and bake it in the center of the 350°F oven for 14 to 15 minutes, or until the pastry is golden brown; it will bake much more quickly than the pie, so keep peeking and remove it when the color is right. Slide the foil containing the lattice off the cookie sheet onto a wire rack on the counter to cool completely. After the baked pie has cooled at least 20 minutes, it is ready to receive the lattice topping. To do this, carefully slide a flat edge of the cookie sheet beneath the lattice, working it free of the foil and lifting it up. Hold the cookie sheet over the pie, and gently slide the lattice off the sheet and into position on top of the pie. *Note:* Because the lattice is baked in one piece, it will break easily after the first slice is cut.

Lemon Meringue Pie

THE FILLING FOR this old favorite is a classic lemon custard pudding cooked on top of the stove. I have taken a few liberties with the top and the bottom of the pie, to guarantee easy success every time. Instead of a traditional pastry, I prefer a crunchy crumb crust with a touch of shredded coconut, which provides a nice contrast to the creamy filling and topping. To ensure stable, picture-perfect meringue, I use a trick I learned from my friend Delores Custer, a successful New York–based food stylist, who adds a little cooked cornstarch to the whites as they are being whipped. For an unusual variation, try Lemon Cloud Pie, in which the lemon pudding is folded into the meringue to make a light creamy lemon mousse.

for good measure

- If you prefer to have a pastry crust, use a store-bought refrigerate crust or the pastry recipe on page 92; since this is only a 9-inch pie, you will have a little dough left over. Bake the pastry shell following steps 1 and 2, pages 92–93.

- If you like an extra-tall meringue topping, use 5 egg whites in the meringue recipe.

- Remove the eggs from the refrigerator before starting the recipe; room temperature whites will whip to greater volume than cold whites.

- You will need 3 to 4 lemons for the filling.

special equipment: 9-inch pie plate; 1½- to 2-quart heavy-bottomed saucepan; small saucepan; large metal spoon; electric mixer

advance preparation: Pie should be baked the same day it is served; the bottom crust of any type may soften on standing. Remove the eggs from refrigerator so they can come to room temperature before starting the pie.

temperature and time: Crumb crust: 350°F for 8 minutes; stove-top custard: 10 to 13 minutes; meringue: 350°F for 12 to 15 minutes

yield: 9-inch pie; 8 to 10 servings

crumb crust

1¼ cups graham cracker crumbs

2 tablespoons granulated sugar

½ cup shredded sweetened coconut (or ½ cup additional graham cracker crumbs)

6 tablespoons (¾ stick) unsalted butter, melted (use 7 tablespoons with 1¼ cups graham cracker crumbs)

filling

1 cup granulated sugar

⅓ cup cornstarch

¼ teaspoon salt

1½ cups water

Grated zest from 1 lemon (about 1½ tablespoons)

½ cup fresh lemon juice

4 large egg yolks, at room temperature

2 tablespoons unsalted butter, at room temperature, cut up, optional

meringue stabilizer and meringue topping

½ cup granulated or superfine sugar, divided (2 tablespoons and 6 tablespoons)

1 tablespoon cornstarch

½ cup water

4 or 5 large egg whites, at room temperature

⅛ teaspoon salt

¼ teaspoon cream of tartar

½ teaspoon vanilla extract

1. Position a rack in the center of the oven and preheat it to 350°F. In a bowl, toss together the crumbs, sugar, coconut, and melted butter. Turn out the crumbs into the pie plate and use the back of a large metal spoon to press the crumbs in an even layer against the pan sides, then flat on the bottom. Bake the crust 8 minutes. Remove the pan from the oven and set it aside.

2. Prepare the filling: In a medium heavy-bottomed saucepan, whisk together the sugar, cornstarch, and salt. Whisk in the water, lemon zest, and juice; scrape into the pan corners to incorporate all the dry ingredients. Place over medium heat and cook, stirring, 7 to 8 minutes, until it comes to a boil. Whisk constantly while boiling 1 full minute (count to 60), until it thickens, looks clear, and generously coats a spoon. Remove from the heat.

3. In a medium bowl, whisk the yolks well, then whisk in about ½ cup of the hot lemon pudding to warm the yolks (work quickly so yolks do not poach). Scrape the warm yolks into the hot lemon pudding in the pot, while simultaneously whisking hard to blend in the yolk mixture before the eggs begin to set.

Return the lemon pudding to the stove over the very lowest heat, and stir continually about 4 minutes to cook the yolks and ensure a stable pudding. Remove the pudding from the heat and stir in the butter, if using, mixing until it melts. Leave the pudding in the pan but set it aside.

4. Prepare the meringue stabilizer: In a small saucepan, stir together 2 tablespoons of the sugar, the cornstarch, and the water until the cornstarch dissolves. Stir constantly over medium-high heat for 2 to 3 minutes until the mixture bubbles up into a boil; it will immediately start to thicken and look almost clear. Quickly remove the pan from the heat and set it aside.

5. Prepare the meringue: Place the egg whites into the largest grease-free bowl of an electric mixer. Combine the egg whites with the salt and cream of tartar. With the electric mixer on medium speed, whip the whites until foamy, then gradually add the 6 remaining tablespoons sugar while beating continuously. When the whites look thick and foamy, increase the speed to high and beat until the whites look smooth and satiny, and you begin to see beater

tracks on the surface. When the mixer is turned off and the beater is lifted, the foam should make a soft, slightly droopy peak. Add the vanilla, turn the mixer on medium speed, and begin beating in spoonfuls of the cooked cornstarch mixture from step 4. Beat on high a little longer, until the whites are smooth, satiny, and hold very stiff peaks.

6. Rewarm the lemon pudding by stirring it over very low heat just until it is *almost* hot to the touch; it must be warm enough to cook the surface of the meringue which rests on it. Spoon the warmed pudding into the pie shell. Add about half the meringue, spreading it out onto the edges of the crust to seal it and prevent shrinking. Pile on the remaining meringue and shape medium-high swirls with the back of a big spoon. Bake the pie at 350°F for 12 to 15 minutes, or just until the meringue begins to look golden brown. Cool the pie on a wire rack, and serve at room temperature. Refrigerate leftovers.

Lemon Cloud Pie: To make this light lemon mousse filling, fold together the lemon pudding and the meringue. The volume of this filling (6 cups) requires a 10-inch regular or 10-inch deep-dish pie plate, preferably Pyrex. Prepare the basic recipe above, making the crust as described, but use 7 tablespoons melted butter and 1¾ cups crumbs; it will fit in the 10-inch pie plate but be slightly thinner than usual; bake as directed. Prepare the lemon pudding as directed. Prepare the meringue with only 4 egg whites; *omit the stabilizer* (step 4) and the water-cornstarch-sugar mixture it requires. Instead, follow step 5 to whip 4 whites with salt and cream of tartar, then slowly whip in the full ½ cup sugar (8 tablespoons) making stiff peaks. Add vanilla extract and whip to very stiff peaks. Finally, fold the lemon custard into the bowl of whipped meringue in several additions; don't worry if some streaks are visible. Pile the mixture into the crust and bake at 350°F for about 15 minutes, until just beginning to look golden on top. Cool on a wire rack, then chill. Serve at room temperature.

No-Bake Berry Pie

TO BE PERFECTLY honest, the no-bake part is just the filling. The pastry crust does need baking, but that's not hard (especially if it is store-bought, and who's telling?). In fact, this pie is so quick that it is one of my summer standards—I use blueberries, raspberries, blackberries, blueberries with peaches, nectarines with blueberries and plums . . . whatever combination of berries and ripe fruit is available. The time-saving technique involves cooking some of the fruit into a thick sauce, then stirring in the remaining fresh fruit and chilling it all together in the shell. You can put it together in minutes and be off to the beach. On the Fourth of July, use red and blue berries topped with whipped cream . . . call them patriotic calories.

for good measure

- To prevent the bottom pastry crust from becoming soggy, brush a layer of apricot or other fruit preserves over the shell before adding the fruit mixture.
- A 9-inch springform pan can be substituted for the pie plate.
- Any crumb crust can be used for this pie instead of a pastry shell (see Index).

special equipment: 9-inch pie plate, preferably heat-proof glass; wax paper; rolling pin; pastry brush; aluminum foil; pie weights or dry rice or beans reserved for this purpose; 2- to 3-quart heavy-bottomed saucepan

advance preparation: Pie should be prepared and served the same day; it needs about 3 hours for the filling to set. The prebaked pastry shell can be made a day in advance, or store-bought.

temperature and time: Pastry: 425°F for 12 minutes, then 350°F for 10 to 15 minutes; stove top: about 10 minutes; refrigerator: about 3 hours

yield: 9-inch pie; 8 to 10 servings

(choose one) pastry

Store-bought refrigerated crust for 9-inch pie shell

or flaky pastry (for one 9-inch shell)

1½ cups unsifted all-purpose flour

1 tablespoon granulated sugar

½ teaspoon salt

6 tablespoons (¾ stick) chilled unsalted butter, cup up

3 tablespoons chilled shortening (Crisco) or solid stick margarine, cut up

1 large egg yolk

3 to 4 tablespoons iced orange juice or water, or as needed

filling

⅔ to 1 cup granulated sugar

3 tablespoons cornstarch

1 cup orange juice or water

4 cups any combination fresh berries, picked over, hulled, rinsed, and blotted dry; or peeled, pitted, cut-up fresh fruit

1 tablespoon fresh lemon juice

2 tablespoons unsalted butter, cut up

1. If making your own pastry, mix and bake it before starting the filling. (If using store-bought pastry, go to step 2.) In a food processor or the bowl of electric mixer, pulse or beat the flour, sugar, and salt to blend, then add the butter and shortening. Pulse or beat just until the mixture is cut into pieces the size of small peas. Add the yolk and 1 or 2 tablespoons of juice. Pulse or beat a few seconds, then add more liquid, 1 tablespoon at a time, until the dough just begins to look clumpy. The amount of water needed will vary; it is best to add more by hand after the dough is out of the bowl. Do not allow a dough ball to form in the machine. Turn the clumpy dough out onto a piece of wax paper, gather it into a ball, and wrap and refrigerate it about 30 minutes, or longer, if time permits. On a lightly floured surface, with a floured rolling pin, roll out the dough until it measures about 1 inch larger around the pie plate (invert the plate on the dough to measure it).

2. Fold the homemade or store-bought pastry dough into quarters and fit it into the pie plate, positioning the folded point at the center (see sketch, page 85). Unfold and gently drape the pastry over the pan; do not stretch it. Allow the dough to extend about ¾ inch beyond the plate rim, then cut off excess. Fold under the extra dough, then pinch it up into points or "flutes" on the rim using your fingertips. Or, press the dough flat on the rim with the floured tines of a fork. Position a rack in the lower third of the oven and preheat it to 425°F.

3. To completely prebake the empty pastry shell, line it with a piece of aluminum foil, shiny side down, and cover with pie weights or dry rice (see sketch, page 111). Bake for about 12 minutes, then reduce the heat to 350°F and bake another 10 to 15 minutes. Remove the pan from the oven, lift out the foil and the weights, and inspect the pastry. It should be a light golden color, completely baked. If the dough still looks pale or translucent, bake it a few more minutes without the foil and weights. Set the baked shell on a wire rack to cool completely.

4. In a large saucepan, combine the sugar, cornstarch, and juice. Whisk until smooth. Add about 1½ cups of the berries or mixed fruit and mash it gently against the side of the pan with a big spoon, releasing some juice. Cook the mixture over medium-low heat 7 to 10 minutes, stirring on and off, until the sauce is thick and clear. Stir in the lemon juice. Taste and adjust the sauce; add more sugar or lemon juice if needed.

5. Stir in the butter and the remaining 2½ cups fresh berries. Chill the mixture until partially thickened (stir over ice water if you are in a hurry) then pour it into the pastry shell and refrigerate about 3 hours to set the filling. Serve with sweetened whipped cream or vanilla ice cream.

Three-Nut Thanksgiving Pie

A VARIATION ON classic pecan pie, this taste combination is delicious and unexpected. The original sweetness is reduced and cut with lemon juice, and the different nuts add their own flavors. Use your favorite nuts . . . feel free to substitute toasted hazelnuts, almonds, dry-roasted peanuts, black walnuts, or pine nuts (pignoli), as well as traditional pecans. To make Bourbon-Pecan Pie, see the variation following.

for good measure

- Because this is basically a custard pie, the bottom crust tends to get soft unless the pastry is partially baked before the filling is added.
- Nut pastry can be pressed into the pie plate with the fingertips instead of being rolled out.

special equipment: 9-inch pie plate, preferably heat-proof glass; wax paper; rolling pin; pastry brush; aluminum foil; pie weights or dry rice or beans reserved for this purpose

advance preparation: Pastry can be prepared 1 or 2 days in advance, wrapped, and refrigerated. The pie is best baked the day it is served or no more than 1 day in advance.

temperature and time: Prebaked pastry shell: 425°F for 10 to 12 minutes; filled pie: 350°F for 30 to 35 minutes

yield: 9-inch pie; 8 to 10 servings

nut pastry

1½ cups unsifted all-purpose flour

1 tablespoon granulated sugar

½ teaspoon salt

½ cup (generous 2 ounces) walnuts, pecans, or other nuts

6 tablespoons (¾ stick) chilled unsalted butter, cut up

3 tablespoons chilled solid shortening (Crisco) or solid stick margarine, cut up

1 large egg yolk

1 tablespoon fresh lemon juice or white vinegar

3 to 4 tablespoons ice water, or more as needed

filling

¾ cup packed dark brown sugar

3 large eggs, at room temperature

6 tablespoons (¾ stick) unsalted butter, melted

⅔ cup dark corn syrup

1 tablespoon unsulfured molasses

1½ teaspoons fresh lemon juice

1 teaspoon vanilla extract

¼ teaspoon salt

½ cup (2 ounces) halved pecans

½ cup (2 ounces) halved or broken walnuts

½ cup (2 ounces) macadamia nuts

1. Prepare and partially prebake the pastry shell: In the workbowl of a food processor fitted with the steel blade, pulse the flour, sugar, salt, and nuts until the nuts are finely chopped. Add the butter and shortening and pulse just until the mixture resembles coarse meal. Through the feed tube, add the yolk, lemon juice, and 1 or 2 tablespoons of ice water. Pulse a few times, stopping as soon as the dough begins to look clumpy. Add more water, 1 tablespoon at a time if needed, but do not allow a dough ball to form. Turn the clumpy dough out onto a piece of wax paper and gather it into a ball. Refrigerate it 30 minutes, or overnight, if time permits. Using a lightly floured rolling pin, roll out the dough until it measures about 1 inch larger around than the pie plate (set it on top of the dough to measure it).

Fold the dough into quarters and fit it into the pie plate, positioning the folded point at the center (see sketch, page 85). Unfold and gently drape the pastry over the pan; do not stretch it. Allow the dough to extend about ¾ inch beyond the plate rim, then cut off excess. Fold under the extra dough, then pinch it up into points or flutes on the rim using your fingertips. Refrigerate the pastry-lined pan until the dough feels firm.

2. Position a rack in the lower third of the oven and preheat it to 425°F. Line the dough with a 12-inch square of foil, shiny side down, and cover it with pie weights or dry rice (see sketch, page 111). Bake the weighted pastry shell for about 12 minutes. Remove it from the oven, lift out the foil with all the weights, and cool the pastry shell on a wire rack. Reduce the oven heat to 350°F and position a rack in the center of the oven.

3. In the bowl of an electric mixer or food processor fitted with a steel blade, combine and beat together the brown sugar and eggs. Mix in the all remaining ingredients except the nuts. Pour the filling into the pastry shell. Arrange the nuts on top, either mixing and scattering them or carefully positioning them in concentric circles of alternating nut types and colors.

4. Bake the pie in the center of the oven for 30 to 35 minutes, or until a table knife stuck into the center comes out clean. Cool on a wire rack. Serve at room temperature.

> **Bourbon-Pecan Pie:** Prepare the basic pie filling but omit the lemon juice; add 1 tablespoon bourbon, and use only pecans (1½ cups).

Pumpkin Chiffon Pie with Gingersnap Crumb Crust

THANKSGIVING ISN'T THE same without pumpkin pie, and in my home this is our favorite. This pumpkin chiffon, with its well-balanced quintessentially spiced flavor, is simple and fearless—the crumb crust is, literally, a snap, and the filling sets in the refrigerator so you don't have to worry about baking a temperamental custard with a soggy bottom crust. The best part of all is that you can prepare this a day in advance, to leave time for the other holiday "fixings."

for good measure

- My mother originally developed this recipe, and I remember her putting a few tablespoons of dark rum in the filling, a good idea.

- Remove the eggs from the refrigerator before starting the recipe; room temperature whites whip to greater volume than cold whites.

special equipment: 9-inch pie plate, preferably heat-proof glass; large metal spoon; double boiler or metal bowl set over a larger pan; small saucepan; large mixing bowl containing ice cubes and cold water, optional; chilled bowl and beater; toothpicks, optional

advance preparation: Crumb crust can be prepared a day in advance. The complete pie can be made a day ahead, and the whipped cream, if using, can be added shortly before serving.

temperature and time: Refrigerator: 30 minutes minimum for crust; 3 hours minimum or overnight for filled pie

yield: 9-inch pie; 8 to 10 servings

gingersnap crumb crust

25 store-bought gingersnap cookies (2-inch diameter) or 1⅓ cups gingersnap crumbs

2 tablespoons granulated sugar

6 tablespoons (¾ stick) unsalted butter, melted

filling

3 large eggs, at room temperature

2¾ teaspoons unflavored gelatin

¼ cup hot water

⅔ cup granulated sugar, divided (⅓ cup and ⅓ cup)

½ teaspoon salt

¾ teaspoon ground cinnamon

¾ teaspoon ground nutmeg

¾ teaspoon ground ginger

1¼ cups canned plain pumpkin puree

½ cup heavy cream (36% butterfat), chilled

garnish, optional

½ cup heavy cream, chilled and whipped with 1 tablespoon sugar

Pinch of ground nutmeg

1. Prepare the crumb crust: To make gingersnap crumbs, pulse the cookies in a food processor, or put them in a sealed plastic bag and crush them with a rolling pin. In the pie plate, toss together the crumbs, sugar, and butter. With the back of a large metal spoon, spread the crumbs into an even layer on the sides and bottom of the pan. Refrigerate the pie while you prepare the filling.

2. Separate the eggs, putting the yolks in the top of a double boiler and the whites in the large grease-free bowl of an electric mixer.

In a small saucepan, sprinkle the gelatin over the water, let it sit about 2 minutes to soften, then stir it over low heat for 2 to 3 minutes just until the gelatin dissolves (pinch it between your fingers to see if it is still grainy); don't let it boil. Remove it from the heat and set it aside to cool.

3. Whisk ⅓ cup of granulated sugar into the yolks, beating until they are thick and light in color. Whisk in the salt, spices, and the dissolved gelatin, and beat well.

Place the yolk mixture over (but not touching) water that is simmering in the bottom part of the double boiler. Whisk the yolk mixture constantly over the simmering water until the mixture becomes very thick, like a pudding, and generously coats a spoon. Remove the yolk mixture from the heat and stir in the pumpkin puree, whisking to blend it well.

4. Turn the pumpkin custard out into a metal (heat-proof) mixing bowl. If you are not in a hurry, place the mixture in the refrigerator for about 45 minutes, until it cools and thickens, but check it once in a while and don't let it gel completely. Or, to speed the process, set out a large bowl of ice mixed with cold water and place the bowl of hot custard in it. Whisk on and off about 15 minutes to cool the custard until it feels thick, mounds on the spoon, and is just beginning to set; don't let it gel. When the custard is cooled and partially thickened, remove it from the refrigerator or ice water bath and set it aside.

5. With the mixer on medium speed, whip the whites until foamy. Gradually add the remaining ⅓ cup sugar while beating continuously. When the whites look thick and foamy, increase the speed to high and beat until the whites look smooth and satiny, and you begin to see beater tracks on the surface. Beat a little longer until, when the mixer is turned off and the beater is lifted, the foam makes a peak that stands up straight on the tip.

With the chilled bowl and chilled beater, whip the heavy cream until medium-stiff peaks form.

6. Using a flexible spatula, fold the pumpkin custard into the whipped cream, then into the whipped whites. To do this, cut a flexible spatula down through the center of the foam, turn it, and draw it up along the side of the bowl. Give the bowl a quarter turn and repeat. Keep cutting through the mass but don't stir or deflate the foam.

Spoon the pumpkin chiffon into the crumb shell and refrigerate at least 3 hours to set. Once the filling is set, stand up 3 or 4 toothpicks in it and cover the pie with plastic wrap or foil (the picks hold the cover away from the top). Before serving, if you wish you can garnish the top with more whipped cream, spooned into a ring around the edge of the pie, and sprinkle a pinch of nutmeg over the cream.

Sour Cream Apple Crumb Pie

I FIRST MET Florence and Alvin Bloch, summer neighbors in northern Vermont, when we kept turning up at the same local bake sales, church luncheons, and the Craftsbury Common Library Silver Tea. It didn't take long to discover that we shared a love of home baking as well as an affection for Vermont's Northeast Kingdom. I treasure the afternoon I spent in their sunny living room overlooking the mountains and lake while poring over a notebook of family recipes. This unusual creamy apple pie topped with crunchy crumbs is my adaptation of one of Florence's favorites; she suggests using Golden Delicious or a similar medium-hard eating apple, which will bake more quickly than a green cooking apple. While you can use any pastry recipe you prefer, I suggest using this especially tender one made with sour cream, an ingredient you already have on hand for the filling.

for good measure

To make the crumb topping quickly and easily, put cold butter in the microwave on "defrost" for about 1 minute, until barely softened; use a pastry blender to cut together all the ingredients into crumbs. *Note:* As written, the crumbs melt together into a crackly crisp topping; however, if you prefer sandy crumbs, don't add them to the pie until the last 15 minutes of the baking time.

special equipment: 9-inch pie plate, preferably heat-proof glass; pastry blender, optional; wax paper

advance preparation: Pastry can be prepared ahead and frozen, or made a day ahead and refrigerated. Pie is best served warm on the day it is baked.

temperature and time: 425°F for 15 minutes, then 350°F for 35 to 40 minutes

yield: 9-inch pie; 8 to 10 servings

sour cream pastry

1 cup unsifted all-purpose flour

2 tablespoons granulated sugar

½ teaspoon salt

⅓ cup (5⅓ tablespoons) chilled unsalted butter, cut up

3 to 4 tablespoons sour cream (or plain yogurt, top liquid drained off), as needed

topping

⅓ cup unsifted all-purpose flour

⅓ cup granulated sugar

¼ cup (½ stick) unsalted butter, cut up

1 teaspoon ground cinnamon

filling

1 large egg, at room temperature

1 cup sour cream

1 teaspoon vanilla extract

¼ teaspoon ground nutmeg

½ cup granulated sugar

2 tablespoons unsifted all-purpose flour

⅛ teaspoon salt

2 tablespoons crumbs made from graham crackers, stale bread, or any crushed cereal

3 large or 4 medium apples, peeled, cored, diced or thinly sliced (preferably Golden Delicious; 3½ to 4 cups)

1. Prepare the pastry: In a bowl, whisk together the flour, sugar, and salt. Pinch in the butter using your fingertips or cut in with a pastry blender or 2 cross-cutting table knives until the mixture is cut into pieces the size of small peas. Add the sour cream one tablespoon at a time, using just enough to make the dough begin to clump together. Turn the dough out onto a piece of wax paper and gather it into a ball; refrigerate about 30 minutes, then roll the dough out between 2 lightly floured pieces of wax paper and fit it into the pie plate. Fold over any overhanging dough pieces and pinch up the rim into points or flutes or press flat with a floured fork. Refrigerate the dough while making the filling.

2. Position a rack in the lower third of the oven and preheat it to 425°F. Prepare the crumb topping: In a bowl, pinch together all the topping ingredients with your fingertips or a pastry blender to make crumbs.

3. Prepare the filling: In a large mixing bowl, whisk together the egg, sour cream, vanilla, and nutmeg, then the sugar, flour, and salt.

Scatter cracker crumbs evenly over the pastry shell (to absorb excess moisture). Add the apple pieces, spoon on the cream filling, and spread on the topping crumbs. Bake 15 minutes, then reduce the heat to 350°F and bake 30 to 35 minutes longer, until the filling is puffed up and a sharp paring knife stuck into the pie center easily pierces the apple slices. Cool the pie on a wire rack. Serve warm or at room temperature. Refrigerate leftovers.

Strawberry-Rhubarb Streusel Pie

WHEN THIS PIE appears, you know spring has arrived. Strawberries and rhubarb are natural partners, and their sweet/tart flavors complement each other perfectly. In this pie, the soft filling is set off by a crunchy crumb topping to make a fine family dessert. You will get rave reviews, especially if you serve it warm with vanilla ice cream on the side.

This recipe has a special bonus for the baker: a no-rolling-pin pastry that is a cinch to prepare and tender to taste. It may become your favorite recipe in the book.

for good measure

> To prevent the moist filling from softening the pastry crust, brush the dough with an egg glaze before adding the filling and be sure to begin baking in a 425°F oven.

special equipment: 9-inch pie plate, preferably heat-proof glass; pastry cutter, optional; plastic wrap; aluminum foil

advance preparation: Pie is best served freshly baked and warm from the oven. The crumb topping can be prepared several hours in advance and refrigerated.

temperature and time: 425°F for 15 minutes, then 350°F for 35 to 40 minutes

yield: 9-inch pie; 8 to 10 servings

press-in-place pastry

2 cups unsifted all-purpose flour

1 teaspoon granulated sugar

1 teaspoon salt

Scant ⅔ cup canola oil

3 tablespoons milk, or as needed

streusel topping

⅓ cup unsifted all-purpose flour

¼ cup granulated sugar

¼ cup packed dark or light brown sugar

½ cup old-fashioned rolled oats (not instant)

¼ cup toasted wheat germ, optional

Pinch of salt

½ teaspoon ground cinnamon

½ teaspoon ground nutmeg

⅓ cup (5⅓ tablespoons) unsalted butter, at room temperature, cut up

strawberry-rhubarb filling

2 cups fresh strawberries, rinsed, blotted dry, hulled and halved or 12 ounces whole frozen berries, partially thawed

2 cups (¾ pound) fresh rhubarb stalks, rinsed, dried, and cut in 1-inch pieces, or same quantity frozen rhubarb pieces, partially thawed

1¼ cups granulated sugar

¼ cup unsifted all-purpose flour

½ teaspoon ground cinnamon

Pinch of salt

½ teaspoon vanilla extract

glaze

1 large egg, at room temperature, lightly beaten with 1 teaspoon water

1. Prepare the pastry: In a mixing bowl, combine the flour, sugar, and salt. Stir with a fork, drizzling in the oil and milk. Mix until the crumbs hold their shape when pressed. Turn out about ¾ of the mixture into the pie plate and cover it with a piece of plastic wrap. Pressing through the wrap, spread out the dough crumbs with your fingertips, making an even layer. Build up the edges enough to crimp or pinch into flutes on the rim of the plate. Use more pastry if needed; you will have a little dough left over. Cover and refrigerate the pastry-lined pan while making the filling.

2. Prepare the streusel topping: In a mixing bowl, combine the flour, both sugars, oats, wheat germ, salt, and spices. With a pastry cutter or your fingertips, pinch the butter into the dry ingredients until crumbs form. Add a few drops of water if too dry. Crumble in any leftover pastry dough if you wish. Set the crumbs aside or refrigerate.

3. Position a rack in the lower third of the oven and preheat it to 425°F. Place a piece of foil, shiny side up, on the oven floor to catch potential drips.

4. Prepare the filling: In a large bowl, toss together the strawberries, rhubarb, sugar, flour, cinnamon, salt, and vanilla extract. Lightly brush the pie shell with the egg glaze, then spoon in the filling. Spread on the streusel topping.

5. Bake the pie for 15 minutes, then reduce the heat to 350°F and bake an additional 35 to 40 minutes, or longer if needed, until the filling is bubbly and the crumbs are golden brown. Cool on a wire rack and serve warm.

Plum Crumb Pie

THIS IS A foolproof method to make a quick pie using whatever fruit is in season—plums, nectarines, peaches, pears, rhubarb, or a combination of these. Simply toss together a bunch of buttery crumbs, then divide them into two layers with fruit in the middle.

This recipe is dedicated to its creator, my late friend Lauren Lieberman, a marvelous and enthusiastic cook who believed that as long as you baked with sweet butter, all was right with the world. The success of this popular recipe is a tribute to her culinary creativity and to her personal strength.

for good measure

- Instead of all-purpose flour, you can substitute half whole wheat flour.

- Nuts add a pleasant crunch to the topping crumbs, but can be omitted if you prefer.

special equipment: 9-inch pie plate, preferably heat-proof glass

advance preparation: Crumbs can be prepared a day ahead, covered, and refrigerated. The pie is best served the day it is baked.

temperature and time: 400°F for 35 to 40 minutes

yield: 4 cups fruit; 2⅔ cups crumbs; 9-inch pie; 8 to 10 servings

fruit

4 cups unpeeled, pitted, sliced plums (about 1¼ pounds, any type, such as Santa Rosa, Damson, or Italian prune plums)

½ cup granulated or packed light brown sugar

2 tablespoons cornstarch

2 tablespoon fresh lemon juice

½ teaspoon ground cinnamon

crumbs

1 cup unsifted all-purpose flour

½ cup granulated sugar

¼ teaspoon salt

½ teaspoon ground cinnamon

½ cup (1 stick) unsalted butter, at room temperature

½ cup (2 ounces) chopped walnuts

1. Position a rack in the middle of the oven and preheat it to 400°F.

2. In a large mixing bowl, toss together the sliced fruit, sugar, cornstarch, lemon juice, and cinnamon.

3. Prepare the crumbs: In a large bowl, toss together the flour, sugar, salt, cinnamon, butter, and nuts. In a food processor or using a pastry blender, 2 cross-cutting knives, or your fingertips, work the butter into the dry ingredients until the mixture forms quite powdery crumbs. Measure 1½ cups of crumbs into the pie plate and press them flat with the back of a big spoon. Reserve the remaining crumbs.

4. Spread the fruit mixture over the crumbs in the pie plate, then top with the reserved crumbs. Bake 35 to 40 minutes, or slightly longer depending upon the type of fruit used, until the fruit is tender when pierced with the tip of a knife and the top crumbs are a rich golden brown. Cool the pie on a wire rack. Serve warm or at room temperature, topped with sweetened whipped cream or ice cream.

Peanut Butter Pie with Chocolate Icing

EARLY FORMS OF this pie began to appear after commercial peanut butter became available in the late nineteenth century. This version, with its creamy no-bake filling sandwiched between a crisp chocolate crumb crust and a rich chocolate icing, will remind you of peanut butter cup candies, although it is a little less sweet than the candy because I prefer to use semisweet instead of milk chocolate.

for good measure

- This crust and filling can also be prepared in a 9-inch square pan and cut into bar cookies.
- Graham cracker crumbs can be substituted for the chocolate wafer crumbs.
- The best peanut butter to use is supermarket store-bought instead of natural-foods style or homemade, which can be too thick to blend properly.

special equipment: 9-inch pie plate; double boiler or metal bowl set over a larger pan

advance preparation: Pie needs to chill at least 3 hours to set properly. It is fine if made 1 day in advance and refrigerated until served. It can also be double-wrapped and frozen up to 1 month; thaw in the original wrapper overnight in the refrigerator.

temperature and time: Crumb crust: 350°F for 8 minutes; stove-top melting chocolate: 5 minutes; refrigerator: 3 hours

yield: 9-inch pie; 8 to 10 servings

chocolate filling and icing

12 ounces (2 cups) semisweet chocolate, chopped, or chips

½ cup heavy cream

chocolate crumb crust

1½ cups chocolate wafer or Oreo cookie crumbs (or 8 ounces chocolate wafer cookies, finely crushed)

6 tablespoons (¾ stick) unsalted butter, melted

peanut butter filling

1 cup commercial peanut butter, chunky or creamy

8 ounces (1 large package) cream cheese (not low-fat), softened

2 tablespoons unsalted butter, softened

¼ teaspoon salt

1 cup sifted confectioners' sugar

1 tablespoon vanilla extract

garnish

2 tablespoons chopped peanuts

1. Position a rack in the center of the oven and preheat it to 350°F. Combine the chopped chocolate and heavy cream in the top of a double boiler set over, not touching, simmering water. Stir on and off until melted; whisk to blend smooth, remove from the heat, and set aside to cool while you prepare the crust.

2. Prepare the crumb crust: In a bowl, toss together the crumbs with the melted butter, then press them into the pie plate with the back of a large spoon, making an even layer on the sides and bottom of the pan. Bake the crust 8 minutes. Remove the pan from the oven and set it aside until cool. Spoon about ½ cup of the melted chocolate mixture onto the crumb shell, spreading it in an even layer.

3. Prepare the peanut butter filling: In a food processor or electric mixer, beat together the peanut butter, cream cheese, and butter until very soft and creamy. Add the salt, sugar, and vanilla and blend thoroughly. Spread the filling over the chocolate layer in the pie plate and top with the remaining melted chocolate (stir it over heat for a minute if it thickened as it cooled). Sprinkle the chopped peanuts on top and refrigerate the pie at least 3 hours to set.

Apple Pie Pizza

WHAT TASTES LIKE apple pie, looks like a pizza, and is easier to make than either one? This free-form tart—simply cream cheese pastry topped with apple pie filling baked on a cookie sheet. Unanimously loved by adults as well as kids, who like to help with this because it is so quick, easy, and delicious. Don't be put off by the lengthy directions; once you see how the stages go together, it's a snap.

for good measure

This pizza does not bake as long as a regular apple pie; select softer eating apples like Jonathan or Golden Delicious instead of hard green apples, which take too long to bake. If you only have green apples, slice them very thinly.

special equipment: Heavy-duty aluminum foil or baking parchment cut into an 18-inch square; rolling pin; cookie sheet with only 1 edge; pastry brush

advance preparation: Pastry can be made 1 or 2 days in advance and chilled. Roll out just before using. Apple pizza is best when baked fresh, but will stand 4 or 5 hours without getting soggy. Unbaked pizza can be double-wrapped and frozen up to 1 month. Bake without thawing for about 5 minutes longer than when fresh.

temperature and time: 425°F for 15 minutes, then 350°F for 25 to 30 minutes

yield: 12-inch pizza; 10 to 12 servings

cream cheese pastry

8 ounces (1 large package) cream cheese (not low-fat)

1 cup (2 sticks) unsalted butter, at room temperature, cut up

2 cups unsifted all-purpose flour

½ teaspoon salt

fruit filling

4 or 5 large Golden Delicious apples (or other medium-soft eating apple), peeled, cored, and sliced about ⅛ inch thick (about 2 pounds, generous 4 cups slices)

2 tablespoons fresh lemon juice

⅓ cup granulated sugar or packed dark brown sugar, or more depending upon sweetness of fruit

¾ teaspoon ground cinnamon

¾ teaspoon ground nutmeg

2 tablespoons unsifted all-purpose flour, plus extra for preparing foil

¾ cup apple jelly or apricot preserves, or other preserves with complementary flavor

⅓ cup graham cracker crumbs, or crushed wheat or rice flake cereal

egg glaze

1 large egg, at room temperature, beaten with 2 teaspoons water

pastry topping

1 tablespoon granulated sugar

1. Prepare the pastry: In the large bowl of an electric mixer or a food processor fitted with a steel blade, beat or pulse the cream cheese and butter until completely smooth. Add the flour and salt and slowly work together only until blended in and just beginning to clump together.

Remove the dough from the machine; on a lightly floured surface, form a dough ball. The warmth of your hands will help the dough to come together. Add a tiny bit more flour if the dough feels sticky. Form the dough into a flat disk about 1 × 5 inches. Wrap and chill it at least 30 minutes, or while you prepare the fruit.

2. Position a rack in the lower third of the oven and preheat it to 425°F. In a large bowl, toss together the apples, lemon juice, sugar, spices, and flour.

3. Measure an 18-inch square of foil. Turn the foil shiny side down, and sprinkle lightly with flour. With your fingernail or a toothpick, draw a circle on the foil approximately 16 to 17 inches in diameter as a guide for rolling out the dough. Place the dough disk in the center of the foil and roll it out like a pie crust, using a lightly floured rolling pin. Lift the dough and flour under it now and then so it doesn't stick. Roll the dough until it fills the marked circle, allowing the edges to be ragged. If working with kids, cover the dough with plastic wrap and let them press the dough into place with their fingertips.

4. Slide the foil, with the dough in place, onto a cookie sheet. With your fingertips or a toothpick, lightly mark a 2-inch border in from the edge of the dough; this border will later be folded up over the fruit.

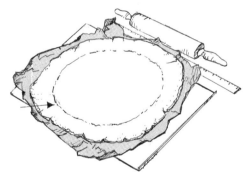

Mark the border

5. Make the egg glaze: In a cup, beat the egg and water together, then use a pastry brush to paint it over the rolled dough. Spread on the fruit preserves, sprinkle on the crumbs, then top with the fruit mixture, spreading it out to fill just the marked area.

6. To shape the dough border, slide your hand beneath the foil or parchment and lift it just beneath the outer edge of the pastry. Use the foil as a pusher to flip the dough over onto the edge of the fruit. Allow the dough to fold over on itself naturally, like fabric making pleats, as it goes around the

circle. Brush the egg glaze over any pastry cracks and pinch them with your fingers to seal. Fold up the edges of the foil to make a lip to catch any drips as the pizza bakes.

7. Brush the egg glaze over the top of the pastry border, then sprinkle on the granulated sugar topping.

Fold over the dough border

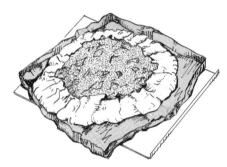

Fold up the foil edges

Slide the foil onto a cookie sheet. Bake for 15 minutes, then reduce the heat to 350°F and bake another 25 to 30 minutes or just until the pastry is golden brown and the fruit can easily be pierced with the tip of a sharp paring knife. Slide the foil holding the pizza off the baking sheet and onto a wire rack to cool. Cut the pizza into wedges to serve.

> **Plum, Pear, or Peach Pizza:** Prepare the recipe above but replace apples with about 4 cups unpeeled pitted, sliced plums or peeled, cored, sliced pears or peeled sliced peaches. Before adding fruit, spread dough with ½ cup plum, apricot, or other preserves, then add some crushed cereal crumbs.

Cranberry Pizza

THIS RUSTIC, FREE-FORM fruit pizza, or—in this case—pan-less cranberry tart, is really easier than pie! Its ruby red color brightens any table and is perfect for holiday entertaining, especially since it can be made ahead and frozen. Children love to help shape the dough and spread the filling—the more help, the sweeter the taste.

for good measure

- If you want the top to look very shiny, add the glaze; otherwise, forget it. Golden raisins are best for the filling because they are brighter; black raisins are too dark, but Craisins or dried cherries or cranberries can be substituted.

- Nuts add crunch but are optional.

- In the filling, use any type of preserves you prefer— seedless raspberry, plum, orange marmalade, or currant jelly. In a pinch, substitute for the cranberry filling 2 cans of whole-berry cranberry sauce mixed with the raisins, spices, and chopped nuts.

special equipment: Heavy-duty aluminum foil or baking parchment cut into an 18-inch square; rolling pin; cookie sheet with only 1 edge; pastry brush

advance preparation: Pastry can be made 1 or 2 days in advance and chilled. Roll out just before using. Pizza is best when baked fresh, but will stand 4 or 5 hours without getting soggy. Unbaked pizza can be double-wrapped and frozen up to 1 month. Bake without thawing for 5 to 10 minutes longer than when fresh.

temperature and time: 425°F for 15 minutes, then 350°F for 25 to 30 minutes

yield: 12-inch pizza; 10 to 12 servings

cream cheese pastry

8 ounces (1 large package) cream cheese (not low-fat)

1 cup (2 sticks) unsalted butter, at room temperature, cut up

2 cups unsifted all-purpose flour, plus extra for preparing foil

½ teaspoon salt

cranberry filling

3 cups (12-ounce bag) whole fresh or frozen (unthawed) cranberries, picked over, rinsed, and blotted dry

½ cup packed golden raisins

2 teaspoons grated orange zest

1 cup granulated or packed light brown sugar

½ teaspoon ground cinnamon

½ teaspoon ground nutmeg

½ cup (2 ounces) walnut or pecan pieces

½ cup orange marmalade or other fruit preserves

⅓ cup orange juice

2 tablespoons cornstarch

egg glaze

1 large egg, at room temperature, beaten with 2 teaspoons water

pastry topping

1 tablespoon granulated sugar

pizza glaze

½ cup seedless raspberry or red currant jam, optional

1. Prepare the pastry: In the large bowl of an electric mixer or a food processor fitted with a steel blade, beat or pulse the cream cheese and butter until completely smooth. Add the flour and salt and slowly work together only until blended in and just beginning to clump together.

Remove the dough from the machine; on a lightly floured surface, form a dough ball. The warmth of your hands will help the dough to come together. Add a tiny bit more flour if the dough feels sticky. Form the dough into a flat disk about 1 × 5 inches. Wrap and chill it at least 30 minutes, or while you prepare the fruit.

2. Position a rack in the lower third of the oven and preheat it to 425°F.

3. Make the cranberry filling: In a large bowl, toss together all the filling ingredients except the cornstarch and orange juice. Stir the juice and cornstarch together until the cornstarch dissolves, then stir into the fruit mixture.

4. Measure an 18-inch square of foil, turn it shiny side down and sprinkle lightly with flour. With your fingernail or a toothpick, draw a circle on the foil approximately 16 to 17 inches in diameter as a guide for rolling out the dough. Place the dough disk in the center of the foil and roll it out like a pie crust, using a lightly floured rolling pin. Roll the dough until it fits inside the marked circle, allowing the edges to be ragged. If working with kids, cover the dough with plastic wrap and let them press the dough into place with their fingertips.

Slide the foil, with the dough in place, onto a cookie sheet. With your fingertip or a toothpick, lightly mark a 2-inch border in from the edge of the dough; this border will later be folded up over the fruit (see all sketches, page 105).

5. Make the glaze: In a cup, beat together the egg and water, then use a pastry brush to paint it over the rolled dough. Spread the cranberry mixture inside the marked circle.

6. To shape the dough border, slide your hand beneath the foil or parchment and lift it just beneath the outer edge of the pastry, using the foil as a pusher to flip the dough over onto the edge of the fruit. Allow the dough to fold over on itself naturally, like fabric making pleats, as it goes around the circle. Brush the egg glaze over any pastry cracks and pinch them with your fingers to seal.

7. Fold up the edges of the foil to make a lip to catch any drips as the pizza bakes. Slide the foil onto the cookie sheet. Brush the egg glaze over the top of the pastry border, then sprinkle on the topping sugar. Bake for 15 minutes. Reduce the heat to 350°F and bake another 25 to 30 minutes or just until the pastry is golden brown. Peek in the oven after about 15 minutes and, if the pastry is browning too much or the berries are looking too dark, cover it with foil (see page 231). Slide the foil holding the pizza off the baking sheet onto a wire rack to cool.

8. If you want to use the glaze: In a small saucepan, stir the jam a minute or two on low heat until liquefied. Brush the glaze over the *fruit* area of the baked pizza to give it a bright shine. The glaze will set as it cools. Cut the pizza into wedges to serve.

Strawberry Angel Pie

ANGEL PIES ARE so named because they are delicious enough to tease the angels out of the heavens. This inspired creation proves the point. Most angel pies have meringue shells, but this one is unique: a pie plate filled to the brim with crisp-baked meringue cut into wedges, then piled high with sweetened berries and whipped cream. It was a specialty of Louvene Allford, of McAlester, Oklahoma, the mother of my friend and neighbor Jerry Allford. Jerry remembers growing up with this family favorite: "My brother and I loved it," he told me as we stood in his kitchen exchanging recipes, "the crisp sweet taste of the meringue contrasted with the sweet/tart juicy berries and the luscious whipped cream . . . it just drove us wild!"

Louvene had a trick for getting this meringue texture right: She believed the meringue should be baked in a glass pie plate (so you could see the color of the bottom) until the top and bottom were a pale tan–beige color, not pure white. This slight coloring meant the sugar had caramelized to give the meringue its special flavor. The inside of the meringue, however, should still be white, but firm and dried out.

special equipment: 9-inch pie plate, preferably heat-proof glass; electric mixer; chilled bowl and beater for whipping cream

advance preparation: In dry weather, you can prepare the meringue pie 1 or 2 days in advance and keep covered, at room temperature. Or, it can be kept in an airtight box in the freezer for about 2 weeks.

temperature and time: 275°F for 1 hour and 20 to 30 minutes, then in oven with heat off and door closed for 1 more hour

yield: 9-inch pie; 6 to 8 servings

for good measure

- The meringue will rise at least an inch above the plate while baking, then sink back and crack as it cools. This is okay. Let it cool completely before cutting and serving.

- Oven temperature is important to the success of this pie. To be sure your oven is the correct temperature, get an auxiliary oven thermometer at a hardware store and adjust your oven to the internal temperature.

- Remove eggs from the refrigerator before starting the recipe; room temperature whites whip to greater volume than cold whites. The presence of any fat will impede the whipping of egg whites. Be sure your bowl and beater are absolutely grease free by wiping them with a towel dampened with white vinegar.

- Humidity softens meringue; bake this on a clear, dry day.

meringue

Unsalted butter for preparing the pan

5 large egg whites, at room temperature

⅛ teaspoon salt

¼ teaspoon cream of tartar

1 cup granulated sugar, preferably superfine

½ teaspoon vanilla extract

fruit

1 quart ripe strawberries, rinsed, hulled, blotted dry on paper towels

2 to 3 tablespoons granulated sugar

whipped cream

1½ cups heavy cream (36% butterfat), chilled

2 tablespoons granulated or superfine sugar

½ teaspoon vanilla extract

1. Position a rack in the center of the oven and preheat it to 275°F. Butter the pie plate.

2. Prepare the meringue: Put the egg whites into the largest grease-free bowl of an electric mixer. Add the salt and cream of tartar. With the mixer on medium speed, whip the whites until foamy, then gradually add the sugar while beating continuously. When the whites look thick and foamy, increase the speed to high and beat until the whites look smooth and satiny, and you begin to see beater tracks on the surface. Beat just a little longer until when the mixer is turned off and the beater is lifted, the foam makes a peak that stands straight up on the tip. Add the vanilla, beat a few seconds to blend, then retest.

3. Mound the whites into the prepared pie plate, then spread them fairly evenly on top. The meringue should touch the pan edges all around so it doesn't shrink. It is not necessary to make peaks or designs. Bake about 1 hour and 20 minutes, but look in the oven after the first 40 minutes and reduce the heat if the meringue is browning too much; you may have to adjust the heat as baking progresses, depending upon your oven temperature. When the meringue looks pale beige-light tan on the top and bottom, turn off the heat but leave the pan in the oven with the door closed for 1 hour longer so the interior of the meringue can dry out completely.

4. Shortly before serving, slice the strawberries into a bowl and stir in the sugar. In a medium-size bowl, whip the cream to soft peaks, add the sugar and vanilla, and whip to medium-stiff peaks. To serve, put a wedge of the cold meringue on each plate, spoon on a generous helping of juicy sweetened berries, and top with whipped cream. Pass leftover berries and cream at the table.

Favorite Fresh Fruit Tart

THIS IS ONE of the three essential recipes in my life, right up there with Mom's Apple Pie and To-Live-For Chocolate Mousse Cake. No-rolling-pin, press-in-place pastry is a snap to make and the filling is simply orange-flavored cream cheese covered with berries. This tart is a perfect example of *Baking for Bluffers,* a title suggested to me for this book by my friend, British writer Val Corbett, who loves stylish, but effortless, entertaining.

for good measure

- You can bake this in a tart pan or pie plate.

- You can substitute for this pastry any crumb crust (see Index), prebaked at 350°F for 8 minutes to make it firm, or a store-bought and then prebaked pie shell.

- The cream cheese filling can be flavored with frozen lemonade or strawberry daiquiri mix concentrate, or any other frozen juice concentrate instead of orange juice.

special equipment: 10½- or 11-inch removable-bottom tart pan or 10-inch pie plate, preferably heat-proof glass; plastic wrap; aluminum foil; pie weights or dry rice or beans reserved for this purpose; paper towels; paring knife; small saucepan; strainer; pastry brush

advance preparation: Tart can be prepared early on the day it is to be served. Refrigerate and add glaze no more than 2 hours before serving.

temperature and time: Pastry: 425°F for 12 minutes, then 350°F for 10 to 15 minutes

yield: 10½- or 11-inch tart or 10-inch pie; 1½ cups filling; 10 to 12 servings

orange press-in-place pastry

Butter for preparing pan and foil

2 cups unsifted all-purpose flour

1 teaspoon granulated sugar

1 teaspoon salt

1 teaspoon grated orange zest

Scant ⅔ cup canola oil

3 tablespoons milk, or as needed

orange cream filling

12 ounces (1½ large packages) cream cheese, at room temperature

⅓ cup granulated sugar, or to taste

1 tablespoon grated orange zest

1½ tablespoons frozen orange juice concentrate, undiluted, or other frozen juice drink concentrate

2 tablespoons orange-flavored liqueur or white rum, optional

fruit (about 4 cups total)

1 kiwi fruit

1 ripe peach or nectarine

2 tablespoons fresh lemon juice

1 cup fresh whole raspberries

1 cup fresh whole blueberries

1 cup fresh whole blackberries

1 small bunch seedless red or green grapes

glaze

⅔ cup apricot preserves

2 tablespoons orange-flavored liqueur or white rum, optional

1. Position a rack in the lower third of the oven and preheat it to 425°F.

Prepare the pastry: Generously butter the inside of a removable bottom tart pan or pie plate. In a mixing bowl, combine the flour, sugar, salt, and orange zest. Stir with a fork, drizzling in the oil and milk. Mix until the crumbs hold their shape when pressed. Turn out the mixture into the tart pan or pie plate, and cover it with a piece of plastic wrap. Pressing through the wrap, spread out the dough crumbs with your fingertips, making an even layer on the bottom and up the sides of the pan.

2. To completely prebake the empty pastry shell, line it with a piece of aluminum foil, shiny side down, and cover with the pie weights or dry rice (see sketch below). Bake for about 12 minutes, then reduce heat to 350°F and bake another 10 to 15 minutes. Remove the pan from the oven, lift out the foil and all the weights, and inspect the pastry. It should be a light golden color and completely baked. If the dough still looks pale or translucent, bake it a few more minutes without the foil and weights. Set the baked shell on a wire rack to cool completely.

3. Prepare the filling: In a food processor or an electric mixer, beat the cream cheese until completely soft and smooth. Add all the remaining filling ingredients and blend until absolutely smooth. Taste and add sugar if needed. Spread the cream in the cooled pastry shell and smooth the top. Refrigerate the tart.

4. Prepare the fruit: Peel and thinly slice the kiwi and peach into a bowl and coat the slices with lemon juice to prevent discoloration. Rinse the berries and grapes and gently blot them dry on paper towels. Arrange the berries and fruit slices in an attractive pattern on top of the cream.

5. No more than 2 hours before serving (or the glaze may melt), warm the apricot preserves and liqueur, if using, in a small saucepan, strain it to remove fruit pieces, and allow it to cool slightly. With a pastry brush, gently coat the tops of the berries and fruit. Refrigerate the tart to set the glaze. Bring the tart to room temperature before serving. Refrigerate leftovers.

Note: To remove the sides of a tart pan, set the metal pan bottom on a wide-topped jar for support and let the pan sides slide down. Serve the tart on pan bottom.

Mocha Walnut Tart with Walnut Pastry

EASY TO MAKE and divine to taste, the tart filling is a buttery blend of chocolate, coffee, and toasted walnuts coated with a satin smooth icing glaze garnished with a ring of chocolate-coated coffee beans. It is simple but elegant, a perfect dinner party dessert. For the quickest preparation, make the crust and filling in a food processor (an electric mixer can be substituted). Bake it either in a tart pan or a pie plate.

for good measure

- Hazelnuts can be substituted for walnuts. Chocolate-coated coffee beans are sold in gourmet shops or by mail order (see Mail-Order Sources and Suppliers, page 240); nuts can also be used as a garnish.

- For the best flavor, be sure to toast nuts before using them. You need a total of about 2¾ cups (10 ounces) nuts for the pastry, filling, and garnish; toast them all together before starting the recipe: Spread nuts in a jelly roll or roasting pan and bake them at 325°F for 10 to 12 minutes, tossing them a few times, until aromatic. If using hazelnuts, rub them in a towel to remove most of the skins after toasting.

- To ensure a smooth finish on the glaze, be sure to put it on the filling while it is still very warm. After glazing, don't touch the top; fingerprints show.

special equipment: 10½- or 11-inch removable-bottom tart pan or 10-inch pie plate, preferably heatproof glass; jelly roll or roasting pan for toasting nuts; food processor or nut chopper; rolling pin; pastry brush

advance preparation: Pastry can be made a day in advance and refrigerated. Prepare the filling and bake the tart the day it will be served, or no more than 1 day in advance.

temperature and time: 425°F for 12 minutes, then 375°F for 15 to 18 minutes

yield: 10½- or 11-inch tart or 10-inch pie; 12 to 14 servings

walnut pastry

½ cup (generous 2 ounces) walnuts or hazelnuts

1½ cups unsifted all-purpose flour

½ teaspoon salt

6 tablespoons (¾ stick) chilled unsalted butter, plus extra for preparing pan

3 tablespoons chilled solid shortening (Crisco) or solid stick margarine

1 large egg yolk

2 tablespoons fresh lemon juice or white vinegar

3 to 4 tablespoons ice water, or as needed

filling

1⅓ cups (5 ounces) toasted walnut pieces or hazelnuts

¾ cup granulated sugar

8 tablespoons (1 stick) sweet butter, at room temperature, cut up

2 tablespoons instant espresso coffee powder (such as Medaglia d'Oro; regular instant coffee can be substituted)

2 tablespoons unsweetened cocoa powder, any type

¼ cup boiling water

2 large eggs, at room temperature

1 teaspoon vanilla extract

¼ teaspoon salt

icing glaze

1¼ cups confectioners' sugar

1 tablespoon unsweetened cocoa powder

1 teaspoon vanilla extract

garnish

20 to 28 chocolate-coated coffee beans or walnut pieces (halves if available) or whole toasted hazelnuts

1. Toast the walnuts (see For Good Measure). Butter the tart pan or pie plate.

2. Prepare the pastry: In the workbowl of a food processor fitted with the steel blade, pulse the flour, salt, and nuts until the nuts are finely chopped. Add the butter and shortening and pulse just until the texture resembles coarse meal. Through the feed tube, add the yolk, lemon juice, and 1 or 2 tablespoons of ice water. Pulse a few times, stopping as soon as the dough begins to look clumpy. Add more water, 1 tablespoon at a time, if needed, but do not allow a dough ball to form. Turn the clumpy dough out onto a lightly floured board and gather it into a ball. Refrigerate it 30 minutes, or overnight, if time permits. Using a lightly floured rolling pin, roll out the dough until it measures about 1 inch larger around than the baking pan (set it upside down on top of the dough to measure it).

3. Fold the dough into quarters and fit it into the prepared pan, positioning the folded point at the center (see sketch, page 85). Unfold and gently drape the pastry over the pan; do not stretch it. Trim the edges to fit the tart pan or, for a pie plate, fold the pastry edges under and press them into a fluted or pinched rim on the pan lip. Refrigerate the pastry-lined pan while you make the filling. Return the processor workbowl to the base without washing it.

4. Position a shelf in the lower third of the oven and preheat it to 425°F.

Prepare the filling: In the food processor, pulse the toasted walnuts with the sugar until the nuts are chopped medium-fine. Add the butter and blend until a paste forms. Turn off the machine and scrape down the bowl.

In a cup, mix together the coffee powder and cocoa, then stir in the boiling water until the coffee dissolves. Reserve 2 tablespoons of this mocha essence for the glaze and pour the remaining 2 tablespoons through the feed tube into the processor, pulsing to blend it with the nut paste. Add the eggs, vanilla, and salt and pulse to blend.

5. Spoon the filling into the prepared pastry shell, smooth the top, and bake it for 12 minutes. Then reduce the heat to 375°F and bake an additional 15 to 18 minutes, or until the top of the filling begins to puff slightly; the pastry edges will look golden and a knife inserted in the filling center should come out clean. While the tart bakes, prepare the icing glaze. Set the baked tart on a wire rack to cool.

6. Make the icing glaze: In a bowl, sift together the confectioners' sugar and cocoa, then whisk in the vanilla and the reserved 2 tablespoons of mocha essence from step 4, making a glaze that has the consistency of softly whipped cream; add a drop or two of water if it feels too thick.

7. Allow the tart to cool on the rack about 5 minutes, until the filling settles and flattens out. While the tart is still very warm, spoon the icing glaze on top and use a pastry brush to spread it into an even coating; the warmth of the tart will melt the glaze so it flows on evenly. Arrange the coffee beans in a ring around the edge of the tart. Let the tart sit at room temperature, or refrigerate, at least 30 minutes, to set the glaze. Bring the tart to room temperature before serving.

COFFEE CAKES, COBBLERS, CRISPS? If you are wondering what these categories have in common, my answer is "attitude." They are all casual, quick to prepare with little fuss, and homey. Desserts or treats to share with family and good friends. Little labor, tremendous taste, garnished with their own crumbs, juices, and golden dough rather than flowers and frosting. Simply the best.

COFFEE CAKES ARE EVERYONE'S FAVORITE. These are simple, quick-to-put-together recipes you will want to make your personal standbys. Blueberry Buckle and Cape Cod Coffee Cake are so elementary you can prepare them with any fruit or berries you happen to have on hand, and if you are like me, a slice of Gladys Martin's Sour Cream Cake with a steaming mug of tea will quickly become the *only* way you can start your day. This recipe is a bake-sale winner, as well.

Coffee cakes, COBBLERS, AND crisps

COBBLERS, ALSO KNOWN AS GRUNTS, slumps, or spoon pies, consist of a simple blend of sweetened fruit slices or berries topped by a biscuit dough. You will love my Golden Harvest Apple Honey Cobbler as well as Peach-Plum Cobbler and its Ginger-Peach variation.

CRISPS ARE NAMED FOR THEIR TOPPING, which ideally is a crunchy golden brown jumble of crumbs (often with oats and nuts added) set atop a bubbling bed of juicy sweetened fruit. Many crisps are really deep-dish pies, usually without a lower crust; the emphasis here is on the contrast between the soft, warm fruit and the crisp topping. You can use Apple-Pear-Cranberry Crisp as a master recipe, mixing together whatever fruit is available and topping it with the crumbs—it is always a hit, especially when served with vanilla ice cream.

Gladys Martin's Sour Cream Coffee Cake

RICH, MOIST, PACKED with flavor and laced with nutty crumbs—you absolutely *need* a thick slab of this old-fashioned favorite alongside your steaming mug of morning coffee or tea. Perfect for a brunch, picnic, or bake sale, this big, easy-to-prepare Bundt cake will keep at least a week (if it is alone in the house).

There are many versions of basic sour cream coffee cake, but this one is special. I discovered it recently at an auction in Vermont when Gladys Martin, a summertime neighbor, passed away and the contents of her home were sold. While antique hunters eyed the chests and china, my daughter and I searched for cookbooks, leafing through a jumble of boxes stacked near the barn. Beside shovels and rakes, we spied a couple of battered cartons we considered pure gold. Though a relative assured us the family had long since taken what they wanted from the house, we waited through the long hot July day, sure that someone would want the recipes. By the time the sun set, when most of the furnishings and crowd had gone, the two bedraggled boxes of handwritten recipes and well-used cookbooks reached the podium. I raised my numbered bidding card. "Sold!" cried the auctioneer. Over in a heartbeat— the treasure of a lifetime in the kitchen. This heirloom recipe, handwritten in blue ink on a pink file card, is one you will want to pass on to your family.

for good measure

> For a delightful flavor variation, replace 2 teaspoons vanilla in the original recipe with ½ teaspoon each: vanilla, lemon, and almond extract.

special equipment: 9- to 9½-inch (10- to 12-cup capacity) Bundt or tube pan; 2 flat platters or cardboard cake disks

advance preparation: Cake keeps a week, covered at room temperature, or can be double-wrapped and frozen up to 2 months.

temperature and time: 350°F for 50 to 55 minutes

yield: 5¾ cups batter; 14 to 16 servings

filling/topping

1 cup (4 ounces) chopped walnuts

½ cup granulated sugar

1 teaspoon ground cinnamon

cake

Solid shortening for preparing pan

3 cups sifted all-purpose flour, plus extra for preparing pan

1½ teaspoons baking powder

1 teaspoon baking soda

1 teaspoon salt

¾ cup (1½ sticks) unsalted butter, softened

1½ cups granulated sugar

4 large eggs, at room temperature

1½ cups sour cream

2 teaspoons vanilla extract

1. Position a rack in the center of the oven and preheat it to 350°F. Coat the baking pan with shortening, taking special care to generously coat the tube and all indentations if using a decorative Bundt. Dust flour all over the inside of the pan, especially directing it onto the tube; tap out excess flour.

2. To prepare the filling/topping: Toss together in a bowl the chopped nuts, sugar, and cinnamon. Set it aside.

3. In a medium bowl, whisk together the flour, baking powder, baking soda, and salt.

In the large bowl of an electric mixer or in a bowl with a sturdy spoon, beat together the butter and sugar until smooth and well blended. Beat in the eggs, sour cream, and vanilla. Slowly mix in the dry ingredients, stirring just until thoroughly incorporated and no flour is visible.

4. Spoon about half the batter into the baking pan, sprinkle on about half the nut filling, cover with the remaining batter, and top with the remaining filling; lightly press this mixture onto the batter.

Bake for 50 to 55 minutes, until the top is well risen, golden brown and springy to the touch, and a cake tester inserted in the center comes out dry or with just a few moist crumbs attached. Cool the cake in its pan on a wire rack for 15 minutes, then top with a plate or cardboard disk, invert, and lift off the baking pan. Leave a decorative Bundt in this position; for a plain tube, top again with a plate or disk and invert, so the crumb topping is up. Yes, a little of the topping falls off during this procedure, but not much, so don't worry.

Cape Cod Coffee Cake

ONE OF THE quickest and easiest coffee cakes I know, this is a basic recipe to use with whatever fruit or berry is in season—from apples and cranberries to blueberries and peaches. For topping, choose either a simple cinnamon-sugar topping or make my favorite streusel crumb mixture—either is delicious.

I developed this recipe many years ago after tasting a blueberry-raspberry coffee cake in Provincetown, on Cape Cod. Recently, I found a similar cake, made with apples, cranberries, and walnuts, in a 1948 pamphlet of local recipes put out by a Vermont rural electric company. New Englanders have always known you can't go wrong with a simple batter and a lot of fruit.

for good measure

Whole frozen berries, canned peaches (drained), or frozen peach slices (unthawed and cut up, ice crystals removed) can be substituted for fresh fruit. Frozen fruit can take up to 10 minutes longer to bake. Craisins or dried cranberries can also be used.

special equipment: 9 × 9 × 1½- or 2-inch baking pan

advance preparation: Cake keeps several days, covered at room temperature, or can be double-wrapped and frozen up to 2 months.

temperature and time: 350°F for 40 to 45 minutes

yield: 4 cups batter; 9-inch cake; 9 servings (3-inch squares)

(choose one topping) cinnamon sugar

2 tablespoons granulated sugar

½ teaspoon cinnamon

or streusel crumbs

½ cup unsifted all-purpose flour

⅓ cup granulated sugar

Pinch of salt

½ teaspoon ground cinnamon

¼ cup (½ stick) unsalted butter, at room temperature, cut up

Coffee cakes, cobblers, and crisps

cake

Butter-flavor no-stick vegetable spray or solid shortening for preparing pan

3 cups fruit, total: 2 large apples, such as Golden Delicious, peeled, cored, and coarsely chopped (½-inch cubes) plus 1 cup fresh or whole frozen cranberries (or peeled, pitted, and cut up peaches and blueberries, or unpeeled, pitted, chopped plums, or nectarines)

¾ cup (3 ounces) walnuts, coarsely chopped, (optional; for use with apples and cranberries)

1 cup unsifted all-purpose flour

1 teaspoon baking powder

½ teaspoon salt

½ teaspoon ground cinnamon

2 large eggs, at room temperature

½ cup (1 stick) unsalted butter, melted and cooled

1 teaspoon vanilla extract

1 cup granulated sugar

1. Position a rack in the center of the oven and preheat it to 350°F. Coat the pan with vegetable spray or shortening.

2. Prepare one topping: *Either* toss together cinnamon and sugar in a cup *or* make streusel by pinching together all the ingredients with your fingers or a fork until crumbs are formed.

Prepare the cake: In a large bowl, mix all the fruit and add the nuts, if using.

3. In a medium bowl, whisk together the flour, baking powder, salt, and cinnamon.

In a large bowl with a whisk or an electric mixer, beat together the eggs, butter, vanilla, and sugar. Stir in all the dry ingredients and mix only until combined. Gently mix the fruit into the batter, stirring only once or twice; do not overbeat. The batter will be thick.

4. Spread the batter into the baking pan, sprinkle on the topping, and bake for 40 to 45 minutes, until golden brown and a cake tester inserted in the center comes out dry. Cool the cake on a wire rack; cut it into squares and serve it from the pan.

Blueberry Buckle

EARLY SETTLERS IN New England made a version of this simple cake with wild berries and named it after the fact that the berries, batter, and crumbly topping buckle, or bubble up and bump into each other, as they bake. Serve this warm for breakfast or brunch, or top it with vanilla ice cream for a family dessert.

for good measure

- To vary the flavor and texture, you can replace blueberries with raspberries, huckleberries, strawberries, or fresh sweet cherries, pitted.
- The lemon flavor best complements blueberries; omit if using other berries.

special equipment: 9 × 9 × 1½- or 2-inch pan

advance preparation: Cake is best served warm from the oven; it keeps at room temperature 1 or 2 days.

temperature and time: 375°F for 40 to 45 minutes; 50 minutes if using frozen berries

yield: 2½ cups batter; 9-inch cake; 9 servings (3-inch squares)

crumbs

Butter-flavor no-stick vegetable spray or butter for preparing pan

½ cup unsifted all-purpose flour

⅓ cup granulated sugar

Pinch of salt

½ teaspoon ground cinnamon

¼ cup (½ stick) unsalted butter, at room temperature, cut up

cake

1½ cups sifted all-purpose flour

1 teaspoon baking powder

¼ teaspoon baking soda

¼ teaspoon salt

⅓ cup (5⅓ tablespoons) unsalted butter, at room temperature

1 cup granulated sugar

2 large eggs, at room temperature

1 teaspoon vanilla extract

¼ cup sour cream or plain yogurt (top liquid drained off)

Grated zest of 1 lemon (about 2 teaspoons)

2 tablespoons fresh lemon juice

¼ cup milk or orange juice

2 cups fresh blueberries, picked over, rinsed, and blotted dry on paper towels (or whole frozen unthawed berries with all ice particles removed)

1. Position a rack in the center of the oven and preheat it to 375°F. Coat the pan with vegetable spray or solid shortening.

2. In a small bowl, combine all the crumb ingredients and pinch them together with your fingertips or a fork, making crumbs. Prepare the cake: In a medium bowl, whisk together the flour, baking powder, baking soda, and salt.

In the large bowl of an electric mixer, beat together the butter and sugar until blended, then beat in the eggs, vanilla, sour cream, lemon zest, and lemon juice. With the mixer on lowest speed, spoon in the flour mixture, then the milk, and beat just until it looks combined.

3. Spread about half the batter in the prepared pan, covering the bottom. Add all the berries. Drop spoonfuls of the remaining batter over the berries in an uneven layer, then scatter on all the crumbs. Bake 40 to 45 minutes (50 minutes if the berries are frozen), until the cake top is golden brown and a cake tester inserted in the center comes out nearly clean. Cool the cake on a wire rack, then cut it into squares. Serve warm from the pan.

Banana Crumb Cake

THIS FLAVORFUL OLD-FASHIONED cake with a light tender crumb and crisp crunchy topping (not to be confused with dense, moist banana bread) is a great brunch, picnic, or lunch-box treat. If you have over-ripe bananas around, this recipe offers an easy way to use them up. Chopped walnuts or pecans are a good, but not essential, addition. For a variation, try Banana-Chocolate-Chip Cake, following.

for good measure

Don't throw away soft, overripe bananas with spotted skins. Instead, pop them whole into the freezer; their skins will turn black, but when defrosted at room temperature, the mushy contents are perfect for this recipe.

special equipment: 9 × 9 × 1½- or 2-inch baking dish or 11¾ × 7½ × 1¾-inch sheet pan

advance preparation: Cake keeps several days at room temperature or double-wrapped and frozen up to 2 months.

temperature and time: 350°F for 45 to 50 minutes; time depends upon type of pan; a glass baking pan takes slightly longer to bake

yield: 4¼ cups batter; 9-inch cake; 9 servings (3-inch squares); sheet cake, 12 servings

crumb topping

½ cup unsifted all-purpose flour

½ cup granulated sugar

Pinch of salt

½ teaspoon ground cinnamon

½ teaspoon ground nutmeg

¼ cup (½ stick) unsalted butter, at room temperature, cut up

cake

Butter or butter-flavor no-stick vegetable spray for preparing pan

2 cups sifted all-purpose flour

1 teaspoon baking powder

½ teaspoon baking soda

½ teaspoon salt

½ teaspoon ground cinnamon

¼ cup wheat germ, preferably toasted, optional

½ cup (1 stick) unsalted butter, at room temperature, cut up

1 cup granulated sugar

2 large eggs, at room temperature

1 teaspoon vanilla extract

3 large ripe bananas, mashed with a fork (9 ounces; about 1 cup)

½ cup (2 ounces) finely chopped walnuts or pecans

1. Position a rack in the center of the oven and pre-heat it to 350°F. Coat the baking pan with butter or vegetable spray.

2. In a large mixing bowl, combine all the crumb topping ingredients and pinch them together with your fingertips or mash them with a fork until crumbs are formed; part of the mixture may still look granular. Set it aside.

3. In a bowl, whisk together the flour, baking powder, baking soda, salt, cinnamon, and wheat germ.

4. In the large bowl of an electric mixer, cream together the butter and sugar until well blended, then beat in the eggs, vanilla, and mashed banana. Scrape down the bowl and beater. With the mixer on low speed, beat in the flour mixture and the nuts. Don't overbeat.

5. Spoon the cake batter into the prepared pan, top evenly with the crumbs, and bake 45 to 50 minutes, or until the topping is golden brown and a cake tester inserted in the center comes out clean. Cool the cake on a wire rack, cut into squares, and serve from the pan.

Banana–Chocolate-Chip Cake: Add ½ cup (3 ounces) semi-sweet chocolate mini-chips along with the chopped nuts.

Grandpa's Blueberry Muffins, PAGE 12; **Double Corn Muffins,** PAGE 13
Cranberry Walnut Muffins, PAGE 19

Carol's Holiday Stollen, PAGE 30

**Blue Ribbon Cherry Pie
with Quick Lattice Topping,** PAGE 87

Cranberry Pizza, PAGE 106
Apple Pie Pizza, PAGE 104

Three-Layer Chocolate Raspberry Romance Cake
with Chocolate Silk Icing, PAGE 136

Golden Harvest Apple Honey Cobbler

THIS DELECTABLE BLEND of apples, sweet golden raisins, and honey is covered with lemon–scented biscuit dough baked on top of the fruit so it absorbs the juices. Be sure to serve this warm, with some vanilla yogurt or ice cream alongside.

special equipment: 10-inch deep-dish pie plate, preferably heat-proof glass; 3-quart (or larger) saucepan with lid

advance preparation: Cobbler is best served the day it is baked, preferably warm from the oven.

temperature and time: Stove top: 10 to 15 minutes; oven: 375°F for 30 minutes

yield: 8 to 10 servings

fruit filling

6 to 7 large Golden Delicious apples, peeled, cored, thinly sliced (6 cups slices)

3 tablespoons fresh lemon juice

½ cup packed golden raisins

½ cup honey

⅓ cup packed light brown sugar

3 tablespoons all-purpose flour

1 teaspoon ground cinnamon

½ teaspoon ground nutmeg

⅓ cup water or apple juice

dough

1 large egg, at room temperature

3 tablespoons unsalted butter, melted

½ cup buttermilk

1 teaspoon grated lemon zest

1¼ cups unsifted all-purpose flour

1 teaspoon baking powder

⅛ teaspoon baking soda

¼ teaspoon salt

3 tablespoons granulated sugar

¾ teaspoon ground nutmeg

topping

Granulated sugar and ground nutmeg

1. In a large saucepan, combine all fruit filling ingredients, stir well, and cover the pan. Place over medium heat and cook about 10 minutes, stirring on and off until the apples are tender when pierced with the tip of a sharp knife. Add 1 or 2 tablespoons of water if apples begin to stick. Remove the pan from the heat and set it aside to cool. Preheat the oven to 375°F.

2. Prepare the dough: In a large bowl, beat together the egg, melted butter, buttermilk, and grated lemon zest. In a medium bowl, whisk together all the remaining dough ingredients, then add them to the egg mixture all at once and stir just until blended; don't overbeat. The dough will be sticky.

3. Spoon the fruit mixture into the *ungreased* pie plate. Drop the dough by the tablespoon on top of the fruit. You will have 9 or 10 mounds of dough, with some space between each. Sprinkle a little sugar and a pinch of nutmeg over the dough.

Bake 30 minutes, or until the topping is golden brown and a cake tester inserted in the dough comes out clean. Cool the cobbler on a wire rack, and serve warm, spooning it from the pan.

Peach-Plum Cobbler

USE FLAVORFUL, RIPE fruit to make this quick, easy, old-fashioned dessert. For a brunch party, double the recipe, bake it in a round or oval earthenware pan, and serve it warm with a little cinnamon- or ginger-flavored whipped cream. Instead of peaches and plums, try other fruit combinations, such as nectarines, mangoes, and blueberries, or make Ginger-Peach Cobbler, following.

for good measure

> Baking time for the cobbler depends upon the size of the baking dish and the thickness of the topping dough. It will bake faster in a pie plate than in a casserole where the dough is crowded.

special equipment: Dutch oven or large pot; slotted spoon; 1½-quart baking dish or 10-inch deep-dish pie plate, preferably heat-proof glass

advance preparation: Cobbler is best served the day it is made, preferably warm from the oven. Before starting the recipe, prepare a large pot of boiling water for peeling peaches.

temperature and time: 375°F for 40 to 55 minutes

yield: 6 to 8 servings

fruit

4 large or 5 medium-size ripe peaches

2 tablespoons fresh lemon juice

3 or 4 whole ripe plums (any type), or 6 to 8 prune plums

⅓ to ½ cup granulated sugar

1 teaspoon ground cinnamon *or* ground nutmeg

topping

1 large egg, at room temperature

¼ cup (½ stick) unsalted butter, melted, or canola oil

¾ cup milk or heavy cream or buttermilk

1½ cups unsifted all-purpose flour

1½ teaspoons baking powder

¼ teaspoon salt

¼ cup plus 1 tablespoon granulated sugar

1. Position a rack in the center of the oven and preheat it to 375°F.

To peel the peaches, gently lower them into a pot of boiling water for 2 minutes, then remove them with a slotted spoon to a bowl of cold water. Drain when cool. The peach skins will slip off easily. Remove the pits, slice the peaches into the ungreased baking dish, and toss them with the lemon juice. Pit and slice the unpeeled plums and add them to the peaches. You should have 3 to 4 cups fruit. Add sugar to taste and cinnamon.

2. In a mixing bowl, whisk together the egg, butter, and milk. Add the flour, baking powder, salt, and ¼ cup of sugar. Slowly stir the mixture together until just blended; do not overbeat.

3. Spoon the batter over the fruit, then sprinkle on the remaining 1 tablespoon of sugar. Bake 40 to 55 minutes, or until golden brown on top and a cake tester inserted into the topping comes out clean. *Note:* See For Good Measure for variations in baking time. Cool on a wire rack. Serve warm, spooning it from the pan.

> **Ginger-Peach Cobbler:** Omit plums. Use 3 to 4 cups *sliced* peaches plus ½ to 1 teaspoon ground ginger or 1 teaspoon freshly grated gingerroot, or more to taste, added to the fruit.

Apple-Pear-Cranberry Crisp

THIS FAMILY-FRIENDLY, DEEP-DISH pie can be made with any combination of fruit—peaches, plums, pears, apricots, or berries, for example. Tart red cranberries or raspberries spark up the apple-pear combination, but chopped dry apricots, Craisins, or dried cherries could be used as well. Serve the warm crisp with vanilla ice cream or ginger-scented whipped cream.

for good measure

The oat-crumb topping is generous and crunchy; I like to add chopped walnuts, but you can use whatever nut you prefer, or leave them out.

special equipment: 10-inch deep-dish pie plate, preferably heat-proof glass, or 2-quart casserole

advance preparation: You can prepare the oat-crumb topping in advance and store it in a jar in the refrigerator up to a week. The crisp is best when freshly baked and served warm from the oven.

temperature and time: 350°F for 45 to 50 minutes

yield: 10-inch deep-dish pie; 2½ cups topping; 8 to 10 servings

fruit

Butter for preparing pan

6 to 6½ cups fruit total: 4 large apples (such as Rome, Jonathan, or Granny Smith), and 2 large ripe pears (Bartlett, Bosc, or Anjou), peeled, cored, and sliced; 1 cup whole fresh cranberries, or whole frozen (unthawed) cranberries or Craisins

¼ cup packed dark brown sugar

½ teaspoon ground cinnamon

½ teaspoon ground nutmeg

2 tablespoons fresh lemon juice

oat-crumb topping

¾ cup unsifted all-purpose flour

¾ cup granulated or packed brown sugar

½ cup old-fashioned rolled oats (not instant)

½ cup (2 ounces) chopped walnuts, optional

Pinch of salt

½ teaspoon ground cinnamon

½ cup (1 stick) unsalted butter, at room temperature, cut up

1. Position a rack in the center of the oven and preheat it to 350°F. Butter the pie plate or casserole and toss in all the fruit filling ingredients.

2. In a bowl, combine all the topping ingredients and pinch them together with your fingertips to make crumbs. Spread the crumbs over the fruit.

3. Bake for 45 to 50 minutes, or until the fruit is tender when pierced with the tip of a sharp knife and the crumbs are golden brown. Cool on a wire rack. Serve warm, spooning it from the pan.

THIS CHAPTER EMBRACES a wide range of cakes, which have several things in common—simplified procedures wherever possible, great taste, and easy-but-attractive presentations. Many of the recipes are quite short; if one appears long to you, it is because I have included extra hints and tips to guarantee success.

THE SHORTCAKES ARE OLD-FASHIONED FAVORITES you can make with any seasonal berries. Pear-Cranberry Upside-Down Cake is for brunch or Sunday night family supper, but there is a special magic about the procedure (and the taste) that makes this a party-pleaser anytime.

Cakes

THE VARIETY OF LAYER AND SHEET CAKES goes from Classic 1-2-3-4 Vanilla Cake and its many variations to a stunning Old-Fashioned Coconut Layer Cake, and two chocolate cakes that are too good and too easy to believe: Easy Devil's Food Cake and Ginnie's One-Pot Chocolate Sheet Cake. Black and White Chocolate Pudding Cake is included because it is my private vice, and I need to know where to find it. It has been known to be a one-serving recipe. For a romantic occasion, celebrate with Three-Layer Chocolate Raspberry Romance Cake or To-Live-For Chocolate Mousse Cake (infinitely better than any To-Die-For cake). For the kids, there are cupcakes plain and fancy (see Clown Cupcakes and Halloween Spider Web Cupcakes). *Note:* When baking cupcakes, add several tablespoons of water to any unused cups in the pan so the heat will be evenly distributed.

BUNDT AND TUBE CAKES ARE GREAT FOR PARTIES and bake sales. Try the classics: Orange Angel, Glazed Orange, and Carrot Cake, or my family's best bet, Swedish Almond Butter Cake, which is sure to become *your* new best friend. For holiday giving, try Applesauce Gift Cake made into small gift loaves, or see the selection of "tea cakes" in the Quick Breads chapter.

Rolled sponge cakes—risen primarily by egg foam—are easier to put together than you might think, and they bake in a matter of minutes. Try the lemon, chocolate, or pumpkin varieties with our simple fillings, or improvise your own creative pudding, jam, or mousse.

Cheesecakes are all basic formulas with flavor variations that will delight you. The easiest, of course, is the Basic No-Bake in a crumb crust, which you can top with any fresh fruit or berries—it takes the cake for effortless elegance.

Old-Fashioned Coconut Layer Cake

THIS GLAMOROUS FOUR-LAYER confection is filled and frosted with Coconut–Cream Cheese Icing sprinkled with toasted coconut. It is a romantic birthday or special occasion cake, well worth the little extra time it takes to prepare.

Because it is so flavorful and moist, I have always loved this recipe, which originally came from my friend Joan Moore. Joan and I used to make it with fresh coconut, draining the milk, cracking the shell, fighting to extract the meat. I know you will be relieved to learn that I have come to my senses; it is just as good, and much easier to make, with packaged coconut and canned coconut milk. You will need a total of 1½ cups coconut milk and 2½ cups shredded coconut; both are available in most supermarkets, Asian markets, and natural food stores. Leftover coconut or coconut milk can be frozen in airtight plastic bags or plastic containers.

for good measure

- Be sure to toast the coconut that will cover the iced cake—it makes the most attractive presentation and enhances the taste. To toast coconut, gently stir it in a large frying pan set over medium-low heat for about 5 minutes, or until golden in color. Set coconut aside on a plate to cool.

- To fill the cake layers, you can substitute any lime or lemon curd (see page 168 or page 162), or use apricot, seedless raspberry, or pineapple preserves. Leftover egg yolks can be mixed with a pinch of salt or sugar and frozen for another use.

- Coconut extract is available in supermarkets or see Mail-Order Sources and Suppliers, page 240.

- Remove eggs from the refrigerator before starting the recipe; room temperature whites will whip to greater volume than cold whites.

special equipment: Two 9 × 1½-inch round cake pans; baking parchment or wax paper; scissors; long-bladed serrated knife; food processor, optional; one 9-inch cardboard cake disk covered in foil, or a flat serving plate

advance preparation: Cake can be baked in advance, wrapped, and kept at room temperature or refrigerated for several days, or double-wrapped and frozen up to 3 months. Frosting can be made up to 2 days in advance and stored, covered, in the refrigerator; to use, bring to room temperature and beat smooth.

temperature and time: 350°F for 35 to 37 minutes

yield: 6 generous cups batter; 4½ cups icing; 4-layer 9-inch cake; 10 to 12 servings

cake

Solid shortening for preparing pans

3 cups sifted cake flour, plus extra for preparing pans

1 tablespoon baking powder

½ teaspoon salt

4 large egg whites, at room temperature

2 cups granulated sugar, divided (¼ cup and 1¾ cups)

1 cup (2 sticks) unsalted butter, at room temperature, cut up

1 teaspoon vanilla extract

2 teaspoons coconut extract

1 cup canned coconut milk (either unsweetened milk or sweet coconut cream such as Coco Lopez)

1 cup shredded sweetened coconut

coconut–cream cheese icing

1½ cups shredded sweetened coconut

24 ounces (three 8-ounce packages) cream cheese (not low-fat), at room temperature

3 cups sifted confectioners' sugar

1 tablespoon coconut extract

Pinch of salt

2 teaspoons dark rum, optional

½ cup canned coconut milk (either unsweetened coconut milk or sweet coconut cream), stirred well

1. Position racks dividing the oven into thirds and preheat it to 350°F. Coat both baking pans with shortening, line the bottoms with baking parchment or wax paper rounds cut to fit, coat the papers with shortening, and dust the pans with flour; tap out excess flour.

2. In a medium bowl, sift together the flour, baking powder, and salt.

3. Place the egg whites in the largest grease-free bowl of your electric mixer. With the mixer on medium speed, whip the whites until foamy, then gradually add ¼ cup of the sugar while beating continuously. When the whites look thick and foamy, increase the speed to high and beat until the whites look smooth and satiny, and you begin to see beater tracks on the surface. Beat just a little longer until, when the mixer is turned off and the beater is lifted, the foam makes a peak that stands straight up on the tip. Remove the bowl from the mixer stand and set it aside. Scrape the beater into the bowl and return it—without washing—to the mixer stand.

4. With another bowl, use this beater to beat together the butter, the remaining 1¾ cups sugar, and both extracts. With the mixer on the lowest speed, alternately add the coconut milk and the flour mixture just until well incorporated. Remove the bowl from the mixer, stir in about 1 cup of the whipped whites to lighten the batter, then fold in the remaining whites along with the well-crumbled coconut. To do this, use a flexible spatula to cut down through the center of the batter, turn it, and draw it up along the side of the bowl. Give the bowl a quarter turn and repeat, adding more whites until all are incorporated. The batter should be quite light and airy.

5. Divide the batter between the prepared pans and bake for about 35 minutes, or until the cake tops are a light golden color and start to pull away from the pan sides; a cake tester inserted in the center will come out clean. Cool the layers on a wire rack about 10 minutes, then slide a knife between the cake sides and the pans, top each with a plate or wire rack, invert, and lift the off pans. Cool the layers completely on wire racks.

6. When the layers are cold, slice each one in half horizontally using a serrated knife with a long blade. Stack the 4 layers, separated by pieces of baking parchment or wax paper.

7. To make the icing: First toast the coconut (see For Good Measure). With an electric mixer or a food processor fitted with a steel blade, blend together the cream cheese and sifted sugar until completely smooth. Scrape down the bowl and beater. Add the extract, salt, rum, if using, and coconut milk and beat smooth. Adjust the sugar or liquid if necessary to reach a smooth spreading consistency. *Note:* Be sure the cake is completely cold before coating it with the icing or the heat will melt the cream cheese.

8. To assemble the cake: Place a dab of icing in the center of the foil-covered cardboard disk or serving plate. Set one layer, cut side up, on the disk. Spread it with about 1 cup of icing, top it with another cake layer, and repeat until all the layers are used. Neatly align the cake sides. Spread icing over the cake sides, then the top. Working over a piece of wax paper or a tray to catch spills, scoop up some of the toasted coconut in the palm of your hand and press it onto the cake sides; rotate the cake and repeat all the way around. Sprinkle the remaining toasted coconut over the cake top. In hot weather, refrigerate the cake.

Classic 1-2-3-4 Vanilla Cake with Orange Frosting

THIS NINETEENTH-CENTURY CLASSIC is the mother of so many American cakes that once you start analyzing recipes, you find more often than not that they fit this basic, easy-to-remember formula: 1 cup butter, 2 cups sugar, 3 cups flour, 4 eggs. If you could have only one cake recipe in your repertoire, this should be it.

Creative variations are infinite; see my suggestions or make up your own. The cake can be filled and frosted with Orange Cream Cheese Frosting, or your favorite buttercream, or you can spread preserves between the layers and sift sugar or cocoa on top.

for good measure

To give the cake a lighter texture, you can separate the eggs. To do this, add the yolks after creaming together the butter and sugar in step 3. In a separate, grease-free bowl beat the whites until stiff but not dry. At the end of step 4, stir about ½ cup of the whites into the batter to lighten it, then fold in the rest.

special equipment: Two 8 or 9 × 1½-inch round pans; or one sheet pan 9 × 13 × 1¾; or two small (6-cup capacity) Bundt pans; wax paper; flat serving plate (10- to 12-inch diameter); icing spatula; food processor, optional

advance preparation: Cake can be made in advance, wrapped, and kept at room temperature for several days, or double-wrapped and frozen up to 3 months. Frosting can be made up to 2 days in advance and refrigerated. Bring to room temperature and beat smooth before using.

temperature and time: 350°F for 30 to 35 minutes for layers or sheet pan; 30 minutes for small Bundt pans

yield: About 6 cups batter; 2-layer 8- or 9-inch cake, or 9 × 13-inch cake, or 2 small Bundt cakes. About 3 cups frosting. Layer cake, 8 or 9 servings; sheet cake, 12 servings; each small Bundt cake, 4 to 6 servings

cake

Solid shortening for preparing pan(s)

3 cups sifted all-purpose flour, plus extra to prepare pan(s)

1 tablespoon baking powder

½ teaspoon salt

1 cup (2 sticks) unsalted butter, at room temperature, cut up

2 cups granulated sugar

4 large eggs, at room temperature

1 teaspoon vanilla extract

1 cup milk

orange cream cheese frosting

8 ounces (1 large package) cream cheese (not low-fat), at room temperature

½ cup (1 stick) unsalted butter, softened but not melted

⅛ teaspoon salt

Grated zest of 1 orange (1½ to 2 tablespoons)

2 tablespoons frozen concentrated orange juice, thawed but not diluted, or 4 tablespoons orange juice

½ teaspoon orange extract or pure orange oil, optional

1 teaspoon vanilla extract

4 cups sifted confectioners' sugar

filling

¾ cup orange marmalade

1. Position a rack in the center of the oven and preheat it to 350°F. Coat the pan(s) with shortening, then dust evenly with flour; tap out excess flour.

2. In a bowl, whisk together the flour, baking powder, and salt.

3. In the large bowl of an electric mixer, beat together the butter and sugar until well blended. Add the eggs and vanilla and beat well. Scrape down the bowl and beater.

4. With the mixer on lowest speed, alternately add the flour mixture and milk. Scrape down the bowl and beater again and beat until thoroughly incorporated.

5. Divide the batter between the prepared pan(s) and bake for 30 to 35 minutes for layers or sheet or 30 minutes for Bundt, or until a cake tester inserted in the center comes out clean and the top is a light golden color and springy to the touch. Cool the cake(s) on a wire rack about 10 minutes, then top with another rack and invert. Lift off the pans. Cool the cake(s) completely on wire racks. You can leave a sheet cake in its pan to cool, and frost and serve it from the pan.

6. To make the frosting most quickly, use a food processor fitted with the steel blade; alternatively, you can use an electric mixer. Blend together the cream cheese, butter, and salt until smooth and creamy, then blend in the grated zest, orange juice concentrate, extract, and vanilla. With the machine on the lowest speed, gradually add the sifted sugar, pulsing or beating until the frosting is smooth and soft enough to spread.

7. To assemble the cake: Place one layer on a flat plate. Slide strips of wax paper under the bottom of the cake to protect the plate during frosting. Spread the first layer with marmalade, top with the second layer, and adjust the cake sides to align neatly. Spread frosting over the cake sides, then the top. In hot weather, refrigerate the cake.

Lemon Cake: Prepare the basic cake. In addition to vanilla extract, add 1 tablespoon grated lemon zest and 1 teaspoon lemon extract. Fill with any lemon or lime curd filling (see page 162 or page 168) or any citrus-flavored marmalade. Frost with Lemon Cream Cheese Frosting: Follow recipe but omit orange concentrate and orange zest; add ½ teaspoon lemon extract and the grated zest of one lemon.

Spice Cake: Prepare the basic cake. Add to dry ingredients 1½ teaspoons cinnamon, ½ teaspoon each nutmeg, ginger, and allspice, ¼ teaspoon ground cloves, and 1 tablespoon unsweetened cocoa. Top with a sifting of confectioners' sugar or cocoa mixed with a pinch of cinnamon.

Walnut Cake: Prepare the basic cake. Stir into the completed batter 1½ cups (6 ounces) finely chopped walnuts and ½ teaspoon cinnamon.

Cupcakes: Prepare the basic recipe or any variation. Coat 24 (2½-inch) muffin cups with no-stick vegetable spray and dust with flour, or line them with paper or foil cups. Fill the cups a little more than three-quarters full. Pour a little water into any unused cups in the pan. Bake cupcakes at 350°F for about 20 minutes, or until risen and a cake tester inserted in the center comes out clean. Cool cupcakes in the pan about 5 minutes, then remove and cool on a wire rack.

continued

Clown Cupcakes: Prepare the basic recipe or any variation. When cooled, frost the tops with Orange Cream Cheese Frosting or change the flavor: To make vanilla, omit all orange and replace orange juice with milk; for chocolate, omit vanilla and add 2 tablespoons sifted unsweetened cocoa and a few drops more liquid; for lemon, see Lemon Cake variation above; see the Index for other icing recipes. To make clown hats, top each cupcake with an upside-down sugar ice cream cone. Make faces with small nut pieces or candies (half a red Life Saver is a good upturned mouth; coconut or shredded wheat cereal makes hair). See sketches. Or, you can melt chocolate chips (see page 197) in a plastic bag or tint frosting different colors, put it in small plastic bags with a tiny hole in one corner, and squeeze out the features. Don't forget to put a ruffle on the bottom of the cone hat.

Ice Cream Cone Cupcakes: You can eat the cake and its container; great for children's parties. Prepare the basic recipe or any variation. Spoon about 2 heaping tablespoons of batter into each flat-bottomed cake-type ice cream cone, filling three-quarters full. Set the filled cones upright on a sturdy baking pan and bake 22 to 25 minutes, until a cake tester inserted in the center comes out clean. When cold, frost cupcakes with Cream Cheese Frosting (see Clowns, above). Decorate the tops with chopped nuts or crushed peppermint or toffee candies (hammer candy in a sealable plastic bag). Makes 20 to 24 cupcakes.

Easy Devil's Food Cake

THIS CAKE, LIKE the devil himself, appears in many forms in its effort to tempt us. This version contains all the traditional ingredients, but I have streamlined and simplified the mixing technique. Fill the layers with the Mocha Buttercream.

for good measure

> Buttermilk makes this cake especially tender; you can substitute powdered buttermilk (see page 10) or use whole milk whisked together with 2 tablespoons plain or vanilla yogurt or sour cream.

special equipment: Two 8 × 1½-inch round pans; one foil-covered 8- or 9-inch cardboard cake disk, optional

advance preparation: Cake can be kept at room temperature several days or double-wrapped and frozen up to 3 months. Frosting can be made up to 2 days ahead; bring to room temperature and beat well before using.

temperature and time: 350°F for 30 to 35 minutes

yield: 4¾ cups batter; scant 3 cups icing; 2-layer 8-inch cake 8 servings

cake

Solid shortening for preparing pans

2¼ cups sifted all-purpose flour

1¼ teaspoons baking soda

¼ teaspoon salt

½ cup sifted regular unsweetened cocoa, plus extra for preparing pans

½ cup (1 stick) unsalted butter, at room temperature

1½ cups granulated sugar

1 teaspoon vanilla extract

2 large eggs, at room temperature

1½ cups buttermilk

mocha buttercream

½ cup (1 stick) unsalted butter, at room temperature

4 to 6 cups sifted confectioners' sugar, as needed

⅓ cup sifted regular unsweetened cocoa

½ cup double-strength regular or espresso coffee or 1 tablespoon instant espresso powder dissolved in ½ cup boiling water

2 teaspoons vanilla extract

1. Position racks to divide the oven into thirds and preheat it to 350°F. Coat the pans with shortening, then sift on a layer of cocoa; tap out excess.

2. In a medium bowl, whisk together the flour, baking soda, salt, and cocoa.

3. In the large bowl of an electric mixer, beat together the butter and sugar until well blended, then beat in the vanilla and eggs. Add all the dry ingredients and the buttermilk and, with the mixer on lowest speed, beat a full 60 seconds. Scrape down the bowl and beater. Beat on high speed about 3 minutes, until the batter is smooth, light, and fluffy. Scrape down the bowl and beater again.

4. Divide the batter between the prepared pans and bake for 30 to 35 minutes, until the top feels springy to the touch and a cake tester inserted in the center comes out clean. Cool the layers in their pans on a wire rack for about 10 minutes, then run a knife between the cake sides and the pans, top each layer with a plate or wax paper–covered wire rack and invert. Lift off pans. Cool the layers completely on wire racks.

5. To prepare the buttercream: In the large bowl of an electric mixer, beat the butter until very soft and creamy. Slowly beat in about 2 cups of the sifted sugar, then scrape down the bowl and beater. Add 2 more cups of the sugar, cocoa, coffee, and vanilla, beating until completely smooth and very creamy. Add the remaining sugar as needed to bring to spreading consistency.

6. To assemble the cake: Place a dab of buttercream in the center of the foil–covered cardboard disk or on a serving plate. Center one layer on the disk. Spread the layer with about 1 cup of the buttercream, top with the second layer, and the align the cake sides. Spread icing over the cake sides, then the top.

Sour Cream Spice Cake with Honey–Cream Cheese Frosting

THIS FLAVORFUL CLASSIC is streamlined for easy preparation. You can bake it as a layer cake, filled and frosted with the Honey–Cream Cheese Frosting, or make it in a 9 × 13-inch sheet pan, frost the top, and cut it into squares. Whatever the shape, this is an easy-to-prepare all-time winner for picnics, bake sales, and family suppers.

special equipment: Two 8 or 9 × 1½-inch round pans and three 8- or 9-inch round cardboard cake disks (one disk should be wrapped with aluminum foil) or a 9- or 10-inch flat round serving platter; or 9 × 13-inch sheet pan

advance preparation: Cake keeps well at room temperature for several days (refrigerate in warm weather), or baked in advance, double-wrapped, and frozen up to 2 months. Frosting can be made a day in advance, covered, and refrigerated; bring it to room temperature, add a drop or two of milk if too stiff, and beat until spreadable.

temperature and time: 350°F for 25 to 30 minutes for layers or sheet pan

yield: 4⅓ cups batter; 2⅔ cups frosting; layer cake, 10 to 12 servings; sheet cake, 24 servings

cake

Solid shortening for preparing pans

Flour for preparing pans

½ cup (1 stick) unsalted butter, at room temperature, cut up

1½ cups packed dark brown sugar

2 large eggs, at room temperature

1 cup sour cream

½ cup water

2 cups sifted all-purpose flour

1 teaspoon baking powder

1¼ teaspoons baking soda

½ teaspoon salt

2 teaspoons ground cinnamon

½ teaspoon ground nutmeg

½ teaspoon ground ginger

½ teaspoon ground cloves

honey–cream cheese frosting

16 ounces (two 8-ounce packages) cream cheese (not low-fat), at room temperature

¼ cup (½ stick) unsalted butter, at room temperature

⅓ cup honey, or as needed

¾ cup sifted confectioners' sugar, or as needed

Pinch of salt

½ teaspoon vanilla extract

½ teaspoon lemon extract

topping, optional

¼ cup (2 ounces) finely chopped walnuts (use ½ cup for sheet cake)

1. Position a rack in the center of the oven and preheat it to 350°F. Coat the pans with shortening, then dust evenly with flour; tap out excess flour.

2. In a large mixing bowl with a sturdy spoon or an electric mixer, beat together the butter and brown sugar until smooth and well blended. Add the eggs, sour cream, and water and beat well.

Measure the flour, baking powder, baking soda, salt, and all spices directly onto the wet ingredients in the bowl and slowly beat (on the lowest speed) until well blended. Scrape down the bowl and beater and beat again for 2 or 3 minutes on medium-high to be sure the batter is smooth.

3. Turn the batter out into the prepared pans and bake 25 to 30 minutes until the cake is golden brown, springy to the touch, and a cake tester inserted in the center comes out clean. Cool the cake in the pans on a wire rack for at least 10 minutes, then top each layer with another rack or a cardboard cake disk and invert. Lift off the baking pans and allow the layers to cool completely. A sheet cake can cool in its baking pan on the wire rack.

4. While the cake bakes and cools, prepare the frosting: In the large bowl of an electric mixer, beat together the cream cheese and butter until completely smooth. Add the honey, sugar, salt, and extracts and beat until fluffy, smooth, and easily spreadable. Adjust the texture if needed by adding a little more honey or sugar.

5. To assemble the layer cake: Dab a little frosting in the center of the foil-covered cardboard disk or the serving platter, then top with one cake layer. Spread some frosting over the layer, top with the second layer, and align the sides neatly. Spread the remaining frosting around the cake sides, then over the top. Sprinkle on the chopped nuts, if using. If making a sheet cake, simply spread as much frosting as desired over the top and freeze the leftovers in a sealed plastic bag; top the cake with chopped nuts if you wish.

Ginnie's One-Pot Chocolate Sheet Cake

WITH ITS TENDER crumb and deep chocolaty taste, this cake has long been a favorite for kids' birthdays, picnics, and bake sales. Also called Texas Sheet Cake or Famous One-Pot Cake, the recipe is popular with cooks because of the speed with which it can be prepared.

This version comes from my Vermont friend Ginnie Sweatt Hagan, an enthusiastic baker who was stirring it up one summer morning when I walked into her kitchen. By the time I found my teacup at the table—after moving several baskets of wild blueberries she had picked that dawn—Ginnie had the cake in the oven and was frying up a batch of donuts. Ginnie admits to baking this easy recipe as often as once a week when all her family is around, which in summer is most of the time. While it bakes, you can whip up the chocolate icing. The batter can also be used to make plain chocolate or Halloween Spider Web Cupcakes.

special equipment: 9 × 13-inch baking pan; 2½- to 3-quart saucepan

advance preparation: Cake can be kept covered at room temperature several days or double-wrapped and frozen up to 2 months.

temperature and time: 350°F for 35 to 40 minutes

yield: 5 cups batter; 1⅓ cups icing; 9 × 13-inch cake; 24 servings

cake

Butter-flavor no-stick vegetable spray or solid shortening for preparing pan

4 ounces (4 squares) unsweetened chocolate, chopped

½ cup (1 stick) unsalted butter or margarine, cut up

1 cup hot water

2 cups unsifted all-purpose flour

1 teaspoon baking soda

½ teaspoon salt

2 cups granulated sugar

½ cup buttermilk or sour cream or plain yogurt

2 large eggs, at room temperature, lightly beaten

one-pot chocolate icing

¼ cup (½ stick) unsalted butter or solid stick margarine, cut up

3 ounces (3 squares) semisweet chocolate, chopped

2 cups sifted confectioners' sugar, or as needed

2 to 3 tablespoons milk, or as needed

mocha flavoring, optional

1 tablespoon instant coffee powder

garnish, optional

½ cup (2 ounces) chopped nuts or (3 ounces) semisweet chocolate chips

1. Position a rack in the center of the oven and preheat it to 350°F. Coat the baking pan with vegetable spray or shortening and set it aside.

2. In a large saucepan set over medium-low heat, melt together the chocolate, butter, and water. Whisk to blend the mixture smooth, then remove it from the heat.

Add the flour, baking soda, salt, and sugar and whisk or beat hard to blend thoroughly. Beat in the buttermilk and eggs. The batter will be a bit runny. *Note:* If you think your pot is too small, you can transfer the chocolate mixture to a large bowl before adding the flour.

3. Pour the batter out into the prepared pan, spread it evenly, and bake 35 to 40 minutes, or until springy to the touch and a cake tester inserted in the center comes out clean. Cool the cake on a wire rack.

4. While the cake bakes, prepare the icing: In a large saucepan, combine the butter and chocolate. Set it over lowest heat and stir continually until melted; don't leave the pan unattended. When the mixture is melted and smooth, remove it from the heat and whisk in 2 cups of sifted sugar, the coffee powder, if using, and 2 tablespoons of milk, beating until the icing is thick and smooth enough to spread. Adjust the sugar or milk if needed. Spread the warm icing evenly over the warm cake; sprinkle on topping nuts or chips, if using. Set the cake aside at room temperature until the icing hardens, then cut it into squares and serve it from the pan.

Halloween Spider Web Cupcakes: Prepare the basic recipe. Coat 12 (2½-inch) muffin cups with no-stick vegetable spray and dust with flour or line them with paper or foil cups. Fill the cups a little more than ¾ full with batter. If you have extra batter, bake two batches of cupcakes. Pour a little water into any unused cups in the pan. Bake at 350°F for 15 to 17 minutes, or until the cupcakes are risen and a cake tester inserted in the center comes out clean. Cool the cupcakes in the pan about 5 minutes, then remove and cool on a wire rack.

To make Spider Web Icing: Prepare a small double boiler by setting a small (2- to 3-cup) metal bowl or pan over a slightly larger pot containing barely simmering water. In the top container, add 4 ounces of best quality white chocolate, chopped (such as Lindt or Baker's Premium White or Ghirardelli Classic White). Stir until melted, creamy, and without lumps; set aside. Prepare One-Pot Chocolate Icing, above, but use 3 tablespoons of milk, making a slightly softer icing than for the cake.

When the chocolate icing is ready, stir the white chocolate again to be sure it is still smooth and creamy; rewarm if needed. Spoon the smooth white chocolate into a pint-size plastic bag, seal the bottom, and cut a very tiny hole in one corner.

Working with one cupcake at a time, coat the top smoothly with a scant tablespoon of chocolate frosting. While this frosting is still warm and soft, make the web by piping out a spiral of melted white chocolate, starting at the center of the frosted cupcake (see sketches). With a toothpick, draw lines through the icing like spokes in a wheel, alternating directions, from the center of the cupcake to the edge, then from the edge to the center—all the way around. As you draw, the icing will be pulled into the web pattern. Repeat with remaining cupcakes. The icing will harden as it cools.

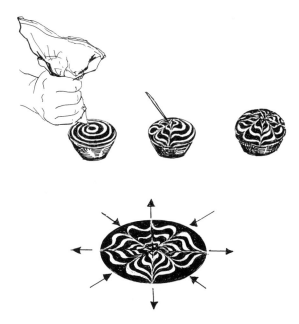

Draw lines through the icing, alternating directions

Three-Layer Chocolate Raspberry Romance Cake with Chocolate Silk Icing

THIS TALL, DRAMATIC (and easy-to-prepare) cake is just the thing for a glamorous birthday party. Raspberry preserves and fresh berries fill the layers, and a rich silky chocolate-cream icing coats the outside with deep voluptuous swirls—what more could you ask? Well, an emerald ring around the middle candle would be a nice touch . . . but only if someone else is making it for *your* birthday.

for good measure

- Coating the prepared pans with cocoa gives a dark color to the finished layers; flour can be substituted.

- If you don't have three 8-inch cake pans, use two 9-inch pans and fill them ¾ full; they will rise high but not overflow; however, reduce the heat to bake them at 325°F for a few minutes longer. To make a 4-layer cake, you can slice each 9-inch layer in half horizontally, using a serrated knife. If you do so, increase quantities for filling ingredients 1½ times.

- For the filling between the layers, you can substitute black cherry preserves and fresh sweet cherries, pitted and chopped.

special equipment: Three 8 × 1½- or 2-inch round cake pans; three 9-inch round cardboard cake disks covered with aluminum foil, 10-inch (or larger) flat serving platter; wax paper; icing spatula; double boiler or metal bowl set over a larger pan

advance preparation: Cake layers will keep, covered, at room temperature up to 2 days, or separated by foil, double-wrapped, and frozen up to 2 months. The filled and frosted cake stays fresh several days but is best served the day it is prepared. The icing needs to cool about an hour in the refrigerator (45 minutes in the freezer) before it is chilled enough to whip; it is best to prepare this before starting the cake. In a pinch, the hot melted chocolate cream can be stirred over a bowl of ice water until cold to the touch before whipping.

temperature and time: 350°F for 35 to 40 minutes

yield: 8 cups batter; 2¾ cups icing; 3-layer 8-inch cake; 10 to 12 servings

chocolate silk icing

8 ounces best-quality semisweet or bittersweet (not unsweetened) chocolate, such as Lindt or Baker's Bittersweet or Tobler Tradition, chopped

1 cup heavy cream

3 tablespoons raspberry liqueur (Chambord), or 2 tablespoons brandy or rum, optional

cake

Solid shortening for preparing pans

1 cup unsifted unsweetened Dutch-processed cocoa, plus extra for preparing pans

2 cups boiling water

2½ cups sifted all-purpose flour

1 teaspoon baking soda

1 teaspoon salt

1½ cups (3 sticks) unsalted butter, at room temperature

2½ cups packed light brown sugar, or granulated sugar

1½ tablespoons vanilla extract

4 large eggs, at room temperature

raspberry filling

2 cups seedless raspberry preserves

2 cups (1 pint) fresh whole raspberries (not frozen), rinsed just before using and blotted dry on paper towels. If fresh berries are not available, leave them out.

1. Prepare the icing: Combine the chopped chocolate and cream in the top of a double boiler set over, not touching, simmering water. Stir occasionally until melted. Remove the chocolate pan from the heat, whisk well to blend the cream and chocolate, and stir in the flavoring, if using. Set the chocolate aside on the counter to cool or, in hot weather, place in the refrigerator to chill while you prepare the cake. The chocolate is ready to whip when it feels cool to the touch (about 80°F on an instant-read thermometer).

2. Position racks to divide the oven into thirds and preheat it to 350°F. Coat the pans with shortening, then sift on an even layer of cocoa; tap out excess cocoa.

3. In a small bowl, whisk together the cocoa and boiling water until smooth, then set it aside to cool. In a medium bowl, whisk together the flour, baking soda, and salt.

4. In the large bowl of an electric mixer, cream together the butter, sugar, and vanilla until well blended. Beat in the eggs. With the mixer on lowest speed, alternately add the flour mixture and cocoa liquid, beating until well blended, about 2 minutes.

5. Divide the batter between the prepared pans, smooth the tops, and bake 35 to 40 minutes, or until the layers are springy to the touch and a cake tester inserted in the center comes out clean. Cool

the layers in their pans on a wire rack about 10 minutes, then top each one with a cardboard disk or rack and invert. Lift off the pans and cool the layers completely.

6. When the layers are cold, assemble the cake. You can leave the bottom layer on a cardboard disk, *or* place it directly on a flat serving platter. Spread 1 cup preserves over the layer, top with 1 cup of fresh berries, then add another cake layer, pressing it down a little to compact the berries slightly. Repeat with the second layer, topping it with the remaining 1 cup preserves and 1 cup of berries. Add the final cake layer and press gently to compact the layers slightly. Align the cake sides. Arrange strips of wax paper around the cake base to protect the platter during icing.

7. Check the temperature of the chocolate icing; it should be cool to the touch. With the electric mixer on medium-high speed, whip the cooled chocolate cream a full 3 to 4 minutes, until it lightens in color and becomes very thick, creamy, and of spreadable consistency. Remove it from the mixer stand.

With an icing spatula, spread frosting on the cake sides, then the top, creating a smooth surface or swirls. Remove the wax paper strips from around the platter.

To-Live-For Chocolate Mousse Cake

I'VE NEVER REALLY understood what people meant when they said a cake was "to die for." Would you risk death, running in front of a bus, for example, just to get a piece? Or is one bite so divine a mere crumb on your tongue would make you keel over in a swoon? It seems to me what you really want is a cake so fabulous that it gives life a richness and purpose, makes life worth living, something worth getting up for in the morning. If that's what you are looking for, this is it.

The flavor is intense, the texture between a soft fudge and creamy mousse; the colder the cake, the more it resembles the soft center of a truffle. The technique may look a little more challenging to you than some others in this book, but it is really not difficult. Serve the cake with fresh raspberries and champagne on an evening you want to remember.

Because the filling is flourless, with a few adjustments you can also serve it on Passover; see the variation.

for good measure

- The flavor of this cake comes primarily from the chocolate, so use the best available.

- To preserve the smooth, creamy texture of this cake, it should be baked in a water bath, which gives an even, gentle heat. To do this, the cake pan is wrapped in a piece of foil to prevent leaks, then set in a slightly larger pan containing hot water.

special equipment: 9½- or 10-inch springform pan; double boiler or metal bowl set over a larger pan; instant-read thermometer, optional; 14-inch square of heavy-duty aluminum foil or double-layer of regular foil; roasting pan large enough to contain the springform pan

advance preparation: Cake needs 4 hours to chill. It is best made a day in advance. It keeps, refrigerated, several days, or double-wrapped (either in its baking pan or after being removed and set on a cardboard disk) and frozen up to 1 month. Thaw overnight in the freezer wrapping. Bring to room temperature to serve.

temperature and time: 325°F for 20 to 25 minutes

yield: 6 cups batter; 9- or 10-inch cake; 14 to 16 servings

crust

3 tablespoons unsalted butter, melted, plus extra for preparing pan

½ cup graham cracker or chocolate wafer crumbs

½ cup (2 ounces) finely chopped walnuts

2 tablespoons granulated sugar

filling

8 large eggs, at room temperature

1 pound (16 ounces) best quality bittersweet (not unsweetened) or semisweet chocolate, such as Lindt or Callebaut Bittersweet or Baker's Bittersweet, chopped

¾ cup (1½ sticks) unsalted butter, room temperature, cut up

¼ cup granulated sugar

2 tablespoons dark rum or Kahlúa or framboise (raspberry eau de vie), optional

1. Coat the inside of the springform pan with softened butter. Prepare the crust: In a mixing bowl, toss together the crumbs, nuts, sugar, and melted butter. Turn the crumbs out into the buttered pan and tilt to allow some crumbs to cling to the pan sides; with the back of a metal spoon, press the remaining crumbs evenly onto the bottom of the pan.

2. Place the square of aluminum foil on the counter, shiny side up, and put the springform pan in the middle. Fold the foil up against the pan sides, making a close-fitting, waterproof jacket that fits comfortably in a roasting pan. Bend down the foil edges, making a thick rim around the top of the pan. Set the jacketed pan aside.

3. Place the whole eggs in their shells in a bowl of very warm water to warm up. Position a rack in the center of the oven and preheat it to 325°F.

In the top of a double boiler set over, not touching, simmering water, melt the chocolate with the butter. Stir on and off, and when nearly melted remove the pan from the heat and whisk the mixture until creamy and smooth. Set the chocolate pan aside to cool; leave the pan containing the water on the stove over the very lowest heat.

4. Break the eggs into the large bowl of an electric mixer. By hand, whisk the eggs slightly, add the sugar, and set the bowl on top of the simmering water on the stove. At once, start whisking the egg mixture over the water; continue for 1 or 2 minutes, or just until the eggs are noticeably warm (not hot) to the touch—98–100°F on an instant-read thermometer. Remove the eggs from the hot water and set the bowl on the mixer stand.

Whip the eggs with the electric mixer on high speed for 5 to 6 minutes, or until the mixture is very thick and pale in color and nearly triple in volume. The bottom of the bowl should feel cool to the touch. When you dip a spoon into the foam, then invert it, you should see a softly drooping foam peak on the tip.

5. Whisk the chocolate mixture a few times, add the rum, if using, and feel its temperature with your fingertip; it should be near room temperature and feel comfortable—neither warm nor hot to the touch.

Fold about one-third of the egg foam into the chocolate with a flexible spatula, cutting down through the center of the batter, turning over the spatula, and drawing it up along the side of the pan. Turn the pan and repeat. Be careful not to stir or deflate the foam too much. Gradually fold the lightened chocolate into the remaining foam in the large

mixer bowl. Be sure to scoop up and fold in the chocolate mixture that sinks to the bottom of the bowl. Don't worry if there are some streaks visible.

6. Pour the batter into the prepared baking pan wrapped in the foil jacket. Set the pan in the center of the roasting pan and place it on the oven rack. Reach in with a pitcher and pour hot water into a corner of the roasting pan until it reaches about 1 inch up the side. Bake 20 to 25 minutes, or a little longer if needed until the top is slightly risen, has a thin crust that is firm and dry to the touch, and the center is softly set; it will move just a little when the pan is touched.

Very carefully, remove the pans from the oven, then lift the cake pan out of the water and set it on a wire rack. Peel off the foil jacket and cool the cake in the pan about 1 hour at room temperature before refrigerating at least 3 hours, or overnight, until cold and firm.

7. To serve, bring the cake to room temperature. Release the cake pan spring and remove the sides of the pan; leave the cake on the pan bottom to serve. To slice neatly, dip the knife in hot water between each cut.

If you prefer to remove the cold cake from the pan bottom, the crust must be softened enough to lift. To do this, set the cake on a dish towel that has been dipped in very hot water, then wrung out and folded flat. After a minute or two, remove the cake from the towel. Work a long, wide spatula or pancake turner beneath the warmed cake bottom and slide it onto a flat platter or foil-covered cardboard disk.

Passover Chocolate Mousse Cake: Prepare the filling in the basic recipe but substitute matzoh meal for the crumbs in the crust.

Black and White Marble Pound Cake

MY FATHER LOVED marble cake, and whenever I bake this I remember how, as a child, I liked to watch my mother making it for him. I find that I am just as intrigued today as I was then by the patterns created by swirling together the vanilla and chocolate batters. Besides nostalgia and intriguing appearance, the cake's other virtues include its ease of preparation and keeping quality—both the flavor and texture are even better a few days after baking. For Vanilla Pound Cake and Hazlenut Pound Cake, see the variations following.

for good measure

> Be sure to use cake flour for the most tender crumb. To substitute all-purpose flour: For each cup needed put 2 tablespoons cornstarch in the bottom of a cup then fill with all-purpose flour and level off.

special equipment: One 9-inch tube pan (6½-cup capacity) or a 9 × 5 × 3-inch loaf pan; flat paddle attachment for electric mixer, if available; double boiler or metal bowl set over a larger pan; sifter, optional

advance preparation: Cake can be baked in advance, wrapped, and kept at room temperature a week or double-wrapped and frozen up to 2 months.

temperature and time: 325°F for 45 to 50 minutes for tube pan; 1 hour 15 minutes for loaf

yield: 4½ cups batter; tube cake, 8 to 10 servings; loaf cake, 12 servings (¾-inch slices)

Solid shortening for preparing pan

½ cup (3 ounces) semisweet chocolate chips or chopped chocolate

2 cups sifted cake flour, plus extra for preparing pan

1 teaspoon baking powder

½ teaspoon salt

1 cup (2 sticks) unsalted butter, softened

1⅔ cups granulated sugar

1 tablespoon vanilla extract

5 large eggs, at room temperature

1. Position a rack in the center of the oven and preheat it to 325°F. Coat the baking pan with shortening, then dust evenly with flour; tap out excess flour.

2. Melt the chocolate in the top of a double boiler set over, not touching, simmering water. Stir until creamy, then remove the chocolate bowl from the water below it and set it aside to cool (don't let it harden).

3. In a medium bowl, whisk together the flour, baking powder, and salt.

In a mixing bowl with a sturdy spoon or in an electric mixer fitted with a paddle attachment if available, beat the butter until it is very soft and creamy, then beat in the sugar and vanilla. Scrape down the bowl and beater. Add the eggs a couple at a time, beating after each addition. Scrape down the bowl and beater again.

With the mixer on the lowest speed, or slowly by hand, gradually blend in the flour mixture. Scrape down the bowl and beater, then beat once or twice again to be sure the batter is well blended, very creamy, and without lumps. Pour slightly less than half the batter into the melted and cooled chocolate and mix well.

4. Alternately spoon generous tablespoons of the vanilla and chocolate batters into the prepared pan. To create the marbleized pattern, gently swirl the blade of a table knife once or twice through the batter without touching the pan sides or bottom.

5. Bake a tube cake for 45 to 50 minutes or a loaf cake 1 hour and 15 minutes, or until the cake rises, looks golden on top, and a cake tester inserted in the center comes out clean. Cool the cake in its pan on a wire rack for 20 minutes, then slide a knife between the cake and pan sides to loosen it. Top the cake with another rack or platter and invert. Lift off the baking pan. Leave a tube pan inverted but turn a loaf over once more so the baked top is up. Allow the cake to cool completely.

Vanilla Pound Cake: Prepare the basic recipe but omit the chocolate.

Hazelnut Pound Cake: Prepare the basic recipe but omit the chocolate and at the end stir in 1 teaspoon hazelnut extract and 1 cup toasted and finely chopped hazelnuts.

Cocoa Walnut Torte

THIS FLAVORFUL, MOIST cake is suitable for Passover because unleavened matzoh meal replaces finely ground dry cracker or bread crumbs which, at other times of the year, can be used with equally good results. To make Plain Walnut Torte, see the variation following.

This recipe was developed by a long-time Connecticut friend, Anne Maidman, who gave the original (non-cocoa) version to my mother years ago. We have shared friendship and recipes for so long that both Anne and her cake feel like part of our family.

for good measure

- For best flavor, toast the walnuts before using them. Spread the nuts in a jelly roll or roasting pan and bake them at 325°F for 10 to 12 minutes, tossing them a few times, until aromatic.

- To give the cake the lightest texture, the nuts should ideally be ground into a fine dry powder using a drum-type rotary nut mill (available at specialty cookware shops and by mail order, see page 240). Alternatively, you can chop the nuts finely with some matzoh meal in a food processor or blender.

- Remove the eggs from the refrigerator before starting the recipe; room temperature whites will whip to greater volume than cold whites.

special equipment: 9-inch plain tube or angel food pan (8- to 10-cup capacity); food processor or drum-type rotary nut mill; wax paper or baking parchment

advance preparation: Walnuts can be toasted and ground up to 1 week in advance. Torte is most tender when baked fresh, but it can be prepared ahead, double-wrapped, and frozen up to 1 month. Thaw overnight in its wrapping, and bring to room temperature before serving.

temperature and time: 350°F for 35 to 40 minutes

yield: 6 cups batter; 9-inch cake; 10 to 12 servings

cake

Solid shortening for preparing the pan

2 to 3 tablespoons matzoh meal for preparing the pan

1¼ cups (5 ounces) walnut pieces, toasted

1¼ cups matzoh meal, divided (¼ cup and 1 cup)

¼ cup sifted unsweetened cocoa, any type

½ teaspoon ground cinnamon

6 large eggs, at room temperature

½ teaspoon salt

1 cup granulated sugar, divided (½ cup and ½ cup)

⅓ cup honey

½ cup orange juice

topping

1 tablespoon confectioners' sugar or unsweetened cocoa

1. Position a rack in the center of the oven and preheat it to 350°F. Coat the pan with shortening, taking particular care to cover the sides of the tube. Line the bottom of the tube pan with overlapping 2-inch-wide strips of wax paper or cut a baking parchment ring to fit the pan bottom. Spread shortening on the paper, then sprinkle the inside of the pan with 2 or 3 tablespoons of matzoh meal, coating the pan sides as well as the tube; tap out excess meal.

2. Toast nuts as described in For Good Measure. To grind the nuts, either pass them through a drum-type rotary nut mill or combine them with ¼ cup of matzoh meal in a food processor and pulse fine. In a medium bowl, toss together the nuts, 1 cup remaining matzoh meal, cocoa, and cinnamon.

3. Separate the eggs, placing the yolks in a medium bowl and the whites in the largest grease-free bowl of your electric mixer. Add the salt to the whites and, with the mixer on medium speed, whip the whites until foamy, then gradually add ½ cup sugar

while beating continuously. When the whites look thick and foamy, increase the speed to high and beat until the whites look smooth and satiny, and you begin to see beater tracks on the surface. Beat just a little longer until, when the mixer is turned off and the beater is lifted, the foam makes a peak that stands straight up on the tip.

Remove the bowl from the mixer, scrape the beater into the bowl, and set the whipped whites aside. Without washing the beater, return it to the mixer.

4. With the mixer and the same beater, now whip the yolks with the remaining ½ cup sugar until they are thick, light-colored, and at least double in volume. Stop the machine and scrape down the bowl and beater. Add the honey and orange juice and blend them in with the mixer on its lowest speed.

5. Stir about 1 cup of the whipped whites into the yolk batter. Sprinkle on some of the nut mixture and some more whipped whites and fold them into the batter. To do this, cut the spatula down through the center of the batter, turn it, and draw it up along the side of the bowl. Give the bowl a quarter turn and repeat; alternately fold in the nut mixture and whites until they are all incorporated. This cake is leavened entirely by the whipped whites so be careful to maintain their volume when folding the batter.

6. Turn the batter into the prepared pan and bake 35 to 40 minutes, or until the top is springy to the touch and a cake tester inserted in the center comes out with just a few crumbs attached. Cool the cake in its pan on a wire rack for about 15 minutes, then slide a knife between the cake and pan sides. Top the cake with a rack or flat plate and invert. Lift off the pan and peel off the paper. Cool the cake completely, then sift on a topping of confectioners' sugar or cocoa.

Plain Walnut Torte: Prepare the basic recipe but omit the cocoa.

Orange Angel Cake

ANGEL FOOD CAKE was created in the nineteenth century and has been a favorite ever since. Vanilla is the classic flavor, but this orange version is even more delicious and slightly less sweet. The success of this heavenly tall, light sponge cake depends upon knowing a few tricks about beating and handling egg whites. Don't be put off by the length of the recipe—it includes extra technique pointers you'll be glad to have.

You can garnish this cake with a light sifting of confectioners' sugar topped by thin slivers of orange zest. For variations, try Lime Angel Cake or Classic Vanilla Angel Cake.

for good measure

- Cake flour gives a more tender crumb than all-purpose in this recipe.

- To make your own superfine sugar, whirl granulated sugar in the food processor. Superfine dissolves slightly faster than regular granulated sugar but either will work.

- Separate eggs while cold (reserving yolks to be frozen with a pinch of salt or sugar for another use).

- Before beating the whites, be sure your beater and bowl (metal or glass, not plastic) are absolutely free of grease. For insurance, before using, wipe bowl and beater with a paper towel dampened with white vinegar.

- Do not grease the baking pan. As soon as batter is put into the pan, set the cake in the preheated oven; the egg white foam will deflate if it stands around too long before baking.

- As soon as the cake is baked, turn it upside down to cool so gravity can help prevent it from collapsing before its structure is set.

special equipment: 10 × 4-inch angel cake or tube pan with removable bottom; sifter; largest size electric mixer bowl and another even larger bowl (11- to 14-inch diameter, 5 to 6 quarts); tall narrow-necked bottle, such as wine bottle for suspending tube pan while cooling; cake tester; narrow spatula.

advance preparation: Cake can be double-wrapped and kept fresh at room temperature several days or double-wrapped and frozen about 2 weeks.

temperature and time: 350°F for 45 to 50 minutes

yield: 11 cups batter; 10-inch tube cake; 12 to 14 servings

cake

1¼ cups sifted cake flour

½ teaspoon ground cinnamon

1¾ cups superfine or granulated sugar, divided (¾ cup and 1 cup)

Grated zest of 2 oranges (at least 4 to 5 tablespoons)

2 teaspoons orange extract

1 teaspoon vanilla extract

14 large egg whites (about 2 cups), at room temperature

½ teaspoon salt

1½ teaspoons cream of tartar

topping

1 tablespoon confectioners' sugar

Long thin curls of orange zest, optional

1. Position a rack in the center of the oven and preheat it to 350°F. Place a sifter over a large bowl and measure into it the flour, cinnamon, and ¾ cup sugar. Stir/sift the mixture into the bowl.

2. In a cup, stir together the orange zest, orange extract, and vanilla.

3. Place the egg whites into the largest grease-free bowl of your electric mixer and touch the whites with your fingertip. If they feel cool or cold, set their bowl in a slightly larger bowl of hot (not boiling) water and stir until they feel tepid, or comfortably warm, to the touch. Combine the egg whites with the salt and cream of tartar. With the mixer on medium speed, whip the whites until foamy, then gradually add the remaining 1 cup sugar while beating continuously. When the whites look thick and foamy, increase the speed to high and beat until the whites look smooth and satiny, and you begin to see beater tracks on the surface. Beat just a little longer until, when the mixer is turned off and the beater is lifted, the foam makes a peak that stands straight up on the tip. Add the orange flavoring mixture, beat a few seconds to blend, then retest. If the peak droops, beat a few seconds longer and retest. It is important to catch this stage because overbeaten whites—which look lumpy, dull, and have a watery residue inside the bowl—can cause the cake to fall.

4. Unless your mixer bowl is huge, it will now be filled to the brim. Gently scrape the whipped whites into an even larger bowl in order to combine them comfortably with the other ingredients. With a flexible spatula, gradually fold in the flour mixture: Sprinkle about ¼ cup at a time over the whipped whites, then cut the spatula down through the center of the foam, turn it, and draw it up along the side of the bowl. Give the bowl a quarter turn and repeat, adding a little more flour mixture. With each fold, turn the spatula upside down as it comes over the top, so you rotate it in a light motion and cut through the mass without stirring or deflating the foam.

5. Spoon the batter into the *ungreased* baking pan and set it immediately into the oven to bake 45 to 50 minutes, or until the cake top is golden brown, springy to the touch, and a cake tester inserted in the center comes out clean. Leave the cake in its pan, turn it upside down, and balance it on its elongated neck or pan legs (if it has them) or hang the tube upside down from the neck of a tall bottle several hours until absolutely cold.

6. To remove the cake from the pan, slide the blade of a long thin knife up and down between the cake and the pan sides to loosen. Repeat around the center tube. Top the cake with a flat plate, invert, and lift off the pan. If the pan bottom is removable, it will adhere to the cake; to release it, slide the knife between the pan bottom and the cake. If using a plain tube pan, give a sharp downward rap to the pan to dislodge the cake and it will fall out.

Before serving, sift a little confectioners' sugar over the cake top and, if you wish, garnish it with long thin curls of orange zest. Cut the cake with a serrated knife.

> **Lime Angel Cake:** Prepare cake as above but substitute lime zest for the orange zest and 2 tablespoons fresh lime juice for the orange extract; retain the vanilla extract. Top with Lime Glaze: Beat together 1½ cups sifted confectioners' sugar with 1 teaspoon grated lime zest and 3 to 4 tablespoons lime juice, or as needed to make a soft, spreadable consistency.

> **Classic Vanilla Angel Cake:** Omit orange zest, orange extract, and cinnamon; if you wish, add ½ to 1 teaspoon almond extract.

Glazed Orange Bundt Cake

QUICK AND EASY to prepare, this not-too-sweet cake has a bright, refreshing citrus flavor and moist tender crumb. Make it your bake-sale standby, or bake two and freeze one for unexpected company over the holidays . . . it is everybody's favorite. Note that the glaze is applied while the cake is warm so it soaks in. If you wish, you can garnish the cake with thin orange slices and fresh mint sprigs, or a very light dusting of confectioners' sugar.

for good measure

- Orange zest is the brightest part of the peel, not the inner white layer.
- Cake flour gives a more tender crumb than all-purpose in this recipe.

special equipment: 9 × 3-inch Bundt or plain tube pan (6½-cup capacity); small saucepan; bamboo skewer or toothpick; pastry brush; 12-inch plate with slight edge to catch any glaze drips

advance preparation: Cake can be double-wrapped and kept airtight several days or frozen up to 2 months.

temperature and time: 350°F for 35 to 40 minutes

yield: 4 cups batter; 9-inch tube cake; 10 servings

cake

Solid shortening for preparing pan

2 cups sifted cake flour, plus extra for preparing pan

2 teaspoons baking powder

¼ teaspoon baking soda

½ teaspoon salt

1½ cups granulated sugar

½ cup canola or other mild vegetable oil

5 tablespoons grated orange zest, from 2 to 5 oranges, depending on their size

½ cup orange juice

1 teaspoon vanilla extract

1 teaspoon orange extract

¾ cup milk

2 large eggs, at room temperature

glaze

⅓ cup orange juice

2 tablespoons granulated sugar

1 tablespoon unsalted butter

2 tablespoons orange liqueur or rum, optional

Confectioners' sugar, optional

1. Position a rack in the center of the oven and preheat it to 350°F. Coat the pan with shortening, then dust evenly with flour; tap out excess flour. Be sure to generously coat all depressions of a decorative Bundt pan.

2. In a large bowl, whisk together the flour, baking powder, baking soda, salt, and sugar. Using a sturdy spoon or an electric mixer, beat in the remaining *cake* ingredients except the eggs; beat in the eggs one at a time.

3. Spoon the batter into the prepared pan, smooth the top, and bake 35 to 40 minutes, until the top is golden brown, feels springy to the touch, and a cake tester inserted in the center comes out clean.

4. Prepare the glaze: While the cake bakes, combine the juice, sugar, and butter in a small saucepan, bring to a boil, and stir to dissolve the sugar. Remove from the heat and stir in the liqueur, if using. Set the glaze aside, but warm it just before using.

5. When the cake is baked, set the cake pan on a wire rack to cool about 10 minutes. Slide a knife blade between the cake sides and the pan, then top with a plate, invert, and lift off the pan. While the cake is still very warm, use a skewer or toothpick to poke holes over the cake, then brush on the warm glaze, which sinks right in. Cool the cake completely before serving. The glaze leaves a thin, transparent coating; if you wish, add a very light sifting of confectioners' sugar just before serving.

Lemon Bundt Cake: Substitute lemon zest, juice, and extract for orange in the recipe. Do not use optional liqueur.

Cranberry Gingerbread

A SQUARE OF moist, spicy gingerbread is always a treat. When you add the sparkle of cranberries and serve it with Cinnamon-Ginger Whipped Cream, it becomes festive fare for Thanksgiving or Christmas. For a plain, spicy gingerbread, leave out the cranberries.

for good measure

- For extra "bite," add the fresh gingerroot; it is sold in supermarkets and Asian markets.
- Don't overbake gingerbread or it will dry out.

special equipment: 9 × 9 × 2-inch pan; sifter; chilled bowl and beater for whipping cream, optional

advance preparation: Cake keeps well at room temperature for about 1 week or double-wrapped and frozen up to 2 months.

temperature and time: 350°F for 40 to 45 minutes

yield: 5 cups batter; 9-inch cake; 9 to 12 servings

cake

Solid shortening for preparing pan

½ cup (1 stick) unsalted butter, melted, or canola oil

½ cup packed dark brown sugar

1 large egg, at room temperature

1 cup unsulfured molasses

1 cup boiling water

2½ cups unsifted all-purpose flour, plus extra for preparing pan

1½ teaspoons baking soda

¼ teaspoon salt

1 tablespoon ground ginger

1 teaspoon ground cinnamon

½ teaspoon ground cloves

1 teaspoon grated fresh gingerroot, optional

1 cup cranberries (fresh or whole frozen berries, unthawed)

cinnamon-ginger whipped cream topping, optional

¾ cup heavy cream (36% butterfat), chilled

2 tablespoons granulated sugar

½ teaspoon ground ginger

½ teaspoon ground cinnamon

1. Position a rack in the center of the oven and preheat it to 350°F. Coat the pan with shortening and dust with flour; tap out excess flour.

2. With a bowl and sturdy spoon or in the large bowl of an electric mixer, beat together the melted butter, sugar, egg, molasses, and boiling water.

Place a sifter on top of the bowl and measure into it all the remaining ingredients except the gingerroot and cranberries. Stir/sift the dry ingredients over the molasses mixture below, then stir everything together until thoroughly incorporated. Add the gingerroot if using.

Chop half the cranberries; stir them into the batter with the remaining whole cranberries.

3. Spoon the batter into the pan, smooth the top, and bake 40 to 45 minutes, or until springy on top and a cake tester inserted in the center comes out clean. Cool the cake in the pan or invert and cool on a wire rack.

4. To prepare the topping: Use the chilled bowl and beater to whip the cream until soft peaks form. Add the sugar and spices and whip just to incorporate.

To serve, cut the cake into squares and serve with a dab of whipped cream on the side.

Swedish Almond Butter Cake

ANNA OLSON, A family friend (see page 1), shared this recipe with my mother many years ago. She cautioned us to beat the batter with a wooden spoon to keep the texture as dense as a pound cake. We love to think about Anna whenever we bake her cake, but I confess that we don't always obey her edict; I often use the mixer, though I usually add the paddle attachment to avoid whipping in extra air.

At home we call this Anna's Cake, and it is my family's favorite birthday and special occasion recipe. In fact, this cake makes any day into an occasion. It is easy to prepare, tastes even better after a few days, can be baked in a tube or turned into a layer cake, and can be varied in flavor.

for good measure

If you are using regular beaters on an electric mixer, beat on slow to medium speed for the minimum time needed to incorporate the ingredients; avoid over-whipping the batter.

special equipment: 9-inch tube pan (6½-cup capacity) or two 8 or 9 × 1½-inch layer pans; flat paddle attachment for electric mixer, if available; baking parchment or wax paper, optional

advance preparation: Cake keeps a week at room temperature, covered, or double-wrapped and frozen up to 3 months.

temperature and time: 350°F for 55 to 60 minutes for tube pan; 30 to 35 minutes for layers

yield: 4½ cups batter; 9-inch plain tube or two 8- or 9-inch layers; 8 to 10 servings; recipe can be doubled

cake

Solid shortening for preparing pan(s)

2 cups plus 2 tablespoons sifted all-purpose flour, plus extra for preparing pan(s)

1 teaspoon baking powder

¼ teaspoon salt

1 cup (2 sticks) unsalted butter, at room temperature, cut up

1½ cups granulated sugar

1 teaspoon almond extract, or vanilla extract

2 large eggs, at room temperature

¾ cup milk

filling (choose one; used only between layers, not for tube cake)

⅔ cup canned almond pastry filling (such as Solo brand)

or ⅔ cup apricot preserves, optional

1 cup prepared marzipan (sold in plastic tube or can), optional

topping (choose one)

1 tablespoon confectioners' sugar

or almond icing glaze

1⅓ cups sifted confectioners' sugar

1 or 2 tablespoons cream or milk, as needed

½ teaspoon almond extract

1. Position a rack in the center of the oven and preheat it to 350°F. Generously coat the bottom and sides of the tube pan or layer pans with shortening, then dust evenly with flour; tap out excess flour. Or coat the pan(s) with shortening and line with baking parchment. Coat the parchment with shortening and flour.

2. In a medium bowl, sift together the flour, baking powder, and salt.

3. In a large mixing bowl with a sturdy spoon or in an electric mixer fitted with a paddle attachment if available, beat the butter, sugar, and almond extract until very soft and well blended, then the beat in the eggs one at a time. Scrape down the bowl and beater. Slowly beat in the flour mixture, alternating with the milk. Scrape down the bowl and beater. Don't overbeat.

4. Spoon the batter into the prepared pan(s), level the top, and bake 55 to 60 minutes for a tube or 30 to 35 minutes for layers, until the top is golden brown and a cake tester inserted in the center comes out clean. Cool in pan(s) on a wire rack about 10 minutes. Slide a knife blade between the cake sides and the pan, top with a plate, invert, and lift off the pan(s). Peel off the parchment paper if used. Cool completely. Top a tube cake with a light sifting of confectioners' sugar or prepare the icing glaze, step 6.

5. To fill the layers: Set one layer on a cardboard cake disk or flat plate. Spread evenly with canned almond filling or, alternatively, heat the apricot preserves until spreadable, then brush over the bottom layer and top with a ⅛-inch-thick disk of marzipan rolled out on a board lightly coated with confectioners' sugar. Add the top cake layer.

6. Make the icing glaze: Combine all the glaze ingredients in a bowl and beat well. The glaze should drip from a spatula in a sheet; adjust the consistency by adding more liquid to thin, more sifted sugar to thicken. Spoon the glaze over the tube cake, allowing it to run down the sides, or spread a slightly thicker glaze with a spatula over the top of the stacked layers.

Applesauce Gift Cake with Icing Glaze

I OFTEN MAKE a double batch of this tasty, fruit-filled cake so I can give it to friends as a gift, packed in its baking pan, wrapped in a colorful cloth napkin, and topped with a set of measuring spoons and the recipe. The recipe is absolutely reliable and the taste not too sweet; it appeals to everyone and can be baked and frozen well in advance of the rushed holiday season.

for good measure

- **Creative add-ins:** Vary the type of nuts, or replace the raisins with dried currants, chopped dried cherries, dried or fresh cranberries, or chopped dried pears or apples.

- Use light brown or white sugar but not dark brown, which makes the cake too dark in color.

- Any fruit juice can be substituted for apple juice.

special equipment: 9-inch tube pan (6½-cup capacity) or one 9 × 5 × 3-inch large loaf pan; nut chopper or food processor

advance preparation: Cake keeps well at room temperature about 1 week or double-wrapped and frozen up to 2 months.

temperature and time: 350°F for 50 to 60 minutes

yield: 4 cups batter; 9-inch tube, 10 to 12 servings (2-inch slices); large loaf, about 12 servings (¾-inch slices). Recipe can be doubled to yield 6 "baby" loaves (5½ to 6 × 3½ × 2 inches) which bake 40 to 45 minutes.

cake

Solid shortening or butter for preparing pan

1½ cups sifted all-purpose flour, plus extra for preparing pan

1 teaspoon baking soda

½ teaspoon salt

1 teaspoon ground cinnamon

½ teaspoon ground nutmeg

½ teaspoon ground allspice *or* **cardamom**

¼ teaspoon ground cloves

¼ cup wheat germ, preferably toasted

½ cup (1 stick) unsalted butter, softened

1 cup packed light brown sugar, or granulated sugar

2 tablespoons honey or maple syrup

1 large egg, at room temperature

¼ cup apple juice or apple cider

1 cup thick applesauce, preferably unsweetened

½ cup packed golden raisins

½ cup whole fresh cranberries, coarsely chopped, or dried cranberries or Craisins

1 cup (4 ounces) finely chopped walnuts

icing glaze, optional

½ cup sifted confectioners' sugar

2 to 3 teaspoons milk or water

¼ teaspoon vanilla extract

topping, optional

Nut pieces, dried cherries, or other fruits

1. Position a rack in the center of the oven and preheat it to 350°F. Coat the pan with shortening or butter, then dust evenly with flour; tap out excess flour.

2. In a medium bowl, whisk together the flour, baking soda, salt, all spices, and the wheat germ.

In the large bowl of an electric mixer or in a bowl with a sturdy spoon, cream together the butter and sugar until very well blended and smooth.

Beat in the honey, egg, apple juice, and applesauce. Little by little, beat in the flour mixture, then stir in the raisins, cranberries, and nuts.

3. Spoon the batter into the prepared pan and bake 50 to 60 minutes, or until the top feels springy to the touch and a cake tester inserted in the center comes out clean but wet. Cool the cake in its pan on a wire rack 10 to 15 minutes, then top with another rack and invert. Lift off the baking pan and either leave the cake upside down or invert it once more, so it is baked top-up. Cool the cake completely on the wire rack.

To make the glaze, beat together all the ingredients in a small bowl until the consistency of soft whipped cream. Drizzle or spread glaze on top of the completely cooled cake, then press on a few nut pieces or dried cherries or other fruits before the glaze dries. Wrap and store the cake after the glaze is hard.

Carrot Cake with Cream Cheese Frosting

CLASSIC CARROT CAKE is right up there with chocolate layer cake as everyone's favorite, probably because it's not too sweet and it is easy to prepare. This recipe is a regular on the dessert menu of Max and Mary's Restaurant in New Milford, Connecticut, where my daughter, Cassandra, bakes it with her own touch: She replaces oil with butter. The result is an improvement—the crumb is still moist, but less oily; in fact, it is great either way. And if you are not in the mood for cream cheese icing, the cake is fine with a dusting of confectioners' sugar on top.

for good measure

If you like pineapple, you can add ¾ cup crushed pineapple, drained well, along with the grated carrots.

special equipment: 9-inch tube pan (6½-cup capacity) or one 8 × 2-inch round pan; grater; nut chopper or food processor

advance preparation: Cake stays fresh, covered and refrigerated, for 2 to 3 days. Either plain or frosted, it can be double-wrapped and frozen up to 1 month.

temperature and time: 350°F for 40 to 45 minutes

yield: 4 cups batter; 1¼ cups frosting; 9-inch tube cake; 8 to 10 servings. The cake and frosting recipes can be doubled for a 9-inch (10-cup capacity) tube pan.

cake

Solid shortening for preparing pan

1 cup sifted all-purpose flour, plus extra for preparing pan

1 teaspoon baking soda

½ teaspoon salt

¾ cup (1½ sticks) unsalted butter, at room temperature, or ¾ cup canola oil

1 cup granulated sugar

2 large eggs, at room temperature

1 tablespoon vanilla extract

1 teaspoon ground cinnamon

½ teaspoon ground nutmeg

4 to 5 whole raw carrots, peeled and grated (1½ cups grated; 6 ounces)

½ cup (2 ounces) walnuts, chopped

2 tablespoons toasted wheat germ, optional

cream cheese frosting

4 ounces (½ large package) cream cheese (not low-fat), at room temperature

¼ cup (½ stick) unsalted butter, at room temperature

Pinch of salt

1 teaspoon vanilla extract

2 cups sifted confectioners' sugar

1. Position a rack in the center of the oven and preheat it to 350°F. Coat the baking pan with shortening, then dust evenly with flour; tap out excess flour.

2. In a medium bowl, whisk together the flour, baking soda, and salt. In the large bowl of the electric mixer, beat together the butter and sugar until thoroughly blended, then beat in the eggs, vanilla, and spices. With the mixer on the lowest speed, slowly beat in the flour mixture, just to combine. Remove the bowl from the mixer stand and stir in the carrots, nuts, and wheat germ, if using.

3. Spoon the batter into the prepared pan, level the top, and bake 40 to 45 minutes, until a cake tester inserted in the center comes out clean. Cool the cake in its pan on a wire rack for about 15 minutes, then slide a knife between the cake and the pan sides to loosen it. Top the cake with another rack or a flat platter and invert it; lift off the pan. Cool the cake completely before adding the frosting.

4. While the cake cools, prepare the frosting. In the workbowl of a food processor or an electric mixer, beat the cream cheese and butter together until absolutely smooth and creamy. Beat in the salt and vanilla, then gradually add the sifted sugar, beating until smooth. The longer you beat, the softer the frosting becomes. Apply to the cake when it is a spreadable consistency. Refrigerate the frosted cake in hot weather.

Black and White Chocolate Pudding Cake

THIS IS ONE of the easiest cakes to make, and one of the best. The hardest thing about it is to find a way to keep it all to yourself so you don't have to share. The eggless cake tastes like a brownie crossed with warm chocolate pudding. Not bad. For a bit of color, I like to add big chunks of chopped white chocolate to the batter. Be sure to let the kids help you make this.

for good measure

> If you don't have Dutch-processed cocoa powder, use regular unsweetened cocoa and a pinch of baking soda.

special equipment: 8 × 8 × 1½-inch pan

advance preparation: Cake is best freshly baked and served warm from the pan.

temperature and time: 350°F for 25 to 30 minutes

yield: 8-inch cake; 1 to 4 servings

Butter for preparing pan

1 cup unsifted all-purpose flour

1⅓ cups granulated sugar, divided (⅔ cup and ⅔ cup)

½ cup sifted unsweetened cocoa, preferably Dutch-processed, divided (¼ cup and ¼ cup)

2 teaspoons baking powder

Pinch of ground cinnamon

¼ teaspoon salt

½ cup milk

¼ cup canola or other mild vegetable oil

1 teaspoon vanilla extract

½ cup white chocolate, very coarsely chopped, or white chocolate chips (largest size available) or semisweet chocolate chips

1 cup boiling water

1. Position a rack in the center of the oven and preheat it to 350°F. Butter the baking pan and set it aside.

2. In a mixing bowl, combine the flour, ⅔ cup of sugar, ¼ cup of cocoa, baking powder, cinnamon, and salt. Stir to blend, then mix in the milk, oil, vanilla, and white chocolate. The batter will feel quite stiff. Spread it in the baking pan.

3. In a small bowl, stir together the remaining ¼ cup cocoa with the remaining ⅔ cup sugar. Spread this evenly over the batter in the pan and pour the boiling water on top. Do not stir.

4. Bake the cake 25 to 30 minutes, or until the top looks crisp and crackled and a cake tester inserted in a cakey area comes out clean. Cool the cake a few minutes, then serve warm, spooned directly from the pan. Top with vanilla ice cream or unsweetened heavy cream.

Pear-Cranberry Upside-Down Cake

THIS FRUIT-TOPPED GINGER-SCENTED cake is pretty as a picture—just right for a holiday buffet or brunch spread. For an added treat, accompany the cake with a little sweetened whipped cream flavored with vanilla and a pinch of ground ginger. *Note:* If you cannot find cranberries in the market out of season, substitute frozen whole raspberries, cherries, or bottled maraschino cherries, drained.

for good measure

- Be sure to use frozen cranberries so they will keep their color and appear red even after baking. If yours darken too much after baking, you can cook ¼ cup more whole berries in 1 tablespoon of sugar and 2 tablespoons of water for just a minute or two, then add these brightly colored berries to the finished cake top.

- If you don't have light brown sugar, use all granulated sugar; avoid dark brown sugar because it darkens the pears.

- To add a little extra color, you can warm ⅓ cup apricot preserves and brush them over the pears before serving.

special equipment: Nonreactive 9- or 10-inch oven-proof skillet or 9 × 1½- or 2-inch round metal cake pan; small saucepan; pastry brush; 12-inch flat serving platter with lip

advance preparation: Cake is best made the day it is served, preferably straight from the oven and still warm.

temperature and time: 375°F. Bake fruit alone for 15 minutes, then add batter and bake for 30 to 35 minutes

yield: 2⅓ cups batter; 9-inch cake; 8 to 10 servings

topping

2 large or 3 medium-size ripe but firm pears (Bartlett, Bosc, or Anjou, for example)

2 tablespoons fresh lemon juice

¼ cup (½ stick) unsalted butter

Pinch of salt

⅓ cup packed light brown sugar

⅓ cup granulated sugar

¼ cup pure maple syrup or honey

½ cup whole frozen cranberries, unthawed

cake

⅓ cup (5⅓ tablespoons) unsalted butter, melted

½ cup granulated sugar

¼ cup pure maple syrup or honey

2 large eggs, at room temperature

1 teaspoon vanilla or maple extract

⅓ cup milk or orange juice

1½ cups unsifted all-purpose flour

1½ teaspoons baking powder

¼ teaspoon baking soda

¼ teaspoon salt

2 teaspoons ground ginger

½ teaspoon ground cinnamon

½ teaspoon ground nutmeg

1. Position a rack in the center of the oven and preheat it to 375°F. Prepare the topping: Peel, halve, and core the pears, then cut each half lengthwise into 5 or 6 slices ½ inch thick. Put the pears in a bowl and coat them with lemon juice.

2. In the skillet or baking pan, combine the butter, salt, both sugars, and syrup. Stir on and off over medium heat until the butter and most of the sugar melt and the mixture begins to bubble. Remove the pan from the stove. Arrange a 2-inch cluster of frozen cranberries in the center of the pan, then position the pear slices with their narrow necks to the center touching the cranberries and the ends fanning out like petals of a flower. Make a second layer of pear slices if you have leftovers. Arrange the remaining cranberries around the outside edge of the pan, poking them down between the pears. Carefully (without disturbing the fruit) place the pan in the oven and bake the fruit, uncovered, 15 minutes. Remove the pan from the oven, leave the heat on, and set the pan on a heat-proof surface.

3. Prepare the batter: In a large bowl, whisk together the melted butter, sugar, syrup, eggs, extract, and milk. Directly on top of these wet ingredients, measure in but do not stir together the flour, baking powder, baking soda, salt, and spices. Finally, stir all the ingredients together until well blended; do not overbeat.

4. Spoon dollops of batter over the prebaked fruit and juices in the pan. The batter looks a little sparse in a 10-inch pan but spreads during baking; in a 9 × 1½-inch pan it looks too full but will not overflow as it bakes. To prevent juice spillovers just in case, you can put a piece of foil on the oven floor during baking. Return the pan to the oven to bake, 30 to 35 minutes, until the top is springy to the touch and a cake tester inserted in the center comes out clean. Cool the cake in the pan on a wire rack 2 or 3 minutes, until the juices stop bubbling, then run a knife between the cake and pan sides. Top the pan with a flat serving platter. Hold the pan and platter together and invert with a sharp downward motion. Lift off the baking pan. With a fork, pick off any fruit pieces left in the pan and replace them on the cake. Cool the cake about 5 minutes, then cut into slices and serve warm.

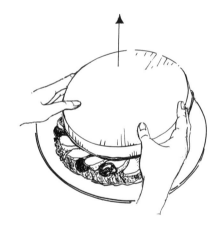

Blueberry Shortcakes

AFTER A HOT summer day picking fresh berries by the side of a dusty country lane, there is no better treat than fresh berry shortcakes. Let the whole family pitch in, from picking to plating.

Scented with lemon and nutmeg, these flavorful shortcakes are best when split and served warm from the oven topped with a pile of freshly picked berries, vanilla whipped cream, and a luscious warm blueberry sauce.

for good measure

Strawberry Shortcake, or any other variation, can be made with any fresh berries in season: blackberries, raspberries, or best of all, a combination of berries and/or peeled, sliced ripe peaches or nectarines.

special equipment: Cookie sheet; baking parchment, optional; pastry blender, optional; serrated knife; 1½- to 2-quart nonreactive saucepan; chilled bowl and beater for whipping cream; pastry brush

advance preparation: Sauce can be made in advance and warmed before using. Whipped cream is best made, just before using, in a chilled bowl and beater (refrigerate both at least 30 minutes in advance). Whip cream stiff no more than 2 hours in advance, then spoon it into a strainer set over a bowl and refrigerate (excess moisture will drain out).

temperature and time: 400°F for 20 to 25 minutes for biscuits; cook sauce berries on stove top for 6 to 7 minutes

yield: 6 shortcakes

shortcakes

Solid shortening or butter-flavor no-stick vegetable spray for preparing pan

2 cups sifted all-purpose flour

1 tablespoon baking powder

Pinch of baking soda

¾ teaspoon salt

3 tablespoons granulated sugar

1 tablespoon grated lemon zest

½ teaspoon freshly grated nutmeg

¼ cup (4 tablespoons) cold unsalted butter, cut up

1 cup buttermilk

glaze

¼ cup buttermilk

2 tablespoons granulated sugar

blueberries and sauce

6 cups (about 2 pounds) blueberries, picked over, rinsed, and blotted dry on paper towels

¼ cup granulated sugar, or to taste

2 tablespoons water

1 teaspoon grated lemon zest

¼ teaspoon freshly grated nutmeg

2 teaspoons fresh lemon juice, or to taste

whipped cream topping

1½ cups heavy cream (36% butterfat), chilled

2 tablespoons sugar

1 teaspoon vanilla extract

1. Position a rack in the center of the oven and preheat it to 400°F. Line a cookie sheet with baking parchment or lightly coat it with shortening or cooking spray. Set it aside.

2. In a large mixing bowl, whisk together the flour, baking powder, baking soda, salt, sugar, lemon zest, and nutmeg. Cut in the butter by pinching it into the flour with your fingertips or mixing it with a pastry blender or 2 cross-cutting table knives until the mixture resembles coarse meal with very small bits of butter visible. Gently stir in the buttermilk until the dough just holds together with no large, dry lumps. Do not overbeat.

3. Divide the dough into 6 equal mounds on the baking sheet. To glaze, brush the top of each mound with a little buttermilk and sprinkle on some sugar. Bake 20 to 25 minutes, or until the tops and the bottoms are golden brown. Let the shortcakes rest a minute or two on the pan, then transfer them to a wire rack to cool. While they are still slightly warm, use a serrated knife to slice them in half horizontally.

4. To make the fruit filling, set aside 2 cups of blueberries. In a medium, nonreactive saucepan, combine the remaining 4 cups blueberries, sugar, water, lemon zest, and nutmeg. Cook uncovered over medium heat for 6 to 7 minutes, stirring frequently until the berries are very soft and juicy. Remove from the heat, add the lemon juice, taste, and add more sugar if desired. If not using immedi-ately, cover and refrigerate. When ready to serve, reheat the blueberry sauce, then stir in the reserved 2 cups of whole berries.

5. To make the whipped cream, use a chilled bowl with a chilled beater. Combine the heavy cream, sugar, and vanilla and whip until medium-stiff peaks form and the beater leaves tracks on the top of the cream.

6. To assemble the shortcakes, put the bottom half of each biscuit on a dessert plate. Spoon on about ½ cup of the blueberry sauce mixture, then a few spoons of whipped cream. Cover with the biscuit top, spoon on a little more sauce, and add a dollop of cream. Serve immediately, passing any remaining blueberry mixture at the table.

Chocolate Sponge Roll with Toffee Cream Filling

THIS IS A basic sponge cake with a strong chocolate flavor and a flexible texture that enables it to roll easily around your favorite filling. My delectable toffee cream is nothing more than whipped cream blended with crushed candy bars, but you might also use softened mint chocolate chip or coffee ice cream and call it a freezer cake.

for good measure

- Coating the prepared pan with cocoa gives a dark color to the finished cake; flour can be substituted.

- This recipe can also be made in two 8-inch round cake pans, coated with shortening and floured. Use the filling between the layers and on the top.

- Cake flour gives a more tender crumb than all-purpose in this recipe.

special equipment: 10 × 15 × 1-inch jelly roll pan; baking parchment or wax paper; sifter; tea towel about 11 × 15 inches; serrated knife; chilled bowl and beater for whipping cream; plastic bag; rolling pin or hammer (to crush candy); icing spatula

advance preparation: Cake can be baked a day in advance and kept refrigerated, rolled in its towel and covered by a plastic bag. Toffee candy can be crushed up to a week in advance and stored in a plastic bag or covered jar. Prepare whipped cream no more than 3 hours before filling and serving the cake.

temperature and time: 350°F for 15 minutes

yield: 4 cups cake batter; 1½ cups toffee cream; 10-inch roll; 10 servings (1-inch slices)

cake

Solid shortening or butter-flavor no-stick vegetable spray for preparing pan

⅓ **cup sifted unsweetened cocoa, preferably Dutch-processed, plus extra for preparing pan**

⅓ **cup sifted cake flour**

2 **tablespoons sifted cornstarch**

½ **teaspoon baking powder**

¼ **teaspoon baking soda**

¼ **teaspoon salt**

Pinch of ground cinnamon

4 **large eggs, at room temperature**

¾ **cup granulated sugar, divided (½ cup and ¼ cup)**

1 **teaspoon vanilla extract**

toffee cream

1 **cup crushed chocolate-covered toffee candy bars (crush four 1.4 ounce Skor bars, for example, or use prechopped Heath Bits or Bits O' Brickle)**

¾ **cup heavy cream (36% butterfat), chilled**

2 **tablespoons sugar, or more to taste**

1 **teaspoon vanilla extract**

¼ **teaspoon almond extract**

topping

⅓ **cup plus 2 teaspoons unsweetened cocoa**

1. Position a rack in the center of the oven and preheat it to 350°F. Lightly coat the pan with solid shortening or vegetable spray, then line it with baking parchment or wax paper. Coat the paper with shortening or spray, dust evenly with sifted cocoa; tap out excess cocoa.

2. In a medium bowl, whisk together the ⅓ cup cocoa, flour, cornstarch, baking powder, baking soda, salt, and cinnamon. Set it aside.

3. Prepare the cake: Separate the eggs, putting the yolks in a large bowl and the whites into a medium grease-free bowl. Touch the whites with your fingertip. If they feel cool or cold, set the bowl in a slightly larger bowl of hot (not boiling) water and stir until the whites feel tepid, or comfortably warm to the touch. With the mixer on medium speed, whip the whites until foamy, then gradually add the ½ cup of sugar while beating continuously. When the whites look thick and foamy, increase the speed to high and beat until the whites look smooth and satiny, and you begin to see beater tracks on the surface. Beat just a little longer until, when the mixer is turned off and the beater is lifted, the foam makes a peak that stands straight up on the tip.

Remove the bowl from the mixer, scrape the beater into the bowl, and set the whipped whites aside. Without washing the beater, return it to the mixer. Don't worry, the whites won't deflate.

4. With the mixer and the same beater, add the vanilla to the yolks and whip on medium high until the yolks become pale in color. Add the ¼ cup remaining sugar and whip about 3 full minutes longer, or until the yolks get even lighter in color and become very thick and foamy.

5. Fold about one-third of the whites into the yolks using a flexible spatula. Sprinkle on about 3 tablespoons of the cocoa mixture and fold: Cut the spatula down through the center of the foam, turn it, then draw it up along the side of the bowl. Give the bowl a quarter turn and repeat, sprinkling on more of the cocoa mixture and adding more whites. With each fold, turn the spatula upside down as it comes over the top, so you rotate it in a light motion and cut through the mass without stirring or deflating the foam. Fold together all the cocoa mixture and all the egg whites. The batter should be light, airy, and smooth; don't worry if there are streaks.

6. Spoon the batter evenly into the prepared pan and spread it to the edge using a flexible spatula. Bake for about 15 minutes, or until the top feels springy to the touch and a cake tester inserted in the center comes out dry. Don't overbake the cake or it will be dry and will not roll easily.

7. While the cake bakes, spread the tea towel flat on the counter and sift on about ⅓ cup cocoa in a rectangle approximately the size of the baking pan, 10 × 15 inches. As soon as the cake is baked, invert the pan over the cocoa area of the towel and lift off the pan; peel off the paper. With a serrated knife, slice off a scant ⅛-inch strip of the crisp edging around the cake sides.

Fold one short end of the towel over a short end of the cake, then roll them together (see sketches, page 164). Place the cake, seam side down, on a wire rack to cool.

8. Once the cake is completely cooled, prepare the toffee cream. Using a rolling pin or hammer, break the toffee bars into a plastic bag and crush them into coarse powdery bits no larger than ¼ inch. With the chilled bowl and chilled beater, whip the heavy cream just until beater tracks begin to show. Add the sugar and both extracts and whip until the cream holds stiff peaks. Remove the bowl from the mixer stand and fold in the crushed toffee. If you plan to spread some cream on top of the roll, reserve about ½ cup now.

9. Unroll the cake, spread it with the toffee cream, and reroll, using the short end of the towel to help lift and push the cake, rolling it over the filling. Place the cake, seam side down, on the serving platter. If you wish, spread a line of reserved cream down the center of the top and sift on 1 or 2 teaspoons of cocoa. Refrigerate the cake. Cut slices with a serrated knife.

Pumpkin Roulade

LIGHTLY SPICED PUMPKIN sponge cake rolled over a sweet pumpkin cream is a welcome dessert for a harvest or Thanksgiving dinner or a Halloween party. The finished cake can be topped either with a little sifted confectioners' sugar or with some of the pumpkin cream garnished with chopped walnuts or pecans.

for good measure

Cake flour gives a more tender crumb than all-purpose in this recipe.

special equipment: 15 × 10 × 1-inch jelly roll pan; baking parchment or wax paper; sifter; cotton tea towel about 10 × 15 inches; serrated knife; chilled bowl and beater for whipping cream

advance preparation: Cake can be baked in advance, rolled up in a cotton cloth, and left to cool several hours or overnight; still rolled, it can go into a heavy-duty plastic bag to be frozen up to 2 weeks. Filling should be prepared no more than 30 minutes before spreading onto the completely cold cake; then the cake should be kept refrigerated. Or, the filled cake can be double-wrapped and frozen up to 2 weeks. Defrost overnight or several hours in its wrapper.

temperature and time: 350°F for 13 to 15 minutes

yield: 5 cups batter; 1½ cups filling; 10-inch filled cake; 12 to 14 servings (¾-inch slices)

cake

Solid shortening or butter-flavor no-stick vegetable spray for preparing pan

All-purpose flour for preparing pan

4 large eggs, at room temperature

¾ cup sifted cake flour (or ½ cup sifted all-purpose flour and ¼ cup cornstarch)

2 teaspoons baking powder

½ teaspoon salt

2 teaspoons ground cinnamon

1 teaspoon ground ginger

½ teaspoon ground nutmeg

½ teaspoon ground allspice

¾ cup granulated sugar, divided (¼ cup and ½ cup)

½ cup plain canned pumpkin puree

1 teaspoon vanilla extract

topping

½ cup unsifted confectioners' sugar

spiced pumpkin cream filling

¾ cup heavy cream (36% butterfat), chilled

5 tablespoons granulated sugar, or to taste

½ teaspoon vanilla extract

½ to 1 teaspoon ground ginger

½ to 1 teaspoon ground cinnamon

½ to 1 teaspoon ground nutmeg

Pinch of ground cloves

⅓ cup plain canned pumpkin puree

1 tablespoon bourbon, optional

Chopped nuts, optional

Dash of nutmeg, optional

1. Position a rack in the center of the oven and preheat it to 350°F. Lightly coat the pan with shortening or vegetable spray, then line it with baking parchment or wax paper. Coat the paper with shortening or spray, dust evenly with flour; tap out excess flour.

2. Prepare the cake: Separate the eggs, putting the yolks in a large mixing bowl and the whites in a medium grease-free bowl. Touch the whites with your fingertip. If they feel cool or cold, set the bowl in a slightly larger bowl of hot (not boiling) water and stir until the whites feel tepid, or comfortably warm to the touch. Set them aside.

In a medium bowl, whisk together the flour, baking powder, salt, and all the spices.

3. With the electric mixer on medium speed, whip the egg whites until foamy, then gradually add ¼ cup of sugar while beating continuously. When the whites look thick and foamy, increase the speed to high and beat until the whites look smooth and satiny, and you begin to see beater tracks on the surface. Beat just a little longer until, when the mixer is turned off and the beater is lifted, the foam makes a peak that stands straight up on the tip.

Remove the bowl from the mixer, scrape the beater into the bowl, and set the whipped whites aside. Without washing the beater, return it to the mixer. Don't worry, the whites won't deflate.

4. With the mixer and the same beater, beat the yolks with the remaining ½ cup sugar, pumpkin, and vanilla. Scrape down the bowl and beater. Remove the bowl from the mixer stand.

5. Fold about one-third of the whites into the yolks using a flexible spatula. Sprinkle on about 3 tablespoons of the flour mixture and fold: Cut the spatula down through the center of the foam, turn it, and draw it up along the side of the bowl. Give the bowl a quarter turn and repeat, sprinkling on more of the flour mixture and adding more whites. With each fold, turn the spatula upside down as it comes over the top, so you rotate it in a light motion and cut through the mass without stirring or deflating the foam. Fold together all the flour mixture and all the egg whites. The batter should be light, airy, and smooth.

6. Spoon the batter into the prepared pan and spread it to the edges using a flexible spatula. Bake the cake 13 to 15 minutes, or just until the top feels springy to the touch and a cake tester inserted in the center comes out dry. Don't overbake the cake or it will be dry and will not roll easily.

7. While the cake bakes, spread the tea towel flat on the counter and sift about ¼ cup of confectioners' sugar into a rectangle approximately the size of the baking pan, 10 × 15 inches.

As soon as the cake is baked, invert the pan over the sugared area of the towel and lift off the pan; peel off the paper. With a serrated knife, slice off a scant ⅛-inch strip of the crisp edging around the cake sides.

Fold one short end of the towel over a short end of the cake, then roll them together (see sketches, page 164). Place the cake, seam side down, on a wire rack to cool.

8. Prepare the filling: In an electric mixer, whip the cream until soft peaks form. Add the sugar, vanilla, and spices, whip several times, then stir in the pumpkin and bourbon, if using, and whip a few seconds longer, just until stiff peaks form. Taste and adjust the spices or sugar if needed. Scrape the filling into a small bowl and refrigerate until ready to use.

9. When the cake is completely cooled, unroll it, spread it with the filling (reserve a generous ⅓ cup if you want to spread a line of it on top of the cake as a garnish) and reroll, using the short end of the towel to help lift and push the cake, rolling it over the filling. Place the cake, seam side down, on the serving platter and sift on a little confectioners' sugar for topping or spoon a narrow row of the reserved cream down the center of the top, lightly comb the tines of a table fork through the cream to give it a decorative shape, then sprinkle on some chopped nuts or a dash of nutmeg. Refrigerate the cake. Cut slices with a serrated knife.

Lemon Sponge Roll with Lemon Curd Filling

THIS ROULADE, OR thin flexible sponge cake, is spread with a rich, creamy lemon curd and rolled up into a log. To make a classic jelly roll, you could fill the cake with a generous cup of fruit preserves—blueberry, seedless raspberry, apricot, or orange marmalade, for example, or any type of thick pudding, plain or studded with fresh whole berries. Jelly rolls and roulades are fun to make, pretty to present, and perfect to serve as a light, flavorful dessert after a festive meal.

for good measure

- This recipe calls for the grated zest (brightly colored part of the peel) of 2 large or 3 medium lemons (4 teaspoons) and the juice of about 3 lemons (½ cup). You can prepare these before beginning the recipe.

- Be sure your beater and bowl (metal or glass, not plastic) are absolutely free of grease before beating the whites. For insurance, before using, wipe the bowl and beater with a paper towel dampened with white vinegar.

- Cake flour gives a more tender crumb than all-purpose in this recipe.

special equipment: 10 × 15 × 1-inch jelly roll pan; baking parchment or wax paper; sifter; tea towel about 11 × 15 inches; serrated knife; chilled bowl and beater for whipping cream

advance preparation: Filling should be prepared ahead, from 2 hours to 2 days, so it can cool. Cake can be baked in advance, rolled up in a cloth, and left to cool several hours or overnight; still rolled, it can go into a heavy-duty plastic bag to be frozen up to 2 weeks. Once it is filled, covered and refrigerated, it will stay fresh 1 or 2 days. Do not freeze the filled roll.

temperature and time: 350°F for 11 to 13 minutes

yield: 4½ cups batter; 1½ cups lemon filling; 10-inch roll; 12 to 14 servings (¾-inch slices)

Solid shortening or butter-flavor no-stick vegetable spray for preparing pan

lemon curd filling

¾ cup granulated sugar

2 tablespoons cornstarch

2 teaspoons all-purpose flour

Pinch of salt

¾ cup orange juice

2 teaspoons grated lemon zest

6 tablespoons fresh lemon juice

3 tablespoons heavy cream or half-and-half

cake

4 large eggs, at room temperature

½ cup sifted cake flour, plus extra for preparing pan

¼ cup sifted cornstarch

Pinch of salt

10 tablespoons granulated sugar, divided (6 tablespoons and 4 tablespoons [¼ cup])

1 teaspoon vanilla extract

Grated zest of 1 lemon (2 to 3 teaspoons)

2 tablespoons fresh lemon juice

topping

½ cup unsifted confectioners' sugar

Lemon peel or slices, optional

Fresh berries, optional

Mint sprigs, optional

1. Position a rack in the center of the oven and preheat it to 350°F. Lightly coat the pan with shortening or vegetable spray, then line it with baking parchment or wax paper. Coat the paper with shortening or spray and dust evenly with flour; tap out excess flour.

2. Prepare the lemon curd filling: In a medium-size nonreactive saucepan, whisk together the sugar, cornstarch, flour, and salt. Whisk in the orange juice, lemon zest, and lemon juice. Set the pan over medium heat and whisk until the mixture comes to a boil. Boil, whisking continuously, for 1 full minute (count to 60) until thickened and clear. Remove from the heat and whisk in the cream. Set aside to cool. If made several hours in advance, refrigerate until ready to use.

3. Prepare the cake: Separate the eggs, putting the yolks in a large mixing bowl and the whites in a grease-free medium bowl. Touch the whites with your fingertip. If they feel cool or cold, set the bowl in a slightly larger bowl of hot (not boiling) water and stir until the whites feel tepid, or comfortably warm to the touch. Sift together the flour and cornstarch into a small bowl.

4. Combine the egg whites with the salt. With the mixer on medium speed, whip the whites until foamy, then gradually add 6 tablespoons of the sugar while beating continuously. When the whites look thick and foamy, increase the speed to high and beat until the whites look smooth and satiny, and you begin to see beater tracks on the surface. Beat just a little longer until, when the mixer is turned off and the beater is lifted, the foam makes a peak that stands straight up on the tip.

Remove the bowl from the mixer and scrape the beater into the bowl. Without washing the beater, return it to the mixer and set the whipped whites aside. Don't worry, the whites won't deflate.

5. With the mixer and same beater, now whip the yolks with the remaining 4 tablespoons sugar until they are thick, light-colored, and at least double in volume. Stop the machine and scrape down the bowl and beater several times. Beat in the vanilla, lemon zest, and juice. Whip until the yolks form a flat ribbon falling back upon itself when the machine is turned off and the beater is lifted (4 to 6 minutes). Remove the bowl from the mixer stand.

6. Fold about one-third of the whites into the yolks using a flexible spatula. Sprinkle on about 3 tablespoons of the flour mixture and fold: Cut the spatula down through the center of the foam, turn it, and draw it up along the side of the bowl. Give the bowl a quarter turn and repeat, sprinkling on more of the flour mixture and adding more whites. With each fold, turn the spatula upside down as it comes over the top, so you rotate it in a light motion and cut through the mass without stirring or deflating the foam. Fold together all the flour mixture and all the egg whites. The batter should be light, airy, and smooth.

7. Spoon the batter into the prepared pan and spread it to the edges using a flexible spatula. Bake the cake 11 to 13 minutes, until the top is barely golden, feels springy to the touch, and a cake tester inserted in the center comes out dry. Don't overbake the cake or it will be dry and will not roll easily.

8. While the cake bakes, spread the tea towel flat on the counter and sift on about ¼ cup of confectioners' sugar in a rectangle approximately the size of the baking pan, 10 × 15 inches.

continued

As soon as the cake is baked, invert the pan over the sugared area of the towel and lift off the pan; peel off the paper. With a serrated knife, slice off a scant ⅛-inch strip of the crisp edging around the cake sides.

Fold one short end of the towel over a short end of the cake, then roll them together. Place the cake, seam side down, on a wire rack to cool.

9. When the cake is completely cooled, unroll it, spread it with the cool lemon filling, and reroll, using the short end of the towel to help lift and push the cake, rolling it over the filling. Place the cake, seam side down, on the serving platter and sift on a little confectioners' sugar for topping. If you wish, garnish with long, curled slivers of lemon peel or a few lemon slices or fresh berries, or mint sprigs. Cut slices with a serrated knife.

Basic No-Bake Cheesecake

THIS DELICIOUS CAKE will bring you praise out of all proportion to the amount of work involved in its preparation. The crumb crust is quick to make and the rich, creamy filling is simply mixed together and chilled until set. The cake tastes lovely plain but can be dressed up in a variety of ways. For example, you can fold fresh whole blueberries or raspberries into the batter or you can add berries on top of the chilled cake—either piling them on or arranging them in a decorative pattern glazed with warm jelly like the top of a fresh fruit tart (see page 155); my favorite is the Honeyed-Blueberry Topping from page 166.

for good measure

Although this recipe is officially in the cake chapter, it is most easily prepared in a 10-inch deep-dish pie plate. If made in a springform pan, the pan sides must be warmed before the cake can be released. To do this, soak a dish towel in the hottest possible tap water; wring it out, and wrap it completely around the pan sides, holding it there for 30 seconds. Remove the towel, release the spring, and ease off the side ring. Leave the cake on the pan bottom for serving.

special equipment: 10-inch deep-dish pie plate, preferably heat-proof glass, or 8-inch springform pan; small saucepan; flat paddle attachment for electric mixer, if available

advance preparation: Cake needs to chill in the refrigerator about 3 hours to set firmly enough to slice. It can be prepared 1 or 2 days in advance and refrigerated, or it can be chilled until set, then double-wrapped and frozen up to 1 month. Defrost overnight in freezer wrapping and leave chilled until ready to serve.

temperature and time: Refrigerator: 3 hours

yield: 4 cups batter; 8- to 10-inch cake; 10 to 12 servings

crust

½ cup (1 stick) unsalted butter, melted, plus extra for preparing pan

1⅓ cups graham cracker (or other cookie) crumbs

2 tablespoons granulated sugar

cake

1 tablespoon fresh lemon juice

3 tablespoons water

3½ teaspoons unflavored gelatin

1 pound (two 8-ounce packages) cream cheese (not low-fat), softened

1 cup granulated sugar

2 cups sour cream, at room temperature

1 teaspoon vanilla extract

1½ cups fresh berries (any type), rinsed, hulled, and blotted dry; optional

1. Lightly coat the pie plate or springform pan with butter. Prepare the crust. In a mixing bowl, toss together the crumbs, sugar, and melted butter. Use the back of a big spoon to press the crumbs onto the pie plate. If using a springform pan, press some of the crumbs about 2 inches up the pan sides, and flatten the rest on the pan bottom.

2. In a small saucepan, combine the lemon juice and water. Sprinkle on the gelatin, stir, then let it sit about 2 minutes to soften. Stir the mixture over very low heat for 2 or 3 minutes, or until the gelatin is dissolved and you no longer see the granules; do not let it boil. Set it aside to cool slightly.

3. In the food processor or large bowl of an electric mixer fitted with a paddle attachment if available, beat the cream cheese until very soft and smooth. Beat in the sugar. Scrape down the bowl and beater. Add the sour cream and vanilla and beat until completely smooth.

Scoop out about ¼ cup of the cheese mixture and whisk it into the dissolved gelatin, beating until creamy. Scrape this mixture into the cheese batter and beat about 1 minute to incorporate the gelatin completely. The batter should be very smooth. If you want to add whole fresh berries, fold them in by hand now.

4. Pour the filling into the prepared pan and refrigerate at least 3 hours, until set. Refrigerate leftovers.

Lemonade Cheesecake with Honeyed-Blueberry Topping

THIS RICH CHEESECAKE has a slightly custardy texture and a bright lemon flavor that comes, effortlessly, from frozen lemonade. The surprise treat here is the topping of fresh blueberries blended with honey, a flavor that perfectly complements the cake.

for good measure

> For the best texture, and to help prevent cracks, avoid whipping excess air into the cheesecake batter, especially after adding the eggs. Use a flat paddle attachment instead of regular beaters for your electric mixer, if available, or, if using regular beaters, beat slowly and for the least time possible to achieve the proper texture; or mix the batter in a food processor.

special equipment: 10-inch springform pan; grater; sturdy flat baking sheet; food processor, or flat paddle attachment for electric mixer, if available

advance preparation: Cake can be made early in the day and, if thoroughly chilled, served that evening, but it is best baked a day in advance and chilled overnight. After it is completely cold (but without the blueberry topping), it can also be double-wrapped and frozen up to 1 month; thaw overnight in the refrigerator in its wrapping. Add the blueberry topping no more than 1 hour before serving.

temperature and time: Cake: 325°F for 30 minutes, then 300°F for 20 minutes; refrigerator: 4 hours

yield: 7½ cups batter; 10-inch cake; 12 to 16 servings

crust

¼ cup (½ stick) unsalted butter, melted, plus extra for preparing pan

1 cup graham cracker crumbs

1 cup (4 ounces) finely chopped walnuts

3 tablespoons packed light brown sugar, or granulated sugar

cake

2 pounds (four 8-ounce packages) cream cheese (not low-fat), at room temperature

1¼ cups granulated sugar

½ cup frozen lemonade concentrate, undiluted

1 teaspoon lemon extract

1 tablespoon grated lemon zest

⅛ teaspoon salt

4 large eggs, at room temperature

topping

½ cup honey

2 cups fresh blueberries (or other fresh berries), rinsed and blotted dry on paper towels (don't use frozen berries)

1. Position a rack in the lower third of the oven and preheat it to 325°F. Coat the inside of the springform pan with softened butter.

Prepare the crust. In a mixing bowl, toss together all the ingredients. Turn the crumbs out into the baking pan. Tilt the pan to allow some crumbs to cling to the pan sides, then with dampened fingers or the back of a large spoon, press the crumbs evenly onto the bottom of the pan. Set the pan aside or refrigerate.

2. In the food processor or large bowl of an electric mixer fitted with a paddle attachment if available, beat the cream cheese until very soft and smooth. Beat in the sugar. Scrape down the bowl and beater. Add the lemonade, lemon extract and zest, and salt and blend until absolutely smooth and free of lumps. Add the eggs, pulsing or beating briefly, just to combine; don't incorporate extra air.

3. Turn the batter out into the prepared pan and place it on a sturdy baking sheet for ease in handling. Bake for 30 minutes, then reduce the heat to 300°F and bake about 20 minutes longer, or until the outer edge begins to puff up and turn light golden brown. The center surface will be firm to the touch though softer than the edges. Don't worry if there are slight cracks around the edges; they close as the cake cools, and the topping covers everything.

Set the baked cake on a wire rack in a draft-free location to cool at least 1 hour, then refrigerate at least 4 hours, or overnight.

4. About 1 hour before serving the cake, prepare the topping. Put the opened jar of honey in a pan filled with very hot water for a few minutes, until the honey is warmed and liquefied. In a bowl, gently stir together the honey and berries, then spread them out on top of the chilled cheesecake. Chill the cake briefly just to set the topping, then serve.

Kristin's Key Lime Cheesecake

THE JUICE OF Florida Key limes gives this creamy tropical cheesecake a bright tangy flavor that cuts its richness. For speed and convenience, this cake is prepared in a food processor, but it can also be made with an electric mixer, preferably fitted with a paddle attachment.

This cake was developed by one of my baking assistants, Kristin Eycleshymer, the talented young pastry chef of The Weston Golf Club, near Boston. For club diners, Kristin prepares small individual cheesecakes coated with lime curd. In addition, she adds her dazzling signature presentation: The cake base is surrounded by a mango sauce and the top is garnished with a jaunty filigreed-caramel bowl, or "nest," containing a dab of whipped cream, a chocolate butterfly, and an edible fresh nasturtium blossom.

At home, you can serve the cake plain or topped with lime curd. Or be creative and finish it with a coating of orange or lime marmalade or a layer of peeled mango slices brushed with warm, strained apricot preserves and a few shreds of lime zest.

for good measure

- Florida Key limes have a pale yellow/cream-colored juice, which is bottled and sold in some supermarkets and gourmet shops or by mail order (see Mail-Order Sources and Suppliers, page 240). The juice of regular fresh green Persian limes found in all markets can be substituted in the cake and the curd, but will have a slightly different taste. If you use regular limes, you will need 4 to 5 medium limes for juice and zest.

- Serve this cake in small pieces because it is very rich.

special equipment: 9- or 10-inch springform pan; food processor or flat paddle attachment for electric mixer, if available; sturdy flat baking sheet; medium heavy-bottomed nonreactive saucepan

advance preparation: Cake can be made early in the day and, if thoroughly chilled, served that evening. It can also, more easily, be baked a day in advance and chilled overnight. After it is completely cold, it can also be double-wrapped and frozen up to 1 month; thaw overnight in the refrigerator in its wrapping. Bring to room temperature before serving.

temperature and time: Crust: 350°F for 8 to 10 minutes; cake: 325°F for 45 to 50 minutes; refrigerator: 3 hours

yield: 7 cups batter; 1 cup lime curd; 10-inch cake; 12 to 16 servings

crust

3 tablespoons unsalted butter, melted, plus extra for preparing pan

½ cup shredded sweetened coconut

¾ cup graham cracker crumbs

cake

2 pounds (four 8-ounce packages) cream cheese (not low-fat), at room temperature

1 cup granulated sugar

1 teaspoon vanilla extract

⅓ cup Key lime juice, or regular lime juice

4 large eggs, at room temperature

lime curd, optional

½ cup granulated sugar

1½ tablespoons cornstarch

1 teaspoon all-purpose flour

Pinch of salt

½ cup hot water

1 tablespoon frozen limeade or orange juice concentrate, undiluted, or 1 tablespoon regular orange juice or water

1 teaspoon grated Key lime or regular lime zest

¼ cup Key lime or regular lime juice

2 tablespoons heavy cream

1. Position a rack in the center of the oven and preheat it to 350°F. Coat the inside of the springform pan with softened butter.

Place the coconut in a small frying pan set over medium heat and stir it 3 or 4 minutes, until it begins to toast and turn golden brown. Put the coconut in a bowl, toss it with the graham cracker crumbs, then stir in the melted butter. Turn the crumbs out into the baking pan and, with dampened fingers or the back of a large spoon, press the crumbs evenly onto the bottom of the pan. Bake the crust 8 to 10 minutes, until golden. Remove the pan from the oven and set it aside; reduce the heat to 325°F.

2. In the food processor or large bowl of an electric mixer fitted with a paddle attachment if available, beat the cream cheese until very soft and smooth. Beat in the sugar. Scrape down the bowl and beater. Add the vanilla and lime juice, pulse or beat just to blend, then add the eggs and pulse or beat just to combine; do not overbeat or incorporate extra air.

3. Turn the batter out into the prepared pan and place on a sturdy baking sheet for ease in handling. Bake 45 to 50 minutes, or until the edges of the cake are slightly puffed and the top has a dull finish that is dry to the touch. When the side of the pan is tapped gently, the cake center should move slightly but not jiggle in waves as if it were liquid. Remove the cake from the oven and set it in a draft-free location for several hours to cool completely. Once it is cold, refrigerate at least 3 hours, or overnight.

4. While the cake chills, prepare the lime curd if you will be using it. In a medium heavy-bottomed nonreactive saucepan, whisk together the sugar, cornstarch, flour, and salt. Whisk in all the remaining ingredients, except the cream, taste and adjust sweetness if necessary, and bring slowly to a boil, whisking constantly. Whisk and boil for 1 full minute, or until thickened and clear. Remove the pan from the heat and whisk in the cream. Set the curd aside to cool, then refrigerate (it thickens as it cools).

5. To unmold the cake, slide a knife blade between the cake sides and the pan, then remove the sides of the springform pan but leave the cake on the pan bottom to serve. Pour on the cooled lime curd, if using, and spread it to within 1 inch of the cake edges. Refrigerate 1 hour to set the curd if it is not completely cold when applied.

THIS CHAPTER IS FOR FUN . . . fun for the adult or care-giver in the kitchen with the kids and, more important, fun for the kids themselves. The recipes are all quick and easy, the results sure to please.

SOME RECIPES, such as Peanut Butter–Honey "Clay Dough," Rice Krispies Candy Cones, or the Ice Cream "Sand" Castle, are actually edible craft projects, to inspire creativity as well as taste buds. No-Bake Chewies and No-Bake Apricot Snowballs will require adult supervision, but since there is no oven involved, these are good classroom projects. The Ice Cream Sundae Party is a great birthday party activity. All the ice cream treats, from the Lemon Cream Sherbet and Ice Cream Sandwiches to Instant Ice Cream Cake, can be made ahead and served at a children's party.

Kids in the kitchen: ice cream, CANDY, AND treats

CHILDREN LOVE TO SHARE WHAT THEY HAVE MADE almost as much as they love to eat it themselves. All the candies in this section make fine gifts from the kitchen: Caramel Nut Turtles, Chocolate Truffles, Butter Mints, Dipped Chips and Pretzel Pops. Let the kids collect a variety of boxes and jars, decorate the labels, and add ribbons and recipes to share the results of their labors. There is no reason kids can't pass on their recipes and start their own traditions just like adults. If you are planning a kitchen project with children, please take the time to read "Kids in the Kitchen" to pick up some ideas about maximizing the experience.

Kids IN THE Kitchen

Since cooking is an essential activity for most adults, we might as well share it with the kids, call it quality time, and while we're at it, make it fun.

Food memories go back very far because they start at a very early age. What are comfort foods, like rice pudding and tapioca, if not the foods of childhood? The memories can be as simple as evocative smells: the perfume of cinnamon and apples, or the taste of a butter cookie or a pumpkin pie, that suddenly reminds you of a favorite aunt or a holiday at home. The foods you recall most powerfully were probably prepared with love by someone who cared for you, and that context renders the image all the more potent. These legacies are every bit as important to pass on as a family quilt or piece of furniture. How can we continue this legacy, and find time for tradition in our busy lives?

Since many adults today work outside the home, it is essential to share whatever skills you do have when you are there. If you don't know how to bake, you and your kids can follow the recipes and learn together. You have to go grocery shopping anyway, so let it become a time to savor the perfume of ripe strawberries, the feel of a ripe peach, the look of a bruised banana. Discuss labels, chemicals added to foods, the relationship between wholesome food, good nutrition, and health. This is the time to learn where foods really come from (farms, orchards, different countries in the world, not boxes or jars or the freezer).

And when you actually get into the kitchen, a lot more will happen—even without trying—than simply mixing and stirring. This is about the process, the participation, personal involvement, and creativity. All the senses are utilized as one sniffs spices, licks a spoon, listens to butter sizzle in a pan, watches a foamy batter transformed into a delicate cake, and pinches together butter, sugar, and flour to make streusel crumbs. In the short time it takes to mix up a batter, a recipe has to be read, procedures analyzed, fractions measured.

In the Kitchen with Kids: Helpful Hints

1. **Cleanliness.** Always emphasize washing hands before handling or eating foods. Rewash hands before touching batter or hand-shaping cookies. Wash cutting boards with hot soapy water after each use.

2. **Safety:** Teach children, even young children, how to use paring knives correctly; always cutting away from themselves on a safe, steady surface. Show them where to store knives, blade down, out of harm's way, and how to wash them (keeping them apart, not dropping them into a bowl of water where an unsuspecting hand could reach in and be cut). Show them how to carry knives and scissors, point down. Keep potholders and hotplates near the stove for hot utensils. Never let youngsters handle pots of boiling water or hot baking pans; devise a system so they work *with* you, or their care-giving adult, who can be called in to do the hot and heavy work. Keep kitchen timers handy, perhaps appointing one child as timer guard—to let the adult know when the bell rings, indicating that the oven should be checked. Be sure, as the responsible adult, to select and assign tasks that are age-appropriate (your decision): two to three-year-olds, with supervision, can learn to measure ingredients and separate eggs. Eight- to ten-year-olds can handle putting things in and out of the oven with supervision.

3. **Baking Is Fun.** Let kids of all ages lick the beaters and the spoon (but not if raw eggs were used). Even the youngest can taste, touch, and smell the spices, herbs, batters, and chocolates. Allow them to stir, squeeze, roll, pound, and wipe the counters. Teach them to decide when something is completely baked; let them taste and critique the results. Get everyone involved, from beginning to end. Remember, the process counts as much as the final result.

4. **Clean-Up.** To make it easier to deal with the mess in the kitchen, put a plastic drop cloth or newspaper under the work table and a bowl of soapy water in the sink. Keep a sponge handy. Drop used utensils (except knives) right into the soapy water to soak and let crumbs land where they will on the drop cloth. Try not to create an atmosphere in which the kids will be so afraid to bother you that they would rather stare passively at the television.

5. **Stove/Oven.** Depending upon the kids' ages, this is generally adult territory. Be sure to have potholders and hotplates nearby to handle hot things on the stove or in the oven.

6. **Microwave.** I use the microwave only occasionally, to warm ingredients, to plump raisins, or to melt butter or chocolate. Many youngsters are accustomed to using it for warming their foods. They should be reminded which dishes are microwave safe (most plastic, glass, or pottery, but never metal or foil). Remember that foil wrappers, such as those on unsalted butter, contain metal and must be removed before butter is put into the microwave. Any food put into the microwave should be pierced if it has a skin (like an apple), and an egg should never be in a microwave while still in its shell. Microwaved foods may be hotter than they look, and contain steam. Avert your face and use potholders when removing containers from the microwave oven. If using plastic wrap, never let it touch food that is being microwaved.

7. **Creativity.** Keep a box of crayons or colored felt pens and a pad of paper in a basket in the kitchen for the times when a junior chef gets bored baking and needs a different diversion. That's the time for coloring a dinner menu, placemats, or name cards. Children too young to care about baking can still make colorful designs on paper for placemats; you can have the brightest ones laminated for reuse or cover them yourself with clear Contac paper from the hardware store. A small star, heart, or teddy bear cookie cutter can cut out a sandwich, cinnamon toast, sliced apple snacks, or leftover pie dough cookies. Older children enjoy fancy napkin folding, fabric-painting an apron, or making a centerpiece by combining fruits, vegetables, flowers, and even colorful toys. Kids of different ages have different attention spans as well as differing interests; it helps the kids—and frees up the adult—if you have a variety of choices on hand.

Lemon Cream Sherbet

THIS RICH CREAM sherbet is so easy the kids can make it: Just blend and freeze it in a plastic container, no ice cream maker required. Since the basic flavor comes from frozen juice concentrate, you can vary the taste by changing the juice—try limeade or pineapple-orange juice concentrate, for example, and replace the lemon zest with orange or lime zest.

for good measure

For a decorative treat, freeze this sherbet in hollowed-out oranges or lemons. To do this, cut the top ¼ off 10 lemons or 8 oranges, and cut a thin slice off the bottoms so they will stand upright. Cut and scoop out the pulp using a serrated grapefruit knife and a teaspoon (reserve it for another use). Pack the empty fruits with the prepared sherbet, cover the top with a piece of aluminum foil, and place on a pan to freeze solid. Save the fruit "lids" to add just before serving.

special equipment: Electric blender or food processor; 1-quart freezer container with lid

advance preparation: Sherbet takes several hours to freeze and is best made the day before it is served.

temperature and time: Freezer: at least 5 hours

yield: About 1 quart; 8 (½-cup) servings

1 pint (2 cups) heavy cream (36% butterfat) or whipping cream

¼ cup plain or lemon yogurt or sour cream

One (6-ounce) can frozen lemonade concentrate, undiluted

⅔ cup granulated sugar

¼ teaspoon salt

Grated zest of 2 lemons (about 3 tablespoons)

1. Measure all the ingredients together in the container of a blender or food processor. Mix or puree about 2 minutes, until thick and smooth.

2. Pour the mixture into a freezer container, cover, and freeze about 2 hours. Remove from the freezer and stir with a fork to break up any ice crystals. Return to the container, cover, and freeze at least 3 hours or overnight, until solid. To serve, let the sherbet sit out at room temperature 15 to 20 minutes until soft enough to scoop.

Baked Banana–Coconut Ice Cream

BANANA ICE CREAM is popular in the Caribbean as well as in Mexico and southern India, where the mellow fruit flavor calms the palate after eating spicy foods. Children love to help make and eat this treat, but the addition of rum, or rum extract, is strictly for grown-ups. Personally, I like it best with the works: vanilla and coconut extract plus rum. This recipe is surprisingly easy to prepare and can be frozen in any type of container; the larger the container the thinner the mixture and the quicker it will freeze. You do not need an ice cream maker.

for good measure

- For best flavor, use ripe bananas with some brown spots. You can save overripe bananas, whole in their skins, in the freezer until ready to use. Peel them before thawing.

- Canned unsweetened coconut milk is sold in many supermarkets and Asian, Thai, or natural foods markets; it should have a fresh coconut taste; do not use it if it is bitter or sour.

- Sweetened canned Coco Lopez can be substituted. Coconut extract is sold in supermarkets or see Mail-Order Sources and Suppliers, page 240.

special equipment: 9- or 10-inch oven-proof baking dish; 1½- to 2-quart saucepan; 1-quart freezer container with lid (or 9 × 13-inch metal pan plus plastic wrap)

advance preparation: Ice cream is best prepared the day before serving; it needs 5 or 6 hours minimum to freeze hard.

temperature and time: Bananas: 425°F for 20 minutes; stove top: about 5 minutes

yield: 3½ cups; 6 to 8 servings

2 or 3 medium bananas (9½ to 10 ounces total, after peeling)

2 teaspoons canola or other mild vegetable oil

One (14-ounce) can unsweetened coconut milk (generous 1¼ cups)

1 cup heavy cream (36% butterfat) or whipping cream

2 tablespoons light corn syrup (Karo)

½ cup granulated sugar (omit if using sweetened coconut milk)

Pinch of salt

Pinch of ground nutmeg

1 teaspoon vanilla extract

1 teaspoon coconut extract, optional

3 tablespoons white or dark rum or 1½ teaspoons rum extract, optional for grown-ups

1. Preheat the oven to 425°F. Place the peeled bananas in an ovenproof dish, drizzle with oil, and bake for about 20 minutes, until softened, browned, and aromatic. Mash the bananas with a fork, then set them aside to cool. You should have about 1 cup.

2. In a saucepan, combine the coconut milk, cream, corn syrup, sugar, if using, salt, and nutmeg. Stir over medium heat 3 to 5 minutes, until the coconut milk solids melt, the sugar dissolves, and the mixture is smooth and creamy. Remove from the heat and stir in the extracts and rum, if using.

3. Put the baked bananas in the workbowl of a food processor fitted with a steel blade or in the bowl of an electric mixer. Add the coconut mixture and process or beat until smooth and creamy. Taste and adjust flavoring if needed. Pour the mixture into a container, cover, and freeze 2 or 3 hours or until it begins to get solid. Remove from the freezer, stir the mixture to break up the ice crystals, then return it to the freezer overnight, or until frozen solid. If the ice cream is too hard to scoop, let it stand at room temperature 15 to 20 minutes or pulse chunks in the food processor to soften slightly, like a sherbet.

Ice Cream "Sand" Castle

ON A HOT summer day when you can't get to the beach or the pool, an ice cream sand castle is a good, cooling substitute. The castle makes a perfect dessert for a summer birthday or pool party, too.

To make the castle, simply fill a plastic sand castle mold with store-bought ice cream. When it is hard-frozen and unmolded, the cinnamon sugar sprinkled on top looks just like sand, especially when garnished with candy seashells, gummy fish, and pebbles sold in candy shops. Be sure to let kids help with this one.

for good measure

If you don't have a castle mold, peel the cardboard container off a quart—or pint—of ice cream. Top it with cinnamon sugar "sand" and decorate with candies or a drawbridge made of graham crackers and string licorice; you can use animal crackers or other cookies instead of seashell candies, but keep the decorations edible.

special equipment: Plastic sand castle mold about 5 inches tall and 5¼ inches wide (sold in novelty or drug stores) or substitute any cylindrical quart-size plastic or cardboard ice cream container; toy flag (or paper triangle decorated and taped to a toothpick); flat plate covered with foil; large platter or serving tray covered with aluminum foil with its edges folded up into a ½-inch lip (to catch "sand" sugar or ice cream drips)

advance preparation: Plan ahead. The castle should be started at least 1 day before you plan to serve it, as it takes least 3 hours, or overnight, to freeze solid in the mold, then another 3 hours to refreeze the unmolded and sand-coated castle. Before serving, let it stand at room temperature about 15 minutes to soften the ice cream.

yield: 1-quart mold; about 8 (½-cup) servings

1 quart vanilla or coffee ice cream

1 cup granulated sugar

2 teaspoons ground cinnamon

Pinch of instant hot chocolate mix, optional

Candies: edible candy seashells, pebbles, and rocks, gummy fish, sharks, and octopuses, available at bulk candy shops or mail order (see Mail-Order Sources and Suppliers, page 240)

1. If you are using a plastic sand castle mold, be sure it has been washed and dried well. Allow the ice cream to soften about 15 minutes at room temperature, then spoon it into the castle mold, packing it down well and filling any crenellations or designs on the bottom of the mold. Cover the top tightly with a piece of plastic wrap or foil and freeze overnight, or until solid.

2. In a medium mixing bowl, stir together the sugar and cinnamon to make beach sand; you can darken the color by adding a little more cinnamon or a pinch of instant hot cocoa mix if you wish.

3. At least 3 hours before serving (or up to several days ahead of time) unmold the castle. Set out a foil-covered plate. Fill a 2- to 3-quart pot with hot tap water. Remove the mold from the freezer. Hold it open end up and carefully but quickly (for no more than 2 seconds) dip it into the hot water to warm the mold without melting more than the

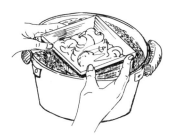

surface of the ice cream. Immediately top the mold with a foil-covered plate and invert. Lift off the mold. Bend up the edges of the foil to catch any ice cream drips.

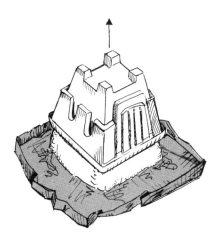

4. Working quickly, sprinkle a generous coating of cinnamon sugar sand onto the mold, coating the sides as well as the top of the castle. Don't worry if some spots remain bare at this point; you will add more sugar later. Gather and reserve any spilled sugar to use later. Immediately return the uncovered castle to the freezer until it is frozen solid again (at least 3 hours). Wrap the castle with plastic wrap or aluminum foil and keep it frozen until shortly before serving time.

5. About 15 minutes before serving, spread the remaining cinnamon sugar on the foil-covered serving tray. Remove the castle from the freezer, unwrap it, and quickly roll the sides in the cinnamon sugar. Set the castle upright in the middle of the "sandy beach" and sprinkle more cinnamon sugar on the top. Scatter the candy shells, fish, sharks, and pebbles around the sandy beach. Finally, top the castle with the toy flag. Serve at once or return the castle on its tray to the freezer until a few minutes before presentation.

Ice Cream Sandwiches

HOMEMADE ICE CREAM sandwiches are as much fun to make as to eat. They are especially delicious when made with homemade cookies, but store-bought are good, too, especially when paired with ice cream mixed with your own add-ins (see page 181). This is not strictly a recipe, but rather a group of suggestions, ideas for how you can make your own ice cream sandwiches by putting together cookies from this book or from the store.

for good measure

- For each sandwich made of two 3-inch-diameter cookies, you will need one scoop (¼ cup) ice cream.

- To be fancy, roll the edges of each ice cream sandwich in one of the following: crushed toffee candy, graham cracker crumbs, instant hot cocoa mix, granola cereal, or chopped nuts (2 tablespoons crumbs coat one cookie). Then wrap and freeze.

special equipment: Plastic wrap or aluminum foil cut into 8-inch squares; ice cream scoop or spoon; large plastic bag

advance preparation: Ice cream sandwiches are best prepared at least 4 hours, or a day, ahead. If hard-frozen, thaw at room temperature about 10 minutes before serving.

yield: 10 ice cream sandwiches (*Note:* smaller cookies take less ice cream filling, so yield will increase.)

20 cookies, 3 inches in diameter

One pint ice cream

To make an ice cream sandwich: Remove the ice cream from the freezer and let it soften about 15 minutes. Cut one 8-inch square of aluminum foil or plastic wrap. Put a cookie in the center, spread with a scoop of ice cream (about ½ inch thick), and top with a second cookie. Wrap completely, set on a tray, and put into the freezer. Repeat, adding wrapped cookies to the tray as they are made. When the batch is complete, transfer all the cookies to a large plastic bag, seal, and label with contents and date.

Good Combinations

Cookie Jar Oatmeal-Raisin Cookies (page 48) with butter-pecan or vanilla ice cream

Classic Peanut Butter Cookies (page 56) with chocolate ice cream

Gingerbread Cut-Outs (page 60) with vanilla or cinnamon ice cream (or stir some cinnamon into vanilla ice cream to make your own cinnamon ice cream)

Glazed Lemon Thins (page 63) with Lemon Cream Sherbet (page 174)

Quick Walnut Slices (page 64) with butter pecan or maple walnut ice cream

Store-Bought Graham Crackers (or chocolate graham crackers) with vanilla fudge or mint chocolate chip ice cream

Brownies (see Index) with Baked Banana–Coconut Ice Cream (page 175)

Instant Ice Cream Cake

THIS IS AN idea rather than a recipe. To make the world's quickest and easiest ice cream cake, simply peel away the cardboard carton from a half-gallon of your favorite ice cream. With a knife dipped in hot water, cut the ice cream block crosswise into ½-inch slices. Sandwich the ice cream between two layers of homemade or store-bought cake of a compatible flavor. If the cake layers are too thick, slice them in half using a serrated knife with a long blade. If preparing the cake in advance, wrap it in plastic wrap and freeze until about 15 minutes before serving time. Sift confectioners' sugar or cocoa on top or serve with homemade ice cream sauces (see Index). To make your own add-in flavors for ice cream, see page 181.

Good Combinations:

Easy Devil's Food Cake (page 131) and peppermint stick, mint chocolate chip, or coffee ice cream

Swedish Almond Butter Cake (page 148) and butter almond or butter pecan ice cream

Orange Angel Cake (page 144) and Lemon Cream Sherbet (page 174)

Sour Cream Spice Cake (page 132) and vanilla or butter pecan ice cream

Classic 1-2-3-4 Vanilla Cake (page 128) and chocolate or vanilla fudge ice cream

Old-Fashioned Coconut Layer Cake (page 126) with Baked Banana–Coconut Ice Cream (page 175)

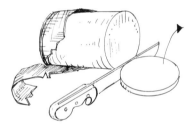

Ice Cream Sundae Party

HERE ARE THE makings for a great party—three classic sauces, four ideas for "smoosh-ins" to create your own flavors of ice cream, and two types of whipped cream. Combine them all to make your own sundaes or banana splits. What's the difference? Nothing but the banana, which can be split and layered beneath the ice cream. Whatever you call it, pile it into a big dish and top it with a cloud of whipped cream, some chopped nuts, and a cherry.

for good measure

The sundae originated in the nineteenth century when some strict believers thought it an unfit luxury to consume ice cream sodas on the Lord's day. "Dry," or uncarbonated treats, named after the day of banning were allowed, however, but the spelling was changed to "sundae" so as not to be sacrilegious.

Butterscotch Sauce

special equipment: 1- to 1½-quart heavy-bottomed saucepan

temperature and time: Stove top: 5 to 7 minutes

yield: 1 cup

¼ cup (½ stick) unsalted butter, cut up

½ cup packed light brown sugar

½ cup heavy cream (36% butterfat)

Pinch of salt

1 teaspoon vanilla extract

In the saucepan, melt the butter over low heat, then stir in the sugar, cream, and salt. Stir well, increase the heat to medium, and bring the mixture to a very gentle boil. Cook, stirring occasionally, for about 5 minutes. Remove the sauce from the heat and stir in the vanilla. Set aside to cool slightly and serve warm over ice cream or store in a covered jar; the sauce thickens as it cools. Serve at room tem-

perature or uncover and rewarm in the microwave 10 seconds on full power; stir well.

All-American Hot Fudge Sauce

THIS RICH, NOT-TOO-SWEET chocolate sauce is absolutely irresistible when served hot over vanilla ice cream. The recipe can be doubled or tripled to give as a much-appreciated holiday gift. It keeps well when refrigerated and can be warmed in the microwave or in an opened jar set in warm water. The recipe is my variation of a specialty that originated with my long-time friend Annabel Stehli, author of *The Sound of a Miracle,* about her daughter Georgiana's remarkable recovery from autism.

special equipment: 1- to 1½-quart heavy-bottomed saucepan

temperature and time: Stove top: 10 to 15 minutes

yield: 1¼ cups

2 ounces unsweetened chocolate, chopped

2 ounces semisweet chocolate, chopped (or ⅓ cup chips)

⅓ cup water

½ cup granulated sugar

Pinch of salt

3 tablespoons unsalted butter, cut up

½ teaspoon vanilla extract

Combine the chocolate, water, sugar, salt, and butter in the saucepan and place over very low heat. Stir 3 to 5 minutes, until the chocolate melts and the sugar dissolves. Whisk to blend well, then reduce the heat to the lowest level possible and whisk the sauce on and off for an additional 10 minutes, keeping it just below a bubbling boil until it is very smooth and thick. Remove the sauce from the heat and stir in the vanilla. Set aside to cool slightly and use warm, or pour it into a jar to cool, then cover and refrigerate. Serve at room temperature or uncover and rewarm in the microwave 15 to 20 seconds on full power; stir well.

Peanut Butter Sauce

special equipment: 1- to 1½-quart heavy-bottomed saucepan

temperature and time: Stove top: 5 to 7 minutes

yield: 1 cup

1 cup peanut butter, chunky or smooth style

1 cup heavy cream (36% butterfat)

¼ cup light corn syrup

In the saucepan, stir together all the ingredients over low heat until completely smooth and creamy. At first the mixture appears to separate, but it smooths out as it is beaten. Serve warm over ice cream. Store in a covered jar; the sauce thickens as it cools. Add a little more cream and if cold, rewarm it in the microwave a few seconds on full power. Stir well before serving.

Four Do-It-Yourself Ice Creams

for good measure

> When adding in flavors, keep the basic ice cream plain. Start with vanilla or orange or lemon sherbet, for example.

special equipment: Rubber spatula

yield: One (1-cup) serving of each flavor

Jam-Boree

1 cup vanilla ice cream, slightly softened

1½ tablespoons seedless raspberry jam (or apricot, blueberry, peach, or strawberry preserves)

In a mixing bowl, use a big spoon to chop the ice cream into tablespoon-size lumps. Add the jam or preserves and stir lightly but don't blend in completely. Spoon into a serving dish.

Berry Good Treat

1 cup vanilla ice cream, slightly softened

½ cup fresh ripe strawberries, rinsed, dried, hulled, and thinly sliced

In a mixing bowl, stir together the ice cream and berries. Spoon into a serving dish.

Candy Crunch

1 cup vanilla, chocolate, or coffee ice cream, slightly softened

¼ cup crushed candy, such as chocolate-covered toffee. For peppermint stick ice cream, crush peppermint sticks and add to vanilla ice cream

To crush the candy, put it in a plastic bag, seal the end, and hit it with a hammer or rolling pin. In a mixing bowl, stir together the ice cream and crushed candy. Spoon it into a serving dish.

Citrus Swirl

1 cup vanilla ice cream, *or* lemon or orange sherbet, slightly softened

1 tablespoon frozen lemonade or orange juice concentrate, thawed but not diluted

In a mixing bowl, use a big spoon to chop the ice cream into tablespoon-size lumps. Drizzle on the frozen juice concentrate and stir lightly but don't blend in completely. Spoon into a serving dish.

continued

Flavored Whipped Cream

for good measure

> Be sure to use "heavy" cream (which contains 36% butterfat and holds its shape when whipped), not "whipping" cream, which does not contain enough butterfat to hold its shape.

special equipment: Chilled bowl and beater for whipping cream

advance preparation: Whipped cream can be prepared up to 3 hours ahead if refrigerated in a strainer set over a bowl.

yield: 2 cups whipped cream; 4 to 6 servings

Vanilla Whipped Cream

1 cup heavy cream (36% butterfat), chilled
2 tablespoons sifted confectioners' sugar
½ teaspoon vanilla extract

In a chilled bowl with chilled beater, whip the cream until soft peaks form. Add the sugar and vanilla and beat until stiff. Refrigerate.

Chocolate Whipped Cream

2 tablespoons confectioners' sugar
1 scant tablespoon unsweetened cocoa powder
Pinch of ground cinnamon
1 cup heavy cream, chilled

In a medium bowl, sift together the confectioners' sugar, cocoa powder, and cinnamon and set it aside. In a chilled bowl with a chilled beater, whip the cream until soft peaks form. Add the sugar mixture and beat until stiff. Refrigerate.

Peanut Butter–Honey "Clay Dough"

NO COOKING IS needed to make this delicious—and nutritious—edible dough that feels and models like clay. Let the kids mix the few ingredients together, then shape it into whatever bugs and critters their imaginations can invent. Add bits of candy, shoestring licorice, raisins, nuts, or chocolate chips for features. Peanut butter bugs are especially fun to make, share, and eat at a Halloween or birthday party.

for good measure

> Nonfat dry milk powder is sold in supermarkets and natural foods stores.

special equipment: Scissors or paring knife to cut licorice; toothpicks, optional; spatula

advance preparation: Edible clay can be made up to 5 days in advance, wrapped in a plastic bag, and refrigerated. Bring to room temperature to make shapes.

yield: About ¾ cup clay; 15 to 18 "creatures"

½ cup peanut butter, chunky or smooth style

2 tablespoons toasted or raw wheat germ

2 tablespoons honey

5 to 6 tablespoons nonfat dry milk, instant or noninstant type, or as needed

Nuts, raisins, dried cranberries or cherries, shoestring licorice, chocolate chips, candies, etc.

1. In a mixing bowl with a sturdy spoon, stir together the peanut butter, wheat germ, honey, and dry milk. Add about 1 tablespoon more dry milk if necessary to make the mixture easy to handle without feeling sticky. If you have time, chill the dough about 15 minutes for a smoother texture.

2. Pinch off 1-inch lumps of the mixture and roll them into balls. Model the balls into any shapes you like: snakes, snails, turtles, bugs. Cut up bits of raisins, other dry fruits, or licorice and poke them into the creatures to make eyes, antennae, legs, or wings. Use a toothpick to help model shapes and a spatula to lift flat designs off the work surface. Display (or eat) the creatures, or refrigerate them on a plate until ready to serve. They harden a little when cold.

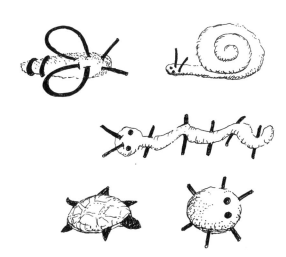

Chocolate Haystacks

THIS RETRO RECIPE is still hanging around from the fifties, and kids of all ages still love it. The recipe was perfected for me by Jesse Nelson, who made haystacks for treats when he was growing up in Stillwater, Minnesota, in the 1970s. A veteran haystack snacker, Jesse cautions that they are easier to eat if flatter in shape, but they look more realistic if tall and roughly cone-shaped.

for good measure

If you don't have butterscotch chips, use all chocolate chips.

special equipment: Double boiler or metal bowl set over a larger pan; wax paper; cookie sheet or tray

advance preparation: Haystacks keep covered about a week at room temperature; refrigerate them in hot weather.

temperature and time: Stove top: about 10 minutes; refrigerator: about 30 minutes

yield: 24 to 26 haystacks (2 × 1½ inches)

2 cups (12 ounces) semisweet chocolate chips

1 cup (6 ounces) butterscotch chips

One (10- to 12-ounce) can crisp chow mein noodles (spaghetti style, not wide flat type)

1. Cover a tray with wax paper and set it aside. Melt together the chocolate and butterscotch chips in the top of a double boiler set over simmering water. Stir occasionally until creamy and smooth.

2. Remove the top of the double boiler, set it on a heat-proof surface, and stir in the noodles, coating them completely with the chocolate mixture.

3. Drop tablespoons of the chocolate noodles onto the prepared tray, making haystacks about 2 inches wide at the base and about 1½ inches tall (or slightly shorter if you want to eat them neatly). Place the tray in the refrigerator for about 30 minutes, or until the chocolate is hard. Store the haystacks in a wax paper–lined box.

Caramel Nut Turtles

EVERYONE LOVES CARAMEL turtle candies and, with adult supervision, they are easy and fun for kids to make. For gifts, you can wrap the turtles in individual packets and layer them in a decorative box tied up with a fancy bow and a recipe.

special equipment: Aluminum foil cut into several 6- to 8-inch squares; jelly roll pan or cookie sheet; paring knife

advance preparation: Turtles take just a few minutes to make and keep several weeks in an airtight container.

temperature and time: 350°F for about 3 minutes

yield: 36 turtles

1½ cups (about 6 ounces) pecan or walnut halves or pieces

18 square individually wrapped caramel candies (sold in supermarkets or candy shops)

½ cup (3 ounces) semisweet chocolate chips, or chopped chocolate

1. Position a rack in the center of the oven and preheat it to 350°F. Set out the foil pieces and the baking pan. Unwrap the caramels and cut each one in half crosswise. Break or cut the nut halves lengthwise to make slivers that will form turtle feet, heads, and tails.

2. Prepare 3 or 4 turtles at a time on a piece of foil set on a cookie sheet. For each turtle, arrange 6 nut slices as shown (see sketches), making 4 feet, a head, and a tail. Place a caramel half in the middle, on top of the nut pieces. Carefully, so as not to disturb the placement of pieces, set the cookie sheet in the oven for 3 to 4 minutes. Peek into the oven often (this is the adult's job). As soon as the caramel melts onto the nuts forming a rounded "shell," remove the pan from the oven and place it on a heat-proof surface. Set a few chocolate chips on top of the caramel "shell" and return the tray to the oven for a few seconds. As soon as the chocolate melts, remove the pan from the oven and use the back of a teaspoon to spread the chocolate into a rounded swirl. Slide the foil containing this group of turtles onto the counter to cool and prepare a new batch on another piece of foil set on the cookie sheet (it shouldn't be too hot to work on, but if you feel it is, use a second cookie sheet). Repeat. Allow all turtles to cool completely before storing between layers of wax paper in a container kept in a cool, dry place.

Arrange the nuts

Add the caramel

Melt the caramel

Melt the chocolate

Chocolate Truffles

THESE CANDIES ARE ACTUALLY modeled after a rare and highly prized fungus with a rounded shape that grows near the roots of certain trees in France and Italy.

Chocolate truffles are much easier to find than the real ones (which must be rooted out of the ground by dogs or pigs). All you have to do is melt some flavored chocolate, then roll it into little balls and dip them in a variety of coatings. Truffles are prized holiday gifts, and the best part is you can make and freeze them in advance. Be sure to plan ahead because the chocolate batter takes an hour or two to chill enough to shape. *Note:* The use of liqueur or brandy is suggested for adults only.

for good measure

- For the best tasting truffles, use the best quality chocolate you can find (see page 220): Lindt or Callebaut, for example, or Baker's Bittersweet or Ghirardelli (sold in supermarkets); Nestlé's semi-sweet chocolate morsels work, too.
- The truffle batter cools most quickly when spread out in a flat metal pan.
- Roll the truffles in a variety of coatings for the most attractive presentation.

special equipment: Double boiler or metal bowl set over a larger pan; 8 or 9 × 1½-inch metal pan; teaspoon melon-baller; wax paper; 2 or 3 small bowls for coatings; wax paper; tray or cookie sheet

advance preparation: The full batch of truffle batter takes about 2 hours in the refrigerator to chill enough to shape (a half batch chills in 1 hour). Truffles can be made up to 2 weeks in advance, layered with wax paper, and refrigerated in an airtight container or double-wrapped and kept frozen up to 1 month in a crush-proof box.

temperature and time: Stove top: about 5 minutes; refrigerator: 1 to 2 hours

yield: About 1½ cups batter; 32 to 36 truffles (¾ to 1 inch)

truffle batter

12 ounces best quality bittersweet (not unsweet-ened) or semisweet chocolate, chopped

¼ cup (½ stick) unsalted butter, cut up

¼ cup heavy cream (36% butterfat)

optional flavoring (choose one or use *half* a recipe for *half* the chocolate mixture)

Orange: Add 2 tablespoons orange liqueur and 1 teaspoon orange extract

Mocha: Add 1 tablespoon instant espresso or regular coffee powder dissolved in 2 tablespoons coffee liqueur (Kahlúa or Tia Maria, for example)

Cognac: Add 2 tablespoons brandy or Cognac

coating (choose one or use *half* the given quantity for *half* the chocolate mixture)

½ cup sifted unsweetened cocoa; ½ cup (about 2 ounces) finely chopped, toasted almonds, pecans, walnuts, or hazelnuts; granulated sugar; chocolate sprinkles (jimmies, shots)

1. Cover a tray or cookie sheet with wax paper and set it aside. Combine the chocolate, butter, and cream in a double boiler set over, not touching, simmering water. Stir or whisk gently until melted and absolutely smooth and creamy. Remove the mixture from the heat and stir in the flavoring of your choice (or leave plain). You can also divide the melted chocolate in half, putting each portion in a bowl and adding *half* the amount of flavoring to each.

2. Spoon the flavored melted chocolate into one or several flat metal pans (one per flavor) and refrigerate 1 to 2 hours, or until the chocolate is stiff enough to scoop with a spoon. Use a teaspoon or a melon-baller to scoop up balls about ¾ inch in diameter, then roll them into irregular, slightly lumpy rounds between the cocoa-covered palms of your hands. Work quickly because the mixture tends to soften easily.

3. Roll the balls in one of the coatings, then set on the prepared tray. Repeat, using a variety of coatings. Store the truffles in a box between layers of wax paper or plastic wrap in the refrigerator or freezer.

Butter Mints

NO COOKING IS needed for this easy-to-make candy—even the youngest cook can help hand-shape the mints, which dry in the air. Butter mints are a favorite at holiday time; add them to a holiday cookie platter or give them as a gift in a decorative box with the recipe attached.

special equipment: Sifter; wax paper; tray or cookie sheet

advance preparation: Mints need at least 4 hours (on a dry day) or overnight to air-dry completely. They remain fresh at room temperature up to 1 month in a covered container.

yield: About 70 mints (1-inch diameter)

¼ **cup (½ stick) unsalted butter, at room temperature**

⅓ **cup light corn syrup (Karo)**

1 teaspoon pure peppermint extract

½ **teaspoon salt**

1 pound (4¼ cups) confectioners' sugar, plus a little extra if needed

Vegetable food colors or substitutes (see step 3)

1. Cover a tray with wax paper and set it aside. In a large mixing bowl with a sturdy spoon or in an electric mixer, beat together the butter, corn syrup, peppermint extract, and salt. Place a sifter over the bowl and add in the sugar. Stir slowly to sift. Blend everything together.

2. Mix the dough together with your hands to form a smooth ball. Add a tiny bit more sugar if needed. Coat your hands with confectioners' sugar if the dough feels sticky.

3. Butter mints are traditionally tinted pastel colors: very pale yellow, green, or pink, plus white; you only need a scant drop of each vegetable color to achieve this. You can use packaged colors or substitute beet or raspberry juice for pink or frozen orange juice concentrate, undiluted, for yellow.

Divide the dough into 4 equal parts on wax paper. Leave 1 part white; add 1 scant drop of food coloring to each of the other portions. Knead the color into the dough until it has an even tone.

4. Pinch off a small lump of the dough and roll it between your palms to form a ball ¾ to 1 inch in diameter. Set the ball on the prepared tray and flatten the top by pressing on it with the tines of a table fork. If the fork sticks, dip it in confectioners' sugar. Repeat. Air-dry the mints on the tray at least 4 hours, or overnight, turning them over once to dry the bottoms. Store the mints between layers of wax paper or plastic wrap in a covered container.

Dipped Chips and Pretzel Pops

IF YOU LIKE the combination of sweet and salty as much as I do, chocolate-dipped potato chips and pretzels are for you. They are so easy to prepare that the kids can do it, but don't let the simplicity of the idea fool you. Tony gourmet shops and elegant confectioners sell these in gilt-edged boxes at holiday time because they make tasty and unusual snacks and gifts. Package yours in decorative glass jars and tie on a bright ribbon. I have given basic proportions in the recipe, but you should adjust them to the quantities you wish to make.

for good measure

For the pretzels, let your creativity go wild: Traditionally, finger-length pretzel "rods" are used, but thinner 3-inch "straws" or "knots" of any size are fun, too. You can also roll the chocolate-coated pretzels in some chopped nuts, toasted coconut, chocolate or multicolored sprinkles, or drizzle on melted white chocolate.

special equipment: 1-quart double boiler or metal bowl set over a larger pan; small spatula or pastry brush; wax paper; tray or cookie sheet

advance preparation: Chocolate-dipped chips and pretzels keep about 2 weeks in an airtight container at room temperature.

temperature and time: Stove top: 5 minutes

yield: 65 to 70 chocolate-dipped potato chips or about 50 (4- to 5-inch) pretzel rods coated with 2 inches of chocolate

chocolate coating

- **6 ounces (1 cup) semisweet chocolate chips, or semisweet or bittersweet chocolate, chopped**
- **1 teaspoon solid shortening (Crisco)**

(choose one) potato chips

- **One (medium-size, 5½-ounce) bag potato chips (containing 60 to 70 whole chips, roughly 2 to 3 inches in diameter)**

or pretzels

- **Two (10-ounce) bags baked pretzel rods (20 to 25 rods per pack, 4 to 7 inches long, depending upon brand; use as is or break off to desired length; 6 ounces of melted chocolate coats about fifty 4- to 5-inch rods)**

garnish, optional, for pretzels

- **1 cup (4 ounces) finely chopped walnuts, or little candies**

1. Melt together the chocolate chips and shortening in the top of a double boiler set over, not touching, simmering water. Stir the chocolate until creamy and smooth. Remove the double boiler from the heat but leave the chocolate mixture over the hot water. If the chocolate begins to thicken, reheat it slightly until thin enough to spread.

Cover a flat tray or cookie sheet with wax paper.

2. Potato chips: Gently turn the potato chips out into a large bowl.

Work with one chip at a time. Holding a chip with your fingers at one end, dip a pastry brush or teaspoon into the melted chocolate, and "paint" a thin layer of chocolate onto about ½ of one end of the chip; turn the chip around and paint chocolate on the opposite side, to the same height. Set the chip flat on the wax paper. Repeat with the remaining chips. *Note:* For gifts, whole chips certainly look nicer, but chocolate-coated broken pieces taste just as good! Depending upon the temperature of your room, the chocolate will harden in 30 minutes to 1 hour (or the tray can be refrigerated). Store the chips between sheets of wax paper or plastic wrap in a crush-proof airtight container.

3. Pretzels: Melt the chocolate as above. In addition, set out ½ to 1 cup of finely chopped walnuts on a piece of wax paper. Work with one pretzel at a time. Holding the pretzel rod at one end dip a pastry brush or teaspoon into the melted chocolate and "paint" one end all around, to a height of 2 to 3 inches, leaving some of the pretzel plain. If you have broken the rods, be sure to hold them on the unbroken end and paint on the chocolate so as to conceal the break. Roll the chocolate-coated pretzel in the chopped nuts or candies, then set it on the wax paper until the chocolate hardens. Store the pretzels between sheets of wax paper or plastic wrap in a crush-proof airtight container.

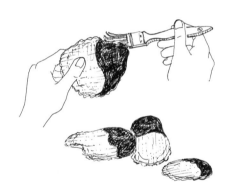

Kids in the kitchen: ice cream, candy, and treats

Rice Krispies Candy Cones

DEFINITELY FOR THE kids, and especially fun to make for birthday parties, these are simply ice cream cones topped with a ball of old-fashioned Kellogg's Rice Krispies Treats, decorated with icing and candies. For a great party activity, let the kids do the whole thing—make the rice candy and icing, then shape and decorate the cones. Be as inventive as you want in adding candies, sprinkles, and a cherry or red candy on the top! This recipe was tested by my friend Jacquie Colman Manley, who prepared a beautiful basket of decorated cones as a centerpiece for the birthday party of her neighbor's seven-year-old daughter. Instead of making cones, you can also hand-form the candy mixture into a variety of shapes, including Christmas trees and cookie cutter forms (see variations).

for good measure

- This does not pretend to be health food, but you can boost the nutritional value of rice cereal candy somewhat by adding ½ cup toasted wheat germ or replacing 1 cup rice cereal with an equal amount of crushed granola cereal.

- Fresh, soft marshmallows melt more easily than stale, hard ones.

- Royal icing can be made with a fresh egg white or—if you are concerned about the possible health hazard of eating uncooked egg whites—you can use meringue (egg white) powder sold in many supermarkets and specialty food shops (see Mail-Order Sources and Suppliers, page 240).

special equipment: 2½- to 3-quart (or larger) saucepan; pint-size plastic bags, scissors; 12 drinking glasses or clean empty jars or mugs to support cones while being decorated; small bowls or 6- to 8-ounce paper cups (to transport cones, optional); wax paper; plastic wrap

advance preparation: Candy balls can be made about a week in advance and refrigerated. The royal icing can be made 1 or 2 hours in advance if completely wrapped and kept airtight so it doesn't dry out. Note that the completed cones get harder as they air-dry, but are fresh enough to eat when kept at room temperature a week.

temperature and time: Stove top: 5 minutes

yield: 12 cones, each topped by a 2½-inch diameter decorated rice candy ball

crisp rice candy cones

- ¼ cup (½ stick) unsalted butter or solid stick margarine
- 10 ounces (40 regular or 4 cups mini) marshmallows
- 6 cups Kellogg's or other brand crisp rice cereal
- 12 ice cream cones (sugar, chocolate, or regular), with 2½- to 3-inch-diameter tops

(choose one) classic royal icing

- 1 large egg white, at room temperature
- ⅛ teaspoon cream of tartar
- ⅛ teaspoon salt
- 1¾ to 2 cups sifted confectioners' sugar
- 1 tablespoon fresh lemon juice, or as needed

or meringue powder royal icing

- 2 tablespoons meringue powder
- 4 tablespoons warm water
- 2 cups sifted confectioners' sugar, or more as needed

candy decorations

Selection of small different colored candies: cinnamon hots, jelly beans, silver dragées, chocolate or colored sprinkles, colored sugars, etc.

1. Melt the butter or margarine in a large saucepan set over low heat. Add the marshmallows and stir to melt completely. Remove the pan from the heat, add all the rice cereal, and stir until all the grains are coated with the marshmallow mixture.

2. Scoop the cereal mixture out onto a piece of wax paper and let it cool a few minutes while you set out the cones, putting one into each glass or other "stand" container. Put out a selection of candies in bowls or cups.

3. When the rice candy is cool enough to handle comfortably, lightly butter or dampen your fingers and divide it into 12 (½-cup) lumps. Shape each one into a ball about 2½ inches in diameter, with a slight point at one end to fit down into the cone. *Note:* Don't compress the candy too tightly or it will be hard to eat. Test a candy ball to see that it fits into a cone. Set the balls on wax paper to air-dry.

4. Prepare either icing: For *Classic Royal Icing,* in the small bowl of an electric mixer, whip the egg white with cream of tartar and salt until foamy, then add about 1 cup of the sugar and the lemon juice and beat well. Add more sugar until the icing reaches the consistency of stiffly whipped cream; adjust the consistency by adding more sugar or lemon juice. Cover immediately with plastic wrap or the icing will air-dry and harden.

For *Meringue Powder Royal Icing*, in a small bowl, whisk together the meringue powder and warm water; let it sit 2 or 3 minutes to soften, then add the sifted sugar. Whip with an electric mixer until the icing forms stiff peaks. Adjust the consistency by adding more sifted sugar or a few drops of warm water if needed. Keep covered with plastic wrap.

5. To complete the cones, spread a little of the stiffest royal icing around the inside top of each cone and gently set in a rice candy ball; the icing acts as a glue. Replace the cone in its stand.

Scoop some of the royal icing into a plastic bag, press out the air, and tightly close the bag. With a scissors, cut a very tiny hole in one corner of the bag; squeeze the icing out of this hole, making decorative designs on the cone top. Stick candies into

the icing. Replace cones in the stands until the icing hardens. *Note:* Depending upon how stiff the icing is, it may take up to a couple of hours to harden completely. If transporting the decorated cones, place each one in a paper cup, wrap the whole thing with plastic wrap, and handle with care until the icing is hard.

Christmas Trees: Hand-shape a tennis-ball-size lump of candy mixture into a cone shape, press on little red-hot cinnamon candies, and sift a little confectioners' sugar over the top for snow.

Christmas tree

Cookie Cutter Shapes: Butter the inside of a cookie cutter (gingerbread men, teddy bears, hearts), pack with candy mixture, then press the shape out of the cutter.

Press the mixture into the cookie cutter

Press out the shape

Stand the figure up

Kids in the kitchen: ice cream, candy, and treats

No-Bake Chewies

THESE ARE FUN for kids to make, pop in a lunch box, or nibble as a snack. Let's not even mention the fact that the nutritious blend of fruits and grains is good for them.

The lightly spiced syrup is prepared on the stove top but can also be made on a hotplate, so this is a good project for a classroom; the recipe is large but may be cut in half. With young children, an adult should carefully supervise the chopping of fruit and the stove-top cooking.

for good measure

- Substitute any of your favorite dried fruits or berries in the batter. The nuts add crunch but can be omitted if you wish.
- The larger the mixing bowl, the easier it will be to toss all the ingredients together.

special equipment: Chopping board and knife or food processor; 1½- to 2-quart saucepan; wax paper; tray or cookie sheet; 4-quart mixing bowl (or larger)

advance preparation: Chewies stay fresh a week at room temperature wrapped in a plastic bag or stored in an airtight container in a cool, dry location.

temperature and time: Stove-top syrup: 3 to 5 minutes

yield: 8 cups fruit-nut mix; 60 to 65 balls (1-inch diameter). The recipe can be halved or doubled.

¼ cup (½ stick) unsalted butter

½ cup packed light or dark brown sugar

¼ cup honey

¼ cup apple or orange juice

1 teaspoon ground nutmeg

½ teaspoon ground cinnamon

1 cup packed soft, moist dried pitted prunes or figs

1 cup packed pitted dates, whole or prechopped

1 cup packed dried apricots

1 cup packed golden raisins or dried cranberries or cherries

1 cup (4 ounces) walnuts, chopped, optional

1 cup granola cereal (any type)

1 cup crisp rice cereal

1½ cups sifted confectioners' sugar, plus extra for storage

1. In a saucepan, combine the butter, sugar, honey, juice, nutmeg, and cinnamon. Set over medium-low heat and stir with a wooden spoon for 3 to 5 minutes, or until the sugar is dissolved. Remove the pan from the heat. Cover a tray or cookie sheet with wax paper.

2. With a knife on a cutting board or in a food processor, chop the dried fruit into coarse pieces. You may find it easier to do this in small batches if using a processor with a small workbowl.

In a large mixing bowl, toss together all the chopped fruit with the nuts, if using, granola, and rice cereal. Pour on the warm sugar syrup and stir well to coat all the pieces. Set the mixture aside until cool enough to touch comfortably. Put the confectioners' sugar in a medium bowl.

3. With *dampened* fingers, pinch off walnut-size lumps of the mixture and press each together to make 1-inch balls. Roll each ball in the sugar, then set it on the covered tray to air-dry. Store the balls in an airtight container with a little sifted confectioners' sugar on top.

No-Bake Apricot Snowballs

THESE EASY-TO-MAKE treats keep so well they can be prepared in advance and given as holiday gifts. Kids of all ages enjoy mixing, shaping, and nibbling on these snowballs. For gift-giving, pack them in a decorative glass jar tied with a festive ribbon and a recipe card.

The recipe requires no cooking and is a good, and nutritious, project for children's groups, Scouts, or a classroom.

special equipment: Food processor or blender or knife and chopping board; wax paper; tray or cookie sheet

advance preparation: Snowballs need 3 or 4 hours to air-dry before they are firm enough to store.

yield: About 40 balls (1-inch diameter)

1¼ cups packed shredded sweetened coconut, divided (¾ cup and ½ cup)

2 cups (about 12 ounces) soft, moist, dried apricots

¼ cup toasted wheat germ

¼ cup instant or noninstant dry milk

¼ cup honey

1. Measure ¾ cup of coconut into a large mixing bowl and put the remaining ½ cup in a small bowl. Cover a tray or cookie sheet with wax paper.

2. Using a food processor (or the blender working with ½-cup batches), finely chop the apricots, then mix them together with the ¾ cup coconut. Stir in the wheat germ, milk, and honey and work the mixture together with a spoon or your hands until thoroughly blended.

3. Pull off lumps of the apricot dough and roll them between your palms to form 1–inch diameter balls. Roll each ball in the reserved shredded coconut, then set it on the covered tray to air-dry for several hours, until firm. Store the dried snowballs in an airtight container.

Easy decorating ideas

Here are a few time-saving suggestions for decorating cake and cupcake tops or adding a decorative garnish alongside any dessert.

SUGARED CRANBERRIES, GRAPES, MINT LEAVES, AND ROSE PETALS

These are dramatic edible garnishes for any dessert or cake top.

Small whole fruits like cranberries and grapes, individually or in small clusters, should be rinsed and completely dried on paper towels. Mint leaves and edible flowers such as nasturtiums, rosebuds, and separate rose petals are especially attractive. Avoid other flowers unless absolutely sure they are edible and have been grown without pesticides. If not certain a flower is edible, consult your local Agricultural Extension Service. Wash flowers carefully to remove any trace of dirt, then blot dry on paper towels. Set nearby a pastry brush, a bowl of granulated sugar, and a tray covered with wax paper.

Beat 1 egg white in a small bowl until slightly foamy. With the pastry brush, lightly coat each berry, grape, leaf, or petal with the egg white, then immediately dip the item into the sugar, coating it well, and place it on the tray to air-dry at least 3 hours, or overnight.

DECORATING CAKES WITH FRESH FLOWERS

Fresh flowers give a decorative finish to any cake and require no effort at all, but be sure to note that these are NOT edible decorations.

Since the flowers will, in some cases, be touching the cake, be sure that they are grown without pesticides and rinsed with water to remove any trace of dirt. Keep the flowers in water while the container is readied. The best bouquet containers are small baby food jars—they can be empty or filled with a little water or with waterlogged florist's foam. Use a serrated grapefruit knife to hollow out a jar-size depression from the top of the cake. Or, to show one or two perfect blossoms, you can use the rubber-stoppered plastic tubes sold by florists to hold individual long-stemmed roses (save them for reuse if you are a lucky recipient). Snip the blossom stems and place the flowers in the container with enough water to cover the stem ends. Poke the tube right into the cake top without making a special hole. Remove the containers before slicing the cake.

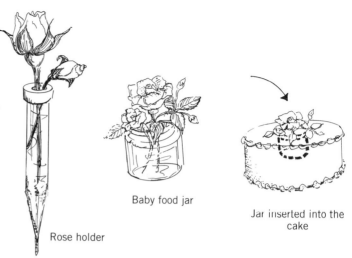

Rose holder

Baby food jar

Jar inserted into the cake

SHAVED OR GRATED CHOCOLATE OR QUICK CHOCOLATE CURLS

With a grater and a chocolate bar, you can make a decorative cake topping.

Use dark, milk, or white chocolate—a candy bar or block or 1-ounce square—at room temperature or slightly warmer. Simply draw the chocolate over the ¼-inch (medium) grater holes, letting the pieces fall directly onto the cake top, or onto a piece of wax paper.

minum foil in an unheated oven with just the pilot light on for about 10 minutes). To make the curls, pull a sharp swivel-type vegetable peeler across the surface of the chocolate. The success of this effort depends largely upon the temperature of the chocolate—if too cold, the chocolate will crack instead of curl. Have patience . . . the results are worth it. Drop the curls directly onto the cake top as they are made, or set them on wax paper and lift them into place by sticking a toothpick in the side as a handle.

If you want to get fancy, make white or dark chocolate curls to garnish a cake. Use block or bar chocolate, warmed slightly more than for shaving or grating (set the chocolate on a piece of alu-

Grated chocolate or chocolate curls can be made in advance and stored in a protective crush-proof box in the refrigerator.

QUICK MELTED CHOCOLATE

To melt chocolate chips quickly without using a double boiler, put them in a self-sealing plastic bag, fasten the end securely, and drop the bag in very hot water (135 to 140°F) for a few minutes. When the chocolate feels soft, dry the outside of the bag carefully, then open the bag and squeeze out the chocolate for spreading, or, alternatively, cut a very small hole in one corner of the bag and squeeze out the chocolate to write a greeting on a cake.

SPEEDY STENCILS

With an X-Acto knife or scissors, cut designs such as hearts, stars, or paper dolls from stiff paper or cardboard. Set the paper on the cake top and sift on confectioners' sugar, or cinnamon, or cocoa. You can also use store-bought doilies as stencils. Place the doily directly on the cake top and sift on the sugar or cocoa, or cut the lacy doily into a different shape (for example, a heart) before placing it on the cake and sifting on the sugar. Carefully remove the doily.

EASY DECORATING TUBES/CONES

When decorating cakes and cupcakes, make quick and easy decorating tubes by putting icing into pint-size plastic bags; freezer-quality bags are best because they are stronger and will not split during use. Cut a tiny hole in one corner of the bag to squeeze out the icing, or, before filling with the icing, drop in a metal decorating tip and arrange it so the point extends out of the hole in the bag. To make your own paper cones, see page 198.

Metal tip

PAPER DECORATING CONES

Decorating bags or cones are available in a variety of materials from paper to plastic or nylon. Disposable paper cones can be purchased in bakeware shops or by mail order (see Mail-Order Sources and Suppliers, page 240) in precut triangles of baking parchment. You can also cut your own from parchment or wax paper. To make a cone, cut a triangle about 12 × 15 inches. Pull one long point around its midpoint, making a cone. Hold the cone tight while wrapping the second point around the middle, and tuck in all the ends. Secure the cone with a piece of tape. Cut a tiny piece off the tip, or cut a hole that permits the nose of a metal decorating tip dropped inside the cone to peek out. Add icing to the cone, fold down the top, and squeeze out the icing.

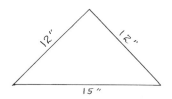 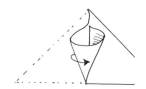 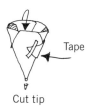

Tape

Cut tip

CANDY "FUNNY FACES" FOR CAKES AND CUPCAKES

To make quick and easy decorations on top of kids' party cakes, you can decorate with icing as above, or, even more quickly, make faces or designs with a variety of candies pressed onto the frosting (the way you might decorate a gingerbread house). Use M & M's (especially the tiny sizes), cinnamon "red hots," silver dragées, shoestring licorice (cut up, for hair), and Life Savers. Shredded wheat cereal, slightly pulled apart, also makes hilarious-looking hair; other breakfast cereals may inspire more ideas.

For a birthday party or Scout troop activity, set out some frosted cupcakes and small dishes containing a selection of candies and cereals. Invite the kids to design their own cupcakes. (See also Clown Cupcakes, page 130.)

DECORATING CAKES WITH COOKIES OR CRUMBS

Home-baked or store-bought cookies can be "glued" to cake tops and sides with jam or jelly spread with the back of a spoon for quick and easy decorations. Animal crackers are fun to put around cake sides, making a kind of parade of the animals.

Chopped nuts or crushed cookie crumbs (put cookies in a plastic bag and roll with a rolling pin) can also be pressed onto jam-covered cake sides and top, as a quick coating.

Spread the jam onto the back of the cookie

CRAZY QUILT GROUP CAKE DECORATING

If your group, club, or brothers and sisters want to present a big sheet cake to someone for a special occasion (a BIG birthday, for example), make one or several sheet cakes, arrange them side-by-side, and frost all together with vanilla icing. Melt some chocolate in a plastic bag (see page 197) and draw thin lines dividing the whole cake top into equal size squares. Prepare frosting in a variety of colors in plastic bags with a tiny hole cut in the corner of each, and let each person decorate his or her own square with a personal greeting. Be sure to have a camera handy!

About bake sales

Who can resist a plate of homemade chocolate chip cookies? A bake sale is a sure-fire way to raise money for any group, from a Scout troop to a library or a ladies' auxiliary. Whether you are in a booth under a striped awning at a village fair or at a cardtable in front of the post office, here are some suggestions and tips that will ensure a successful bake sale.

- **Food Safety:** Unless the sale is to be held in a northern climate in late fall or winter, beware of custard or cream fillings. Avoid anything that might spoil in the heat; ask contributors only to bake goodies that are not weather-sensitive. And nothing should have uncooked egg yolks or egg whites, to avoid any risk of salmonella bacteria. Many people are allergic to wheat, nuts, or other food products. While it is not practical to label everything, it is a good idea if possible to put an "ingredients" label on each item, especially if it contains peanuts or other nuts. Consider reserving one corner of the display for "Special Diet/Reduced-Fat" baked goods.

- **Basic Supplies:** A cash box and change, rolls of plastic wrap, foil, serrated knife, paring knife, scissors, masking tape, paper towels, a jar of water (to clean up spills in case you are outdoors), black oil-base felt pens, an adding machine, and a notebook to keep records.

- **Display Signs:** Have a visible and attractive sign that indicates who is sponsoring the sale and for what purpose the money is being raised. Hang up a bright, legible poster listing the main types of foods you have and the prices: breads, pies, cakes, cupcakes, cookies.

- **General Display:** When setting up the display, consider the overall appearance of the table. Add a bouquet of flowers or a plant, a pumpkin or apples in baskets. Keep it simple and attractive. Don't put everything out at once; store some items in covered containers in the back or under the display table, so you can add and fill in as things are sold. If you can, write the baker's name on the item along with the price; it increases the appeal and spreads goodwill at the same time.

- **Food Display:** First, select baked goods that will look appealing after sitting out several hours. Use a variety of containers just for display, and repackage the items as purchased using paper or plastic bags, plastic wrap, etc., which you have held behind the counter. Purely for display, consider antique baking pans, pottery platters, wooden plates or bowls, straw baskets in many sizes—all to give an old-fashioned country look. Some items may be able to stand up in a big glass cookie jar or apothecary jars. Take-home prewrapped baked goods covered with clear plastic wrap should be arranged on stiff plastic or sturdy paper plates. Bakeshop cake and cookie boxes are available wholesale from party suppliers and are very handy but cost money to start with (so it cuts profits).

Everything should be clearly visible, mouth-watering, and look freshly baked. No store-bought imposters, please.

- **Price Signs:** Use bright, clearly legible price stickers—self-stick labels with colored borders or file cards taped to sticks. Mark the prices legibly with a dark felt pen so customers can read them.

- **Merchandising:** Sell some items whole (pies, cakes, breads), some in a batch (a platter of cookies, three-for-a-dollar cupcakes), and some by the piece (10 cents a cookie; 25 cents a piece of fudge) so kids can buy themselves an inexpensive treat. Display small paper or plastic bags so customers can make up their own mixed selections if they wish, or carry some cookies to eat as they walk along.

- **Mark-Down Time:** As you near closing time, consider doubling up items or offering two-fers or other bargains. You want to sell everything, and giving two loaves for the price of one is better than going home with a box full.

About high altitude baking

When I teach baking at high altitudes in the West, I am always concerned about whether my New England recipes will perform properly. On a recent trip to Denver, for example, I demonstrated the art of pie and cake baking as spokesperson for a national cake flour company. To calm my fears, their high altitude test laboratory checked and adjusted my recipes; the results were instructive. I was right to worry in most cases. Sugar/flour ratios were altered, slightly more liquid was added, baking powder was shaved a tad, and baking times and temperatures increased. If you live and bake at high altitudes, you won't be surprised to hear that some of my recipes required no changes at all but for others the adjustments were different each time, with no all-purpose rules. It is best to try your favorite regular "sea-level" recipes at high altitude once exactly as written to see how they behave before tinkering. Some pie crusts and cookies may work perfectly or need just a few more drops of liquid; cakes may need more help.

In any case, the baker should be aware of the general conditions caused by high altitude and their theoretical remedies. At 3,000 feet above sea level, adjustments must usually be made in baking techniques because of the low humidity in the atmosphere and the decrease in air pressure. The higher the altitude, the more adjustments are needed.

Low humidity makes a dry climate that causes flour to be drier; thus it will absorb more liquid. A recipe may need more or less flour or liquid to maintain proper consistency. Storing flour in moisture-proof containers does not solve this problem.

Decreasing atmospheric pressure causes gases to expand more easily. In cake-baking, decreased atmospheric pressure can have a dramatic effect: Baking powder and baking soda are infused with such enthusiasm they can cause a cake to rise until it literally bursts—and then collapses. To prevent this, try decreasing the amount of leavening slightly. Angel and sponge cakes depend upon whipped air for leavening, which tends to go too far too fast. The remedy: Whip whites to medium-soft peaks instead of stiff peaks. You may also add strength with a bit more flour and a bit less sugar. If you also increase the baking temperature 15–25°F, the batter may be able to set before the air bubbles or leavening gases become too expansive.

As altitude increases, both air pressure and the boiling point of water decrease. At sea level, water boils at 212°F; at 3,000 feet above sea level, at 207°F; at 5,000 feet, at 203°F. The result is that more water evaporates during the baking process so baked goods tend to dry out. In a cake, this can mean too little moisture and too much sugar, which can weaken cell structure; in extreme cases this alone can cause a cake to fall. Cutting back sugar and/or adding a little liquid or an egg usually helps. Rich cakes containing a high ratio of fat may have similar problems because fat can weaken cell structure; try cutting 1 to 2 tablespoons of fat from your recipe. If your cookie recipes are disappointing, try cutting back slightly on leavening, fat, and sugar and/or add a bit of liquid and flour.

To make pudding or cream pie filling above 5,000 feet, a double boiler will not produce temperatures high enough to completely gelatinize starch. Thus, it is best to use direct heat instead of a double boiler.

For specific recommendations for your altitude, consult the Agricultural Extension Service of a nearby university. Your local library, bookstore, or cookware shop probably stocks hometown cookbooks and surely will be a resource for finding cooks and bakers willing to share practical advice.

General tips to guide you in adapting sea-level baking recipes to altitudes above 3,000 feet:

- Reduce the sugar in your recipe 1 to 3 tablespoons per cup of sugar used

- Increase the flour in cakes by 10%

- Increase the liquid by 1 to 4 tablespoons

- Reduce the fat in rich cakes by about 2 tablespoons or up to 20%

- Reduce each teaspoon of baking powder by ⅛ to ¼ teaspoon

- Increase the oven temperature about 25°F and increase baking time slightly

Equivalents **and** substitutions

EQUIVALENTS

BREAD CRUMBS

1 cup fresh bread crumbs = 2 ounces

1 cup dry or toasted crumbs = scant 4 ounces

BUTTER

1 pound butter = 2 cups

¼ pound butter = ½ cup; 1 stick; 8 tablespoons

CHOCOLATE

1 ounce solid
semisweet chocolate = 1 premeasured square

1 ounce regular-size
chocolate chips = ⅛ cup
= 2 tablespoons

½ cup regular
chocolate chips = 3 ounces

1 cup regular
chocolate chips = 6 ounces

1 cup mini-chocolate chips = 5½ ounces

COCONUT

average size coconut, = 3½ cups grated coconut,
4-inch diameter   loose; 2 cups, hard packed

4 ounces coconut, dried
and flaked or shredded = 1 scant cup

CREAM

1 cup heavy cream
(36 to 40% butterfat) = 2 cups whipped cream

EGGS

1 U.S. Grade A large egg = 2 ounces
= 3 tablespoons

1 large egg yolk = 1 generous tablespoon

1 large egg white = 2 tablespoons
= ⅛ cup

2 large eggs = scant ½ cup
= 3 medium eggs

4 to 5 large eggs = 1 cup

6 to 7 large yolks = ½ cup

4 large whites = ½ cup

4 large whites, beaten stiff = 3 cups meringue, enough
to top a 9-inch pie

FLOUR

1 pound all-purpose flour = 4 cups

5 pounds all-purpose flour = 20 cups

1 cup all-purpose flour = 1 cup plus 2 tablespoons
cake flour

EQUIVALENTS

FRUITS

1 8-ounce box dried apricots = 2 cups, packed

1 pound seedless raisins = 3½ cups

1 whole lemon = 2 to 3 tablespoons juice plus 2 to 3 teaspoons grated zest

1 whole orange = 6 to 8 tablespoons juice plus 2 to 3 tablespoons grated zest

1 quart fresh berries = 4 cups

GELATIN

1 envelope unflavored gelatin = 1 scant tablespoon (¼ oz); to hard-set 2 cups liquid

NUTS

1 pound whole almonds, shelled = 3¼ cups

1 cup blanched almonds, shelled = 5 ounces

1 pound walnuts, shelled = 4 cups

1 cup walnuts, shelled = 4 ounces

1 pound whole pecans, shelled = 4½ cups

1 cup shelled pecan halves = 4 ounces

1 cup shelled peanuts = 5 ounces

1 pound whole hazelnuts, shelled = 3¼ cups

1 cup shelled whole hazelnuts = 5 ounces

SUGAR

1 pound granulated sugar = 2¼ cups

5 pounds granulated sugar = 11¼ cups

1 pound brown sugar = 2¼ cups, packed

1 pound confectioners' sugar = 4 to 4¼ cups, unsifted

SUBSTITUTIONS

1 ounce solid chocolate = 3 tablespoons cocoa plus 1 tablespoon solid vegetable shortening or vegetable oil

1 cup sour milk = 1 cup sweet milk plus 1 tablespoon vinegar and let sit for 2 to 3 minutes

1 cup whole sweet milk = 3 to 4 tablespoons dry milk solids plus 1 cup water

1 cup buttermilk = 1 cup plain yogurt, stirred

1 cup crème fraîche = 1 cup heavy cream plus ½ cup sour cream

1 cup all-purpose flour = ⅞ cup rice flour

1 cup granulated sugar = ⅞ cup honey and decrease recipe liquid by 3 tablespoons

1 cup brown sugar = 1 cup granulated white sugar plus 2 tablespoons unsulfured molasses

1 cup cinnamon sugar = 1 cup granulated sugar plus 1 to 2 tablespoons ground cinnamon, to taste

Pan volume **and** serving chart

PAN SHAPE AND SIZE IN INCHES	MAXIMUM CUPS FLUID TO FILL TO CAPACITY	MAXIMUM CUPS BATTER (ALLOWING FOR RISE)	APPROXIMATE NUMBER OF SERVINGS
ROUND LAYERS			
6 × 2	4	2 to 2½	6
8 × 1½ or 8 × 2	4½ to 5	2	8 to 10
9 × 1½ or 9 × 2	6 to 6½	3 to 3½	8 to 10
10 × 2	10	4½ to 6	14
12 × 2	14	7½ to 9	22
14 × 2	19½	10 to 12	36 to 40
SQUARE LAYERS			
8 × 2	8	3½ to 5	9 to 12
9 × 1½	8 to 9	4½ to 5	9 to 12
9 × 2	10	5½	9 to 12
10 × 2	12⅓	6	20
12 × 2	16	10 to 12	36
14 × 2	24	12 to 14	42
RECTANGULAR (SHEET CAKES)			
8 × 12 (7½ × 11¾ × 1¾)	8	4 to 5	12
9 × 13 (8¾ × 13½ × 1¾)	16	8 to 9	20 to 24
11 × 17 (11⅜ × 17¼ × 2¼)	25	14 to 15	24 to 30
10½ × 15½ × 1 (jelly roll pan)	10	4 to 5 for butter cake	24 to 35
HEART			
9 × 1½	5	3 to 3½	14 to 16

PAN SHAPE AND SIZE IN INCHES	MAXIMUM CUPS FLUID TO FILL TO CAPACITY	MAXIMUM CUPS BATTER (ALLOWING FOR RISE)	APPROXIMATE NUMBER OF SERVINGS
TUBE, RING, BUNDT			
9 × 2¾ plain tube	6 to 7	4 to 4½	8 to 10
9 × 2 springform tube	9 to 10	6 to 7	10 to 12
9¼ × 3¼ fluted tube or Bundt	9 to 10	5 to 6	10 to 12
9½ × 3¾ or 10-inch plain tube or springform	12	6 to 7	12 to 14
10 × 3½ Bundt	12	6 to 7	14
10 × 4 angel cake	16	8 to 8½	12 to 14
LOAF PANS			
5½ × 3 × 2⅛ (baby)	2¼	1½ to 1¾	6 to 8
5¾ × 3½ × 2 or 6 × 3½ × 2 (baby)	2 to 2¼	1¼ to 1½	6 to 8
7½ × 3½ × 2	5 to 6	3	7 to 8
8½ × 4½ × 2¾ (average)	5¼	3½ to 3¾	7 to 8
9 × 5 × 3 (large)	8 to 9	4 to 5	9 to 10
MUFFIN PANS/CUPCAKES			
1¾ × ¾ or 1¾ × ⅞ (baby)	2 to 3 tablespoons	1 to 2 tablespoons	1
2 × 1⅛ (mini)	¼ cup	2 to 3 tablespoons	1
2½-inch diameter	⅓ cup	¼ cup	1
2¾-inch diameter	½ cup	⅓ cup	1
3 × 1¼	½ cup	⅓ cup	1
3½-inch diameter	1 cup	generous ¾ cup	1

Pan volume and serving chart

About ingredients

FATS FOR BAKING

Baking fats used in this book include butter, margarine, vegetable shortening, and oil. In baked goods, fats tenderize, moisturize, carry flavors and aromas, add nutrients, and contribute to aeration and flakiness and/or smoothness of the texture. Because fats have different melting points and contain different percentages of water, successful baking depends upon choosing the appropriate type of fat and correctly blending it into the batter or dough.

For greatest aeration of cake batters, best results are achieved with a solid fat such as butter or solid shortening (Crisco). To make flaky pastry, a cold, solid fat is most desirable. The colder the fat, the less it soaks into the flour starch and the more separate it stays, creating little flakes or layers as it is pinched into the flour.

The amount of water released by the fat contributes to the total liquid of a recipe. A fat that contains a lot of water can require more flour and thus result in a tough product. Whipped butter, tub margarine, and margarine spreads (as opposed to solid margarine) contain so much water and/or air that they should never be used in baking.

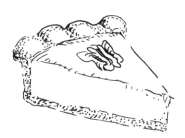

Butter: Butter has the best flavor of all baking fats. I prefer to use unsalted butter because it is (or should be) dated so it will be fresh, or it is sold frozen. Butter, an animal fat, contains cholesterol as well as enzymes that can affect and accelerate rancidity. Producers add salt to butter not only to enhance its flavor, but also to mask off-flavors and to prolong shelf life; different brands of butter contain varying quantities of salt. The best butter should taste sweet and very fresh. When you add the salt yourself, you can control the amount in the recipe.

Margarine: Margarine is made from a variety of oils and solid fats that are blended, heated, and combined with water, milk or milk solids, emulsifying agents, flavorings, preservatives, coloring, and vitamins. Margarine is made from oil that is partially hydrogenated (see below) to make it solid. Soft margarine "spreads," tub margarine, and low-fat margarines can contain as little as 30 to 40 percent oil plus unspecified quantities of water, air, flavoring and other additives, making them absolutely unreliable for baking.

Stick margarine, while it lacks the good taste of butter, has roughly the same fat content, around 80 percent, but is much lower in cholesterol. Many (but not all) brands contain no cholesterol. To satisfy kosher dietary laws, select a solid stick margarine with a high percentage of oil (70 to 80 percent), without milk solids or animal fats; read labels carefully. Fleischmann's unsalted stick margarine is a reliable product for this purpose.

Solid Shortening: To transform liquid vegetable oil into solid or spreadable form (margarine or solid shortening), the oil must be hydrogenated. This is a commercial process by which hydrogen molecules under pressure are forced through the oil. In addition to hardening the fat, hydrogenation increases its stability and prolongs its shelf life. During this process, the molecular structure of the oil is changed; the more an oil is hydrogenated, the greater the change and the more solid the product; squeeze bottle or soft tub margarines are changed less than solid stick margarine.

Hydrogenated shortenings and margarine—once considered the perfect alternative to butter—are now being scrutinized by scientists because, as oil hardens during the hydrogenation process, its molecular formation is changed slightly, creating new structures called trans fatty acids (tfa's). The trans fatty acids help prevent rancidity in the hydrogenated fat, but because tfa's act like other unhealthy saturated fats in the body, many studies recommend that human tfa consumption be reduced, which means cutting down on or not using solid stick margarines, partially hydrogenated vegetable oil, and commercial shortenings and frying oils.

Unlike butter or margarine, solid shortening is designed to go in, not on, food. When selecting a fat for baking, consider that butter, although a saturated fat, has the best taste. Solid margarine is not an ideal substitute—it lacks butter's flavor and contains some saturated fat and trans fatty acids. Its ad-

vantage is that it does not (usually) contain cholesterol, and is available in kosher form. You certainly can bake with margarine, but the recipes in this book were developed for butter (unless another fat is specifically noted in the ingredients list).

Oils: Vegetable oils are the fat of choice for making certain cakes, such as chiffon and carrot. When selecting an oil for baking, choose one with a mild neutral flavor and a light fresh scent (smell the oil before using it), such as canola, safflower, sunflower, peanut, or corn. Vegetable oils contain no cholesterol.

Certain brands of vegetable oil contain silicones to inhibit foaming. Since foaming is essential in most cake batters, select only silicone-free oil.

Which Fat Should I Use to Prepare Baking Pans? After comparative tests with many methods, I still find the most reliable, all-purpose method is to prepare baking pans with solid shortening (Crisco), and I keep a stubby pastry brush in my shortening carton to facilitate application. You can also use a paper towel to smear on the shortening. I prefer shortening instead of butter because shortening is 100 percent fat and contains no water; therefore, it has no moisture that can cause the cake to stick. Batter adheres to the pan and rises more fully when the pan sides are not too slippery; for this reason, I also like to dust the greased surface with flour. To do this, toss about a tablespoon of flour into the greased pan and hold it over the sink while you tilt and rotate it until the inner surface appears coated; if you see a shiny un-greased spot, dab on a little fat and sprinkle on more flour. Turn the pan upside down over the sink and sharply tap the bottom to release excess flour. Whenever there is a possibility that a cake may stick, I place a piece of cut-to-fit baking parchment or wax paper on the pan bottom, and grease and flour the paper. After baking, the paper peels off easily. To cut paper rounds, draw around the pan bottom on a stack of papers, fold the papers in half, aligning the marked lines, and cut out. You can also purchase precut rounds of baking parchment for various pan sizes in many cookware shops.

To coat baking pans with a minimum amount of fat, or when I am too rushed to brush on solid shortening, I sometimes use butter-flavor no-stick vegetable cooking spray. This method produces a somewhat uneven and slightly darker finish on cakes than the shortening-flour method, but it works. Most sprays contain natural antistick soy lecithin, which is an excellent release agent. When I bake muffins, for example, I use this product in-stead of paper or foil muffin cup liners. Bakers' Joy, a vegetable shortening spray mixed with flour, is a similar product available for greasing baking pans; it is sold in most supermarkets.

How to Store Solid Fats and Oils: Fats tend to absorb strong odors; all fats should be stored cov-ered, away from strong-scented ingredients. Butter and margarine should be refrigerated and/or frozen for short-term use; for long-term storage they should be frozen. Oils should be stored in opaque containers in a cool, dark location or re-frigerated. Cold sometimes turns oil cloudy; this is not harmful and clarity returns when the oil is brought back to room temperature. Dark-colored nut oils, such as walnut and hazelnut, are the least stable, with a shelf life of 4 to 6 months. Refined vegetable oils (such as canola, safflower, and corn) should be stored away from air, heat, and light in a cool, dry location; they generally stay fresh 6 to 10 months.

How to Measure Fats: Oil, a liquid fat, is mea-sured in a liquid measuring cup. Solid fats such as butter, margarine, and Crisco are available in quar-ter-pound sticks, marked on the wrapper to indi-cate tablespoon and cup divisions.

solid fat measuring guide

1 stick = 8 tablespoons = ½ cup
⅓ cup = 5⅓ tablespoons
¼ cup = 4 tablespoons

If your butter comes in 1-pound blocks, cut it into 4 equal quarters, or sticks, and use the measure-ments above as a guide. To measure solid fat using measuring spoons or cups, pack it into dry (not liquid) measuring cups or measuring spoons, tak-ing care not to trap air pockets in the bottom. Level the top with a straight edge before use.

FLOUR

Different types of flour have different characteristics depending upon the type of wheat from which they were milled and the geographic and climatic conditions under which they were grown. Bakers are most concerned with the amount of gluten-forming proteins in the flour. Gluten is a stretchy elastic substance that develops when two of wheat's proteins blend with liquid. The flour with the highest protein content will absorb the most water—a factor that is useful in stretchy elastic bread doughs but leads to toughness in delicate cookies and cakes. Since different types of flour produce very different baked results, it is essential to use the flour specified in each recipe in this book in order to achieve the desired results.

White whole wheat flour is made from a particular strain of high protein wheat milled with the bran and germ included so that its nutritional value approximates that of regular whole wheat flour; its protein content is lower than ordinary whole wheat flour, but is similar to bread flour.

Whole wheat flour contains the vitamin- and fiber-rich wheat germ and bran that increase its nutritional value but cause a heavy crumb when baked. For lighter results, it is often combined with a portion of white flour. Whole wheat flour, an excellent product for bread and rolls and some pastries, is sold in 5-pound bags like white flour in most supermarkets and is also available from specialty mills and natural foods stores.

All-purpose flour is sometimes milled from a single type of wheat and sometimes from a blend; it contains fewer stretchy gluten-forming proteins than bread flour and is delicate enough to give good results in most general baking. Most of the time, this is my choice for cakes, cookies, and pie crust.

Cake flour is usually milled from 100 percent soft wheat. It contains still less gluten-forming proteins and is best used for the most tender cakes and pastries. Widely available in 2-pound boxes in supermarkets, cake flour is finely milled and feels like talc. Most cake flour is bleached, giving it a very white appearance and increasing its acidity slightly; this helps cakes set faster and have a finer grain.

Self-rising cake flour is altogether different, containing added leaveners or baking powder and salt. Do not substitute self-rising for other types of flour without adjusting for the presence of leavening in the product; amounts vary depending on the manufacturer, but average about 1½ teaspoons leavening and ½ teaspoon salt per cup flour. I prefer not to use self-rising for two reasons: First, I like to control the amount of salt and leavening in my recipes and second, if the boxed flour is not fresh, the leavening may be old and inactive, causing a cake to fall.

> You can approximate the texture of cake flour by replacing 2 tablespoons of all-purpose flour with 2 tablespoons cornstarch in every cup. Cake flour actually weighs a little less per cup than all-purpose flour; to substitute cake flour for all-purpose flour, use 1 cup plus 2 tablespoons cake flour for each cup of all-purpose.

Pastry flour, milled exclusively from soft wheat, is finer than cake flour and contains even less gluten; generally it is neither chlorinated nor bleached. Good for delicate pastries and pie crust, pastry flour is often sold in 1-pound bags in gourmet or natural foods shops.

Instant-blending flour is processed to be granular so it will mix easily with water without lumping. This is useful for making gravy and some biscuits but not suitable for cakes; do not substitute it for all-purpose or cake flour.

Many types of flour are labeled as bleached, or are conditioned. When flour is exposed to air, oxygen combines with yellowish pigments and whitens them; historically, air-drying was the only so-called bleaching method used. Today, air may still be used as a bleaching agent, but chemical bleaches and oxidants speed up the natural oxidizing process. This oxidation improves baking quality for certain types of cakes by strengthening the stretching and bonding characteristics of the gluten. Many bakers believe unbleached flour is less processed and thus more healthful. However, some so-called unbleached flours have been oxidized or contain dough conditioners; nevertheless, they probably will not have been treated to remove the yellowing pigment. Unbleached flour is my choice for pie crusts, coffee cakes, and cookies, but I prefer to use bleached flour in very delicate, light cakes. The recipes in this book call for either all-purpose or cake flour but do not specify bleached or unbleached; let this paragraph be your guide.

Flour should be stored in a well-ventilated, cool location, off the floor and away from excessive moisture. It can absorb strong off-odors as well as moisture. Flour stored for any length of time in hot weather or a warm location can become a haven for insects. It is best to store flour in the freezer or refrigerator.

Sifting and Measuring Dry Ingredients: Ignore the "presifted" label on store-bought flour. You can be sure the flour bags have been stacked and stored, and the contents certainly have settled. When you open a bag of flour, pour it into a wide-mouth canister with an airtight lid. Before measuring flour from the canister, stir it gently to lighten and aerate the contents.

An important fact to remember about flour is that too much can toughen baked goods; use only as much as a recipe requires. To this end, it is necessary to sift when indicated in a recipe and to measure carefully. Take care not to knock or tap a measuring cup containing flour because the flour will compact and require as much as 2 extra tablespoons to fill it to the top.

When a recipe in this book calls for "½ cup unsifted flour," stir the flour in the canister to loosen it, then lightly spoon the flour into a dry-measuring cup (see sketch below) and level the top with the back of a knife.

When the recipe calls for "½ cup sifted flour," pass the flour through a medium-fine mesh sifter/strainer set over a piece of wax paper or a bowl. Spoon this sifted flour into the dry-measuring cup, heaping it slightly and taking care not to tap the cup. Sweep off the excess, leveling the top with the back of a knife.

SUGAR AND OTHER SWEETENERS

In baking, sugar provides sweetness, helps the creaming and whipping of air into batters, and contributes tenderness, texture, and color. When it is cooked, sugar caramelizes and adds a special flavor. Sugar, sugar syrups (such as Karo), and honey attract and absorb moisture, which helps keep baked goods moist and fresh.

White Sugar: The most common sugar used in baking is sucrose, a natural sugar found in plants. Sucrose is available to the baker as white or brown sugar or molasses. Each type comes from a different stage in the refining process. White sugar comes in crystal sizes ranging from regular granulated to superfine (also called ultrafine or bar sugar) to 10X confectioners'. The size of the sugar crystal is related to the amount of air it can incorporate when beaten into the fat in a batter. The bigger the crystal, the bigger the hole it will cut in the fat and the more air it will allow; granulated sugar, then, is best for creamed butter cakes. Crystal size also determines how fast the sugar will dissolve; superfine dissolves fastest and is thus best for meringues and drinks. You can make your own superfine sugar by whirling regular granulated sugar in a food processor. Granulated and superfine sugar should be sifted if they have become lumpy or caked. Pearl sugar, which has an extra-large crystal size, is desirable for topping cookies and breads. It is available in granulated and opaque-looking confectioners' style and is sold in many gourmet and cookware shops; see page 240 for Mail-Order Sources and Suppliers.

Confectioners' Sugar: This is granulated sugar ground to a specific degree of fineness. 10X is generally the grade for home-baking use (4X and 6X are used commercially). Approximately 3 percent cornstarch is added to each 1-pound box of confectioners' sugar to prevent lumping and crystallization. It is the cornstarch that gives powdered sugar a raw taste, which is best masked with flavorings or cooking. Since it dissolves so quickly, confectioners' sugar is used for meringues, icings, and confections. Confectioners' sugar should always be sifted before use.

Brown Sugar: The darker the sugar, the more molasses and moisture it contains. Turbinado sugar, sold in natural foods shops and supermarkets, has a coarse granulation and a variable moisture content; it is unpredictable as a baking ingredient but can be used as a topping. Both light and dark brown sugars have the same sweetening power as an equal weight of white sugar, although the white sugar is more dense; to achieve equal sweetness, brown sugars must be firmly packed before measuring by volume. The darker brown the color, the more molasses it contains and the more intense the flavor; light brown sugar has a honey-like taste. Brown sugars are added to cakes, cookies, streusel or crumb toppings, and icings to give color, flavor, and moisture. Brown sugars can make baked products heavy and are avoided in light, delicate cakes.

Brown sugars can dry out and become lumpy or hard when exposed to air. To prevent this, store them in a covered glass jar or heavy-duty sealed plastic bag. If the sugar hardens despite your efforts, add a slice of apple to the storage container for a few days or sprinkle on a few drops of water. To make 1 cup of your own brown sugar, add 2 tablespoons unsulfured molasses to 1 cup granulated sugar.

Molasses: Molasses is the liquid separated from sugar during the first stages of refining. The best type of molasses for baking (and the one I recommend in this book) is called "unsulfured" because it is made from sugar cane that has not been treated with sulfur dioxide, a procedure used to clarify and lighten the color of cane juice but which also produces a sulfur taste many find disagreeable.

Honey: Honeys vary depending upon the type of flowers visited by the bees and the areas in which they were produced. Honey contributes moistness, softness, chewiness, and sweetness to a cake or pastry. While honey is not a sugar, it does have the same sweetening power. Honey, however, cannot be used in equal amounts to replace sugar because it is a liquid and will not function like sugar in a batter. Honey caramelizes quickly at a low temperature, giving a dark color to baked goods.

For cake baking, use clear liquefied honey rather than a solid or comb form. To liquefy granular or hardened honey, place the opened jar on a rack in a pot of gently simmering water until the honey clarifies completely; flavor will not be altered.

To substitute honey for 1 cup granulated sugar, use ⅞ cup honey (1 cup minus 2 tablespoons) and decrease the liquid in the recipe by 3 tablespoons.

Maple Syrup: Pure maple syrup comes from the sap of the sugar maple tree boiled down until evaporated and thickened. It takes about 30 gallons of sap to produce 1 gallon of syrup. Store opened syrup in the refrigerator. If you find mold forming on the top, pour the syrup into a saucepan, heat just to boiling, and skim off the mold. Bring to a quick boil, then cool and pour into a clean container.

Corn Syrup: Sweet corn syrup is made when the starch in corn kernels is broken down with acid or various enzymes. Corn syrup, made up of glucose from the corn sugar plus some added fructose and water, is useful in baking because of its sweetness as well as its other physical properties. Its viscosity allows it to help trap air bubbles in a whipped batter, aiding a cake's aeration. Corn syrup adds flavor, and because glucose browns at a lower temperature than other sugars, its presence can cause baked goods to brown quickly.

SALT

Common table salt, or sodium chloride, is the type used in baking. It enhances flavors and improves taste, aids digestibility, and strengthens gluten in yeast products. When salt is completely omitted in baked goods they taste flat; keeping in mind today's health concerns, I have reduced excess salt, but retained the amount necessary for good taste.

Always bake with unsalted butter so you can be in control of the amount of salt added to your baked goods; different brands of butter contain varying amounts of salt.

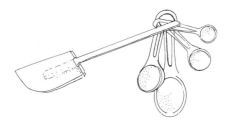

EGGS

In baking, eggs help with leavening, add richness, proteins, vitamins, and minerals, and contribute to the structure, texture, color, and flavor of baked goods. Eggs also help bind batter together.

For the cook, there is no difference between brown and white eggs, but eggs vary in freshness, size, and whipping qualities. For use in cake batters, eggs should be at room temperature. If they are very cold, set them, in the shell, in a bowl of warm water for about 10 minutes.

Storing and Freezing Eggs: Egg whites can be stored, refrigerated, for up to 4 days, covered. Egg yolks can be refrigerated in a covered jar for 1 to 2 days covered with water.

For long-term storage, you can freeze whole or separated eggs. Add a pinch of sugar to yolks to prevent stickiness when thawed. Lightly beaten whole eggs can be blended with a few grains of salt or sugar then frozen in ice cube trays (1 cube equals 1 whole egg) wrapped airtight. Frozen eggs, whole or separated, should be thawed overnight in the refrigerator before use. Never refreeze thawed frozen eggs.

Measuring Eggs: Egg size is very important in baking. In this book, all eggs are U.S. Grade A Large, weighing 2 ounces in the shell. By U.S. law, a dozen large eggs must weigh 24 ounces, although the eggs can vary individually within that dozen.

egg measuring guide

4 to 4½ whole eggs = 1 cup
1 large egg yolk = 1 tablespoon
1 large egg white = 2 tablespoons = ⅛ cup
4 large whites = 8 tablespoons = ½ cup
4 large whites beaten with some sugar until stiff = approximately 4 cups meringue

Separating Eggs: There are several easy techniques: The first and most common is to crack open the egg by sharply tapping its center against the edge of a bowl. Hold the half-shell containing the yolk upright in one hand while you pour the egg white from the other half-shell into a cup. Then, tip the yolk out into the empty half-shell while the white that surrounds it falls into the cup below. Go back and forth once more if necessary, then place the yolk, minus all the white, in another cup. For the second method crack the egg, then hold it over a bowl and pull the halves apart, simultaneously turning one half-shell upright so it will contain the entire egg. Holding this full half-shell upright with one hand, discard the empty half-shell, then turn your clean hand palm-up and dump the whole egg into it. Spread your fingers slightly and let the white slip through them into a bowl below while the yolk remains cradled in your palm; turn the yolk out into another cup.

The third method is to use a separating gadget, a metal or plastic disk with a ring-shaped slot surrounding a central depression. Break the egg onto the disk so that the yolk is trapped on the center pad and hold it upright while the white slides through the slot into a cup below. Place the yolk in another cup.

Whipping Egg Whites: When egg whites are mixed with sugar and whipped into a stiff foam, a meringue is formed. When meringue is exposed to heat in the oven, the molecules of air in the foam cells get warm, expand, and enlarge the cells. To maintain the volume of the meringue during beating and baking, acidic stabilizers are often added in the form of cream of tartar, vinegar, or lemon juice.

There are several important things to remember when whipping whites into meringue. First, keep all utensils scrupulously clean and dry; the smallest speck of fat can prevent the whites from beating to full volume. Don't whip whites in plastic bowls, which are too porous and therefore never completely grease free. To rid any bowl of a hint of grease, wipe the bowl and beater with a paper towel dampened with white vinegar.

Eggs separate most easily when cold, but whip to greatest volume when at room temperature (about 68°F). This paradox can be solved if you separate the eggs as soon as they come from the refrigerator, placing yolks and whites in separate grease free bowls. Place the bowl of whites into a slightly larger bowl of hot (not boiling) water for about 10 minutes, stirring until the whites feel tepid, or comfortably warm to the touch.

To hold its shape, meringue must be properly whipped. For best results with the least effort, use an electric mixer with a balloon-type wire whip and a closely-fitting bowl. The point is to keep the entire mass of whites in constant movement. To begin, add a pinch of cream of tartar (or other acid if called for) and salt to the whites and whip on *low* speed, working up to medium. When the whites are foamy, but not before, begin to add sugar, if using, gradually, while continuing to whip. Whipping on low to medium speed gives smaller bubbles, which are more stable than large bubbles produced if whipped only on high speed. If sugar is added too soon, it will dissolve into the whites and hinder the development of the meringue.

Continue to whip until the meringue looks glossy and smooth, and forms slightly droopy peaks. To test this, turn off the machine and scoop out some whites on a spoon or turn the beater upside down. Then continue to beat a few seconds longer (some bakers prefer to do this final stage by hand with a whisk) until almost-stiff peaks form and you see beater or whisk tracks on the surface of the meringue. This is the moment just before the maximum volume is reached. At this stage, you should be able to turn the bowl of whipped whites completely upside down (over a sink if you are nervous) without the whites moving at all. This is the point referred to as "stiff but not dry."

Avoid overbeating the egg whites. Overbeaten meringue looks lumpy and dry, and a film of liquid forms in the bottom of the bowl. If turned upside down now (this time you need a sink), the mass of whites would slide around precariously.

You can try to salvage and revive overwhipped whites by gently whipping in 1 extra egg white for every 4 in the meringue.

About the Safety of Eggs and Meringue: Egg safety and the possible health hazards of eating uncooked eggs and meringues are significant issues for cooks. Some incidents of contamination from the bacterial organism *Salmonella enteritidis* have been attributed to raw, improperly cooked, or undercooked eggs. The cause and cure are not fully understood. Until the hazard is eliminated, it is prudent to be cautious in baking, although the likelihood of a problem is slim. According to the American Egg Board, studies indicate the chances of a home cook finding an infected egg are about 0.005 percent.

Here are a few simple guidelines:

When shopping, open the cartons and look at

the eggs; avoid any that are cracked or unclean. Be sure the store has well-refrigerated egg cases. At home, refrigerate eggs promptly, storing them inside the refrigerator, where it is colder, rather than on the door. Wash any container or food preparation surface that has come in contact with raw eggs before reusing it. Avoid eating raw eggs or raw egg whites.

Refrigerate cheesecakes and all baked goods containing custards or meringues. Keep cold foods cold (at or below 40°F) and hot foods hot (above 140°F) to prevent growth of salmonella bacteria.

While the bacteria causing the common food poisoning salmonellosis is sometimes present in egg whites, it has also been found on the skins of fruits grown in contaminated soil. Washing produce carefully helps; there is no question, however, that the bacteria cannot survive high temperatures. Commercial food handlers and many restaurants avoid this problem by routinely cooking with pasteurized liquid eggs instead of fresh eggs.

To Cook Raw Yolks for Use in Uncooked Recipes: If a recipe for an unbaked sauce or pudding calls for raw egg yolks, they may be prepared as follows to remove any danger of bacteria: Blend each yolk with at least 2 tablespoons of liquid and cook in a heavy saucepan; over very low heat, stir constantly until the mixture coats a metal spoon

or reaches 160°F. Cool quickly (over an ice water bath if desired), and proceed with the recipe. Don't worry; eggs don't scramble until the temperature reaches 180°F.

To Make Cooked Meringues and Egg White Icings: It is important for the baker to follow instructions carefully when preparing meringues or other puddings such as mousse. While it is highly unlikely that eating a small amount of icing will make you sick, at least you should be informed.

According to the American Egg Board, to destroy the bacteria, egg whites must be held at a temperature of 140°F for 3½ minutes or at some point reach 160°F.

Powdered Egg Whites: To avoid any danger of salmonella bacteria in raw egg whites, many home bakers, like commercial bakeries, are substituting powdered, pasteurized, dried egg whites. There are several products on the market, some available in specialty gourmet shops or baker's catalogues (see Mail-Order Sources and Suppliers, page 240), others in supermarkets. One that I use currently is Wilton Meringue Powder, made by Wilton Industries and sold wherever cake-baking supplies are available. For this product, Wilton recommends using 2 teaspoons of meringue powder plus 2 tablespoons water to make the equivalent of 1 egg white; sugar can be added as desired.

LIQUIDS

For the baker, liquids include eggs, water, milk, cream, sour cream and yogurt, fruit juices, alcohol, honey, molasses, oil, melted butter, and coffee. Liquids have many functions in a batter: They dissolve salt and sugar, create steam to push apart cells, and aerate the structure of the product; they moisten the leavening agent to begin production of carbon dioxide gas, causing rising.

Milk: Milk products add moisture, color, and richness to baked goods and help prolong their freshness. When plain milk is called for in this book, homogenized milk is used. Homogenized milk is treated so the fat and milk are blended and will not separate. Skim milk is regular milk minus the cream content, and low-fat milk contains a small portion of its cream. Shelf-stable, boxed milk, sold in Europe for many years, is now available in most American supermarkets. The sealed product can remain unrefrigerated, though it must be refrigerated after opening. Shelf-stable milk is available in whole and low-fat (1 and 2 percent and skim), but not buttermilk, and may be substituted by the home baker for any fresh milk product, though its taste is very slightly different because of the way it is processed.

Powdered milk is milk with its water evaporated so it is inhospitable to microbes and has a stable storage life. Powdered milk keeps for several months when stored in a cool, dry location. Bakers can use a little dry milk powder (added with dry ingredients) in dough or batter as a nutritional supplement (extra calcium, for example) or reconstitute it with water and use as ordinary milk in any recipe.

Lactose-free milk is available in skim, 1 percent, and 2 percent and may be substituted for regular milk in baking. It is sold alongside regular milk in dairy cases of the supermarket. Lactose intolerance is a physiological inability to digest and absorb lactose (a disaccharide), or so-called milk sugar, in many dairy products. Milk made from soy, rice, or oats can be substituted cup for cup for whole milk if a diet requires it, but baked results will vary.

Buttermilk: The natural acidity of buttermilk slows the development of gluten in wheat flour, tenderizing baked products and, sometimes, giving them a characteristically tangy flavor. Buttermilk is the liquid by-product of churned milk or cream; because the solids and most fats are removed, "regular" buttermilk is actually low-fat; you can also purchase nonfat buttermilk. Cultured buttermilk is pasteurized skim milk mixed with an added lactic-acid bacteria culture. Cultured buttermilk powder, available in the baking sections of supermarkets or from mail-order sources (see page 240), must be reconstituted with water. In a recipe, the powder is added with the flour and dry ingredients and water is added with liquids. I use this frequently and always try to keep a container in the pantry. For the recipes in this book, you can use any type of buttermilk.

As a substitute for buttermilk (though lacking its rich flavor), you can make your own sour milk by adding 1 tablespoon white vinegar or lemon juice to each 1 cup milk; let it sit about 3 minutes before using it. Or, blend 1 cup of milk with 2 or 3 tablespoons yogurt.

Cream: There are many types of cream on the market and all have specific uses for the baker. The butterfat content of the cream is what determines its use, although package labeling information is usually lacking. For all "whipped cream" occasions, use a container labeled "heavy cream" or "heavy whipping cream" (not the same as whipping cream). This is the only type of cream containing at least 36 to 40 percent butterfat, enough to whip properly and hold its shape. Use a chilled bowl and chilled beater for maximum volume. Note that cream doubles in volume when whipped (1 cup heavy cream = 2 cups, whipped).

Fresh cream has a clean, clear taste and is the best choice if available. Ultra-pasteurized cream, which has a slightly different flavor, is more widely available and fine for all uses, but it has been heat-processed to 280°F for at least 2 seconds to kill bacteria. (Normal pasteurization heats cream or milk to 161°F for 15 seconds or 145°F for 30 minutes.)

Sour Cream: Sour cream is basically fermented heavy cream. Commercially marketed sour cream is a rich, tangy product made from 18 percent butterfat cream that is injected with a bacterium, *Streptococcus lactis,* and allowed to thicken. Choose brands made from cultured skim milk (read the label); do not use imitation or nondairy sour creams because they frequently contain highly saturated tropical oils or are made with hydrogenated fat. Well-drained regular or low-fat yogurt can usually be substituted for sour cream.

Yogurt: Yogurt can be made from the milk of cows, horses, sheep, goats, camels, and buffaloes; most of the yogurt made in America today is made from cow's milk, though some small producers use sheep's and goat's milk.

Yogurt is initially made from skim milk, sometimes enriched with extra nonfat milk solids, that is homogenized, pasteurized, and injected with live bacteria, which feed on the milk sugar to produce lactic acid. At this stage the milk is allowed to ferment in order to coagulate into yogurt and develop its characteristic tangy flavor. To keep the cultures alive and active, yogurt at this stage should be chilled and shipped. Live cultures are required by law in the yogurt sold in Europe, but not in the United States. Here, some companies pasteurize the product once more, killing the bacteria. Read the label to tell the difference. The most desirable contain "live, active cultures."

Some manufacturers add vegetable gum, modified food starch, or gelatin to hold or reset the yogurt. Liquid will not drain easily from yogurt containing these additives.

CHOCOLATE AND COCOA

I consider chocolate one of the elements, right up there with earth, air, fire, and water. Not only is it an essential part of the natural world, but it does grow on trees—the *Theobroma cacao* tree, to be exact, a native of South and Central America, and cultivated in Africa and Southeast Asia. Inside the pods of this tree are beans and pulp, which are scooped out, dried, fermented, and cured. The beans are factory-roasted, then hulled, and the inner nibs, which contain about half cocoa butter, are crushed and ground or rolled between steel disks to liquefy and draw off most of the cocoa butter. What remains is chocolate liquor, a dark brown paste that is further refined, churned, and mellowed to improve its quality. This unadulterated chocolate liquor is molded, solidified, and sold as unsweetened or bitter chocolate. Varying proportions of sugar and cocoa butter are combined with this liquor to make blends known as bittersweet, semisweet, and sweet chocolate. When dry milk solids are added, the result is milk chocolate.

Store all chocolate in a cool, dry location at about 60°F. When chocolate is kept at a warmer temperature, you may see a gray or whitish skin appear on its surface. This is called bloom and is the cocoa butter rising to the surface. Bloom does not harm flavor and will disappear when the chocolate is melted. If chocolate is stored at excessively cold temperatures, it may sweat when brought to room temperature, introducing dreaded moisture droplets that will interfere with melting. Do not store baking chocolate in the refrigerator or freezer.

Since the quality of the chocolate is vital to the quality of the dessert containing it, always use pure chocolate, not imitation. Read labels carefully. For fine chocolate, see Mail-Order Sources and Suppliers, page 240. Among my favorite brands are:

Unsweetened Chocolate: Baker's, Nestlé, Guittard; *Semisweet:* Baker's, Nestlé, Guittard, Callebaut, Ghirardelli (Dark Sweet); *Bittersweet:* Callebaut, Lindt (Excellence or Courante), Guittard, Baker's, Tobler Extra Bittersweet.

chocolate measuring guide

2 tablespoons regular-size chocolate chips = 1 ounce solid chocolate chopped = ⅛ cup

1 cup regular-size chocolate chips = 6 ounces

¼ cup unsweetened cocoa = 1 ounce

To substitute cocoa powder for solid unsweetened chocolate, use 3 level tablespoons regular (not Dutch-processed) cocoa plus 1 tablespoon solid vegetable shortening or unsalted butter for each ounce unsweetened chocolate.

White chocolate is not a true chocolate because it does not contain any chocolate liquor. It is actually a blend of whole milk and sugar, cooked, condensed, and solidified. In the best brands, some cocoa butter is added to enhance the flavor. Other additives include whey powder, lecithin, vanilla, and egg whites. The finest quality white chocolate contains the highest proportion of cocoa butter and thus lists that ingredient first on the label. Brands with excellent flavor and smooth melting quality include Ghirardelli Classic White Confection and Ghirardelli Classic White Chips, Baker's Premium White Chocolate Baking Squares (all three available in supermarkets), as well as Guittard Vanilla Milk Chips, Lindt Swiss White Confectionery Bar, Callebaut White Chocolate, and Tobler Narcisse.

To Melt White or Dark Chocolate: Unless handled carefully and melted over a very low heat, chocolate can separate into cocoa butter and solids; it can also take on a cooked flavor. It is best to melt chocolate (which should be finely chopped) in the top of a double boiler set over hot (120°F) water (not boiling). Ideally, melt one-half or two-thirds of the chocolate, then remove it from the heat and stir in the remaining chocolate until it melts. Dark chocolate should not be heated above 120°F or it can separate. White chocolate is much more fragile. It must be stirred until melted, over warm to medium-hot water so it does not get above 110° to 115°F, or it will recrystallize and look lumpy, grainy, and dry.

Be careful not to get a drop of water or other liquid in any chocolate as it melts or the chocolate will seize and harden. This is not always salvageable, but sometimes you can smooth out the mixture by stirring in 1 teaspoon Crisco (solid shortening) for each ounce of chocolate. To avoid the moisture problem, you can melt dark chocolate in a microwave. For each ounce of chopped dark chocolate, heat on medium-low (50 percent) power for 2 to 3 minutes (for milk or white chocolate use 30 percent power), then stir well until smooth. Repeat for a few more seconds if necessary. Pay attention because the chocolate will not lose its shape as it melts in the microwave; you must stir it to observe the consistency.

For an easy way to melt chocolate chips, see page 197.

Cocoa: To make cocoa, chocolate liquor is pressed a second time to remove more than half of the remaining cocoa butter. The result is a dry cake of residue that is pulverized and sifted to make fine unsweetened cocoa powder. This naturally processed cocoa, like chocolate, is acidic and has the fruity flavor of the cocoa bean. To neutralize some of the acid, and to darken and redden the color and give a somewhat richer flavor, some types of cocoa are factory-treated with alkali, or Dutch-processed. This name comes from the fact that a Dutchman, Coenraad van Houten, discovered the process. Popular brands using this method are Droste, Van Houten, Fedora, and Hershey's European (in a gold-colored container). The most widely available American brands, Hershey's regular (in a brown container) and Baker's, are "natural," not alkali-treated, so have a higher acidity. Both types are used in recipes calling for baking soda, which interacts and neutralizes the acidity, but Dutch-processed cocoa requires less baking soda to neutralize it because it contains less acidity. Both types are good, but they are slightly different. It is important to use the specific type of cocoa called for in the recipe. Powdered or granulated instant cocoa drink mixes contain dry milk solids, sugars, and sometimes other additives and should never be substituted for unsweetened baking cocoa.

FLAVORINGS

Flavoring agents enhance taste and bring baked goods to life. For the best results, use fresh aromatic spices, pure extracts, fresh gingerroot, full-flavored citrus zests, and ripe fruits.

Spices: The aroma of any spice is volatile and fades once the spice is ground and/or exposed to air, heat, or sunlight for a period of time. Ground spices should be stored in airtight containers in a cool, dark location. Whole seeds and spices keep better than ground, but should be stored the same way. If you have a choice, select freshly ground spices for greater flavor.

Check the strength of your spices by smelling them before adding them to your perfect batter. A dash of pallid old nutmeg is useless; a grating of fresh nutmeg is pungent.

Extracts: Extracts are the concentrated natural essential oils of a flavoring agent dissolved in alcohol. Some flavors are made from the oils found in the rind of citrus fruits; others are made from the pulp of the fruit.

Most essential oils are volatile and will dissipate when exposed to the heat of baking. For intense flavor in your finished product, start with the best flavoring agent. Pure extracts sometimes cost a little more than imitation, but are worth it. Artificial flavorings are synthetic, often weaker in flavor, and may impart a chemical aftertaste. However, some pure essences and extracts (maple, coconut, or pineapple, for example) are hard to find or nationally unavailable. Ask the manager of your market if a pure form is available from his distributor; if you cannot find a pure extract, of course, use the imitation flavoring. There are several suppliers of fine pure extracts, including Cook Flavoring Company in Tacoma, Washington, and Nielsen-Massey. These and others are available by mail order from Williams-Sonoma and King Arthur Flour Baker's Catalogue (see page 240); they are also sold in gourmet shops. Store all liquid extracts in dark-colored containers, tightly closed, in a cool, dark place.

Vanilla extract varies greatly in quality and strength; quality depends upon where it comes from and how it is processed.

I like to keep a canister of vanilla sugar on hand for baking. Simply stick a vanilla bean into a jar of granulated sugar and use as needed. The flavor perfumes the sugar and can be used in any baked product complemented by vanilla, but it does not replace vanilla in the recipe.

Zests: Zest is the brightly colored outer surface of the peel of citrus fruit. The zest contains all the essential oils or flavors of the peel. When grating a lemon or orange, for example, avoid digging beneath the zest into the white pith, which has a bitter flavor. Usually citrus zest is grated on the small holes of a box or flat grater, a mandoline, or a carpenter's rasp reserved for this purpose. Alternatively, a zester—a small tool with a sharp scooped "eye"—is used to remove shallow strips of the peel, which are then finely minced and substituted for grated peel.

The hardest part of grating zest is removing the pieces that are caught on the sharp teeth of the grater. A trick that solves this problem is to wrap a piece of baking parchment tightly over the "toothed" surface before grating. As the fruit is grated, the zest is caught on the paper. When the paper is lifted off, the zest is easily scraped into your recipe.

Fresh Ginger: Fresh ginger is available in Asian markets and many supermarkets. Look for plump smooth-skinned pieces that are heavy for their size; you should be able to peel the skin with the gentlest scrape of your fingernail. Avoid dried, wrinkled pieces, as they will be fibrous and lack juice. To use ginger, peel it with a paring knife or vegetable peeler, then either grate it on the finest holes of a grater or rub it across the teeth of a porcelain ginger grater (available in Asian markets) or cut the pieces across the grain into very thin rounds, then chop as finely as possible.

Fruits: In baked goods, fresh and dried fruits add flavor, sweetness, fiber, vitamins, and minerals. When purchasing dry fruits, look for those with good color, plumpness, full shape, and soft, moist texture; avoid those that are dry and hard, as baking will not soften them.

Moist dried fruits can be used right from the package. To plump them up, you can soak the fruit (or microwave a few seconds) in fruit juice, herbal tea, or wine (red vermouth gives especially good flavor). Or you can place hard, dry fruits in a strainer set over (not in) boiling water, cover, and steam them for a few minutes until soft.

Dates and prunes are sold either pitted or with pits. I prefer whole, pitted dates because they are softer than those sold prechopped. In any case, dates are easy to chop by hand. Extra-moist "snacking" prunes are also available; some brands are good, others too gooey. Test these before adding to a recipe.

Dried figs come primarily from California, Greece, and Turkey. Select figs that are flexible when pressed rather than hard and dried out. Store dried figs in a covered jar in a dry cupboard. Dried peaches, pears, and apples are available in many supermarkets and in most natural foods stores. These can be chopped and used as creative substitutes for raisins in many recipes.

Raisins are grapes dried either by the sun or artificial heat and usually treated with sulfur dioxide to prevent darkening. The flavor of golden raisins is lighter and sweeter than that of black seedless raisins. Dried currants are actually small raisins made from dried Zante grapes. They are sold in supermarkets next to dried raisins. Do not confuse them with fresh, bush-grown currants. Store raisins and currants in airtight plastic bags or glass jars to prevent drying out.

A few suppliers, like the Chukar Cherry Company in Washington State, offer exciting, intensely flavored, moist "dried" blueberries, strawberries, cherries (tart or sweet), and cranberries. These are sold in some gourmet and natural foods shops and are available through mail order (see Mail-Order Sources and Suppliers, page 240). Dried berries and cherries, as well as Ocean Spray Craisins (sweetened dried cranberries), are good substitutes for raisins in scones, muffins, and cookies. Fresh or frozen whole cranberries add color and flavor to pies, cakes, muffins, and scones. They are widely available in markets from October through December; after that, some stores may have them frozen. Out of season, substitute Craisins (above) or fresh or whole frozen raspberries or pitted cherries. My advice is to buy several extra packages of fresh cranberries, put the bags in the freezer, and use as needed throughout the year.

LEAVENING AGENTS

Leavening agents are added to batters to make baked goods rise and to produce a light and porous structure. Air, steam, and carbon dioxide gas (produced by baking powder and baking soda) are the principal leaveners.

Baking Powder: Baking powder is a chemical leavening agent. It is made up of acid-reacting materials and alkali bicarbonate of soda (1 teaspoon baking powder contains ¼ teaspoon of baking soda). Most brands of baking powder have a starch filler (corn or potato starch) added as a stabilizer and buffer to keep the acid salts from reacting with the bicarbonate of soda and to absorb any moisture that might get into the mixture. As a general rule, use 1 to 1¼ teaspoons baking powder per 1 cup flour.

When baking powder is mixed with the liquid in a batter, it forms a solution, causing a reaction between the acid and the alkali, which begins to release carbon dioxide gas. When the batter is placed in the heat of an oven, the remaining carbon dioxide is released and the "double-acting" baking powder reaction is complete.

Baking powder absorbs moisture from the air and can deteriorate quickly; it can lose strength after about 3 months. The average shelf life of an opened can is about 1 year. Old baking powder can cause cakes to fall! Write the date of purchase on the can so you can keep track, and store baking powder in a cool, dark place.

If you suspect you are dealing with an antique product, perform this simple experiment: Combine 1 teaspoon baking powder with ½ cup hot water; if it bubbles vigorously, it is still usable. If it sits in silence, toss it out.

Baking Soda: Baking soda, also known as bicarbonate of soda, is another common leavening agent. An alkaline product, it is used in baking when there is an acid agent present (such as buttermilk, sour milk, yogurt, molasses, honey, brown sugar, chocolate, or cocoa) to neutralize some of the acidity.

Half a teaspoon of the alkaline soda will neutralize 1 cup of buttermilk, for example. Noted food chemist Shirley Corriher recommends using no more than about ¼ teaspoon of baking soda per cup of flour.

Bicarbonate of soda has other properties as well. Because it is an alkali, it darkens the color of chocolate or cocoa in a cake. It also causes reddening of cocoa, giving devil's food cake its name.

Note that baking soda is four times as strong as baking powder, so it should be used judiciously and never substituted for baking powder. An excess in baked products results in off odors, a soapy taste, and a darkened or yellowed white cake.

Occasionally, a recipe will call for both baking powder and baking soda. The reason is that the baking powder is needed for leavening and the baking soda, which leavens, also acts as a neutralizer for the acidity of certain ingredients.

Cream of Tartar: An acidic by-product of winemaking, cream of tartar is a white powder used in baking to help prevent overbeating of whipped egg whites and to stabilize egg white foam during baking. In addition, it is used when making sugar syrups to inhibit crystallization of the sugar.

Mixtures containing cream of tartar should not be cooked in an unlined aluminum pan because the tartaric acid reacts with the aluminum, discoloring the food being cooked.

NUTS

In baked goods, nuts add unique flavor as well as vitamins, minerals, and fiber. In a cake batter that needs strong flavor, it is best to toast the nuts first; toasting brings out the flavor and darkens the color somewhat. For cookies, meringue cake layers, or crumb toppings where the nuts will be exposed more directly to the heat, they will effectively be toasted during baking so it is unnecessary to do so in advance. When nuts are used as a garnish or pressed onto the top or sides of a cake, they should be toasted first both to bring out their flavor and to give them a richer color.

Be sure the nuts you use are fresh. Nut oils are volatile and lose flavor and/or go rancid when overexposed to heat, moisture, and light. Nuts keep longest when stored in their shells, their original wrappers; next best are whole nuts rather than chopped. Walnuts in their shells can be stored in a cool, dry cupboard. Shelled nuts should be stored in sealed bags or tightly covered jars in the refrigerator or, for long-term storage, the freezer (though I have found that nuts stored in the freezer lose some of their flavor after about 2 months).

To Toast or Skin Nuts: Toasting nuts enhances their flavor and maintains their crispness. To toast nuts instead of simply drying them out, heat the oven to 325°F. Toast the nuts for 10 to 12 minutes, tossing or stirring several times, until they are aromatic and darken slightly. Nuts can also be toasted in a heavy-bottomed frying pan set on medium heat for 3 to 5 minutes, until aromatic and slightly colored; stir or toss continually to avoid burning. To toast walnuts in a microwave, spread a single layer of nuts on a glass plate and microwave on high (100 percent) 5 to 6 minutes, stirring every 2 minutes. Cool.

To remove the skin on hazelnuts after toasting, wrap the hot nuts in a coarsely textured towel and allow to sit a few minutes. Then rub the skins off with the towel. To remove the skins from almonds or pistachios, blanch the shelled nuts (skins still on) about 2 minutes in boiling water, then drain and drop them into cold water. Pinch off the skins with your fingers.

To Dry or Grind Nuts: A food processor or blender does the easiest job of grinding nuts, but may create a paste if the nuts are oily. It is best to dry out or toast the nuts first. Dry them in a shallow pan in a preheated 300°F oven for about 10 minutes, tossing them occasionally. Then combine them with 1 or 2 tablespoons of the measured sugar before pulsing in the food processor. The sugar keeps the nuts spinning and prevents packing, enabling the blades to achieve a finer texture. In a blender, add no more than ½ cup of nuts at a time and empty the jar between additions. To create a dry, shaved nut powder, nuts must be ground in a hand-held food or nut mill that has a presser bar to push the nuts against a rotating cutting disk. This gadget is available in cookware shops and by mail order (see Mail-Order Sources and Suppliers, page 240).

GELATIN

Gelatin is a natural product derived from collagen, the protein found in bones and connective tissue. In the United States, unflavored gelatin is most commonly sold in dry granulated form, in bulk, and in prepackaged envelopes. Each envelope contains 1 very scant tablespoon (actually a generous 2 teaspoons), or ¼ ounce, to set 2 cups of liquid or 1½ cups of solids.

To dissolve granulated gelatin, sprinkle it on top of a small amount of cold liquid (it does not have to be water) in a small saucepan, and let it sit a few minutes so the granules swell. Then, set it over moderately low heat and stir just until the granules dissolve completely; test by rubbing a drop of the mixture between your fingers—it should feel absolutely smooth. Do not let the gelatin boil or it will lose some of its setting strength. Another method is to stir the swollen granules into boiling water until dissolved. To dissolve gelatin in a microwave, sprinkle one envelope over ¼ cup cold water in a glass measuring cup. Let stand 2 minutes to soften, then microwave at full power (high) 40 seconds; stir thoroughly, let stand 2 minutes longer or until gelatin is completely dissolved. If some granules remain, repeat at 5 second intervals, stirring after each interval to test the solution.

Some fresh fruits, such as fresh figs, kiwifruit, papaya, pineapple, and prickly pears cannot be used with gelatin because they contain protease enzymes that soften gelatin and prevent it from setting. However, if these fruits (except kiwi) are boiled for 5 minutes, their enzymes are destroyed and they can be added to gelatin without harming its jelling properties.

Vegetarian substitutes for gelatin are available in natural foods stores. They include agar agar (a gel or crystalized product made from seaweed) and Pomona's Universal Pectin (made from natural pectins, without sugar). For use, follow package directions.

About Equipment

The following general notes are included as a guide to the selection and use of the baking equipment called for in this book.

I assume that your kitchen includes common baking tools such as liquid and dry measuring cups, measuring spoons, knives, whisks, sturdy spoons, and mixing bowls. Every recipe in this book has a Special Equipment list noting *only* the specific pan and size required and any *out-of-the-*ordinary items needed, such as baking parchment, wax paper, grater, cookie cutters, or sifter. In each recipe for a cake or muffin where the pan size may be varied, the Yield includes the number of cups of batter; use this figure to refer to the Pan Volume and Serving Chart, page 206, in order to find a different pan that will successfully bake the amount of batter you have.

MEASURING CUPS AND SPOONS

Dry measuring cups are designed specifically for measuring dry ingredients (e.g., flour, sugar). Fill the cup to the top, then level the ingredient off by passing a straight edge over it. Dry measuring cups are commonly available in nesting sets, in graduated sizes from ⅛ to 2 cups. They do vary in quality; inexpensive plastic or flimsy metal can dent, bend, and hold unpredictable measures. My favorites, available from specialty cookware shops and mail-order sources (page 240), are stainless steel, precisely calibrated in ⅛- (2 tablespoons), ¼-, ⅓-, ½-, 1- and 2-cup sizes. The King Arthur Flour Baker's Catalogue (page 240) also sells odd-size dry measuring cups in ⅔ and ¾-cup sizes, for those who find adding fractions a burden.

Dry and liquid measuring cups should not be used interchangeably. Liquid measuring cups are designed differently, have pouring spouts, and are commonly available in 1-, 2-, and 4-cup sizes. The best are made of heat-tempered glass and are mi-crowave safe. To use, fill the cup to the desired mark, set the cup flat on the counter, and bend down so you can check it at eye level. Don't fill a liquid measuring cup to the brim or you will have too much; the small extra space above the top measuring line is there so the measured liquid can be poured or carried without spilling.

Measuring spoons come in graduated sizes from ⅛ teaspoon to 1 tablespoon; metal spoons are much more accurate than those of inexpensive plastic. My favorites are stainless steel.

MIXING BOWLS

You need only a few mixing bowls. I recommend heavy pottery for hand mixing or stainless steel bowls with flat bottoms (so they don't tip) for use with an electric mixer. Metal bowls are not subject to thermal shock; these are best for mixtures such as mousse, which you whip over heat, then set into an ice bath to chill, or for setting over hot water to make an improvised double boiler.

For general baking, you need a set of bowls sized 1, 1½, 2, and 3 quarts. Heat-tempered glass bowls are useful; one of my favorites is a 2-quart measuring cup/bowl marked in 1-cup increments. Use it to measure the total volume of cake batters.

ELECTRIC MIXERS

Many batters can be beaten by hand with a sturdy wooden spoon and some, such as quick breads and muffins, should only be done that way. Children love to mix ingredients together and should be encouraged to do so with a spoon. Electric mixers, however, save time, energy, and incorporate more air. You can use a hand-held mixer (with cord) or battery-operated cordless type or a standing mixer, such as one made by KitchenAid (I prefer the tilting head model K45SS). Be sure you select one that has a strong enough motor to do the required job. If you are buying a new one, look for one with 175 to 200 watts and a wide range of speeds (more than medium/low/high) so it can go from beating eggs to mixing stiff cookie dough and give you good control. Stand mixers are usually stronger and will beat an extra-stiff dough without overheating. Hand mixers take longer to achieve results than the more powerful stand mixers; depending upon the mixer you are using, adjust your techniques to look for the signs given in the recipe ("beat until well blended and creamy," or "beat until the foam makes a peak that stands straight up on the tip") rather than following beating times.

FOOD PROCESSORS AND BLENDERS

A blender does a good job of chopping, mixing, and pureeing, but overall is not quite as versatile as a processor. The ubiquitous food processor is a great time-saver for making bread crumbs, shredding carrots or apples, or chopping chocolate, nuts, or dried fruits. The processor also does a fine job of mixing creamed icings and glazes that do not need air incorporated. I do not recommend the processor for cake and cookie batters *unless* the recipes are specifically designed for its use, as are some recipes in this book, because its speed and power can quickly overwork the mixture and produce a tough product. In my kitchen, I use both the Cuisinart DLC 7 Superpro and an 11-cup KitchenAid UltraPower food processor.

BAKING PANS

For a basic baker's pantry, a few pan sizes and shapes will suffice. When buying pans, select the best quality you can afford. Look for sturdy, durable pans with smooth seams. Size is obviously an important factor in selection, yet it is frustrating to discover that manufacturers use different measuring systems: Some measure a pan from rim to rim, others across the lip to the outer edges, others across the bottom. I measure across the top inner edge. I also measure the volume of a pan by noting the cups of water needed to fill the pan to the brim (see Pan Volume and Serving Chart, page 206). Many cakes can be baked in pans of a variety of shapes and sizes; recipes that are flexible in this regard have the cup volume of batter indicated in the Yield of my recipes. Select alternate pan sizes from the chart by comparing volumes. Note that pans should be filled about two-thirds full so there is room for the batter to rise. Using the wrong pan size may result in baking failure. Batter that is too thin when poured into a large pan bakes into a cake that is too flat; if the pan is too small, the batter may overflow when it rises.

Nonstick pans are a great help because they require less greasing to prevent baked goods from sticking. However, they still need to be greased; follow recipe instructions as written. Avoid inexpensive nonstick products because their thin coating will wear off quickly.

For cake baking, you need a few basic pans. Buy layer cake pans in pairs or threes in 8- or 9-inch rounds. Also select one or two 8- or 9-inch square pans at least 1½ to 2 inches deep. Look for sturdy aluminum or heavy-gauge tinned steel; for cakes, avoid dark or black pans, which give a dark crust—undesirable in delicate cakes. Springform pans have two pieces: a flat, fluted and/or tubed bottom panel made of metal (some manufacturers use heat-proof glass) and a surrounding hoop fastened with a spring latch. Opening the spring releases the pan sides, and the cake can remain on the pan bottom; these cakes do not have to be turned upside down unless you want to view the decorative design. Springform pans are used for delicate tortes, cheesecakes, and constructed layer cakes built up and then chilled and unmolded.

Tube pans vary in manufacture, size, shape, and name. Whether they are called plain tubes or decorative Bundts or kugelhopf molds, all have a central tube designed to conduct heat to the center of the batter, allowing the dough to rise and bake evenly. When selecting a tube pan, remember that the heavier the metal, the more evenly the cake will bake. Select the sturdiest pans, such as tinned steel (I like the Kaiser pans imported from Germany). Teflon-lined Bundt pans are made of aluminum as well as heavy cast aluminum; both give good results.

Angel food cake pans are also tube pans, but most have removable bottoms as well as small feet sticking up around the rim so the baked cake can be inverted and suspended as it cools. Some pans lack the feet but have a protruding tube for the cake to rest on when inverted. If your pan lacks both, simply invert the pan over the neck of a tall bottle and let it hang upside down until the cake is thoroughly cooled.

A jelly roll pan for home baking commonly measures 10½ × 15½ × 1 inch (not to be confused with a professional "half-sheet" pan of 12¼ × 17½ × 1 inch); it should be of sturdy construction with a good lip all around. Use this for thin sheet cakes, or turn the pan upside down and, in a pinch, use it as an extra cookie sheet. It also makes a fine tray to catch drips when icing a cake or cookies placed on a wire rack.

Sheet cakes can be baked in oblong or rectangular pans 1½ to 2½ inches deep. You can also use a lasagna pan or turkey roasting pan for a sheet cake (see page 206 for pan substitutions by batter volume).

Use cookie sheets made of heavy-gauge metal with a shiny or matte finish; avoid black metal sheets, which I find bake over-browned cookies. The best cookie sheets have only one narrow lip, for a gripping handle, so the hot air can easily circulate around the cookies. Avoid cookie sheets with four edges; they will block the heat. If your cookie sheets are very thin, the cookies will brown too fast on the bottom; to insulate them slide a second flat sheet beneath the first. Another solution is to use a double-layer, self-insulated cookie sheet, which works very well. In a pinch, you can make a cookie sheet from an upside-down roasting pan or jelly roll pan.

Muffin pans come in a variety of sizes, from mini-muffins tins with 1¾-inch-wide cups to giant 3⅓-inch diameters. There are also muffin-top pans that are shallow and only make "high-tops"; any type pan can be used with success if the correct amount of batter is added. The average size used in this book is 2½ inches in diameter. Select a pan with a dull or matte finish, which absorbs heat, rather than a shiny surface, which deflects it; avoid black pans, which overbake. Muffins bake well in heavy or thin pans; weight does not seem critical. To allow for even circulation of oven heat, be sure all baking sheets or pans allow 2 inches of clear air space between them and the oven wall.

Tarts are generally baked in fluted-edge metal or ceramic pans. The ones I prefer are metal, imported from France with a removable flat bottom. They are available in a range of sizes, in round, rectangular, and decorative shapes (flowers, hearts, long narrow strips); for home baking try the 7- to 11-inch rounds. To unmold a tart, set the center of the baked tart on a wide-mouthed canister and press lightly on the edge of the pan. The edging ring will drop away, leaving the tart to be carried and served on its metal bottom. Individual tartlet pans made of the same material as the full size pans, or of heat-proof glass, are also available in cookware shops or from bakeware catalogues.

Pie plates can be made of metal or heat-tempered glass or lead-free pottery. If you prefer metal pie plates, select pans with sloping sides in 9- and 10-inch diameters in aluminum with a dull or dark finish, which absorbs heat quickly. Avoid highly polished metal pans, because the shine tends to deflect heat, causing the crust to bake more slowly. I prefer heat-tempered glass or Pyrex pie pans because they conduct heat quickly and brown crusts nicely, and I can see the color of the bottom crust as it bakes. I could not do without my heat-proof glass pans in 9- and 10-inch diameters, both regular depth and deep-dish, both purchased in hardware stores.

ALUMINUM FOIL / PIE EDGER

To prevent the edges of a pie from over-browning, make your own aluminum foil pie edger. To make a frame to fit a 9-inch pie plate, cut a 10- to 12-inch square of foil and fold it into quarters. Tear out the center, leaving about a 2-inch edge all around. Unfold the foil, flatten it out, and gently curl under the edges. Place the opened foil frame over the pie or tart after about half the baking time, before over-browning has started. Gently crimp the curled edge around the pie plate. Remove the frame during the final few minutes of baking to allow the pastry to color evenly.

Fold

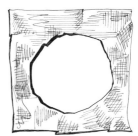

Unfolded frame

NONREACTIVE PANS

Certain sauces and baking mixtures that contain a high proportion of eggs or lemon juice or other acidic ingredients may discolor or absorb a metallic taste when cooked in pans made of nonanodized aluminum, cast iron, or unlined copper. It is preferable to cook these ingredients in so-called nonreactive pans made of stainless steel, enameled cast iron, heat-proof glass, or anodized aluminum.

SPOONS AND WHISKS

Wooden spoons are my favorite tools. They are sturdy, feel good in the hand, look warm and inviting, and do an excellent job of creaming batters because the wood surface actually cuts into the batter and grips it better than a slippery metal spoon. In my kitchen, I use a variety of sizes with long and medium handles. In spite of careful cleaning, wood does absorb flavors and odors so you should keep spoons used for butter-sugar pastries separate from those used for savory garlic-onion preparations, or the tastes might get transferred.

Wire whisks are used for blending, whipping, or folding certain ingredients together. The multiple wires have the effect of opening the batter and incorporating a lot of air when beating. Whisks come in a variety of sizes, from about 3 inches long for making sauce or whipping melted butter in a measuring cup to enormous balloon whisks for whipping egg whites in oversize commercial bowls. For efficiency as well as cleanliness, select a metal whisk that is one piece, with wires that are molded into a metal handle. An all-purpose balloon whisk has a rounded shape, which adds a lot of air for whipping cream and egg whites. A flat whisk (also called a roux whisk) is good for blending or folding ingredients together. When dry ingredients like flour and baking powder do not need sifting, they can be blended sufficiently by whisking them together in a bowl.

SPATULAS

Flexible spatulas (also called rubber scrapers) are invaluable for mixing, stirring, and folding, scraping down bowls and beaters, and turning batters out of bowls into baking pans. Flexible spatulas come in all sizes from 4 or 5 inches to 18 or more for the professional kitchen. I prefer the type having a wooden handle affixed to a flexible blade, which is acid- and high-heat resistant and will neither stain nor deteriorate. Williams-Sonoma and the King Arthur Flour Baker's Catalogue (see page 240) carry these spatulas made of silicone rubber developed for medical equipment, so they are especially durable. For general scooping/stirring tasks, I use a spatula with a scooped head, a cross between a spatula and a spoon (Rubbermaid calls its version the Spoonula).

Straight-edged metal spatulas (also called icing spatulas) are available in flat and offset (stepped-down) form. These are used for spreading icing and cake fillings, for transferring cookies from a baking sheet to a cooling rack, and for leveling off dry ingredients in a measuring cup. I find the 4-inch and 7-inch sizes most useful.

WAX PAPER, BAKING PARCHMENT, NO-STICK BAKING SHEETS

The baker uses wax paper for many purposes, including collecting sifted dry ingredients or grated zests. It is also useful for lining baking pans for cookies and cakes, where it will brown slightly but (in my experience) will not burn. When pans are lined with wax paper, the paper should be greased, and dusted with flour if the recipe so specifies. Baking parchment is a specially formulated non-stick paper designed for lining baking pans. It is sold in rolls like wax paper, as well as in sheets of different sizes. When used for baking most cookies (with the exception of my Mocha Kisses), parchment paper does not have to be greased; for cakes that might stick, I usually grease and flour the parchment. You can draw on baking parchment with a pencil, for ease in following guidelines when making special cookie or meringue shapes. Parchment is more durable than wax paper and thus ideal for making paper decorating cones (see page 198). It is available from some supermarkets, restaurant supply houses, and baking specialty shops (see page 240) in dispenser rolls, in precut triangles (for decorating cones), and in rounds to fit various size cake pans.

A newer no-stick product imported both from Germany and France is a Teflon- or silicone-coated flexible baking sheet, sturdier than either wax paper or parchment. It can be reused over and over and simply rinsed off between baking chores. The sheet can also be cut with scissors to fit your pans. The sheets are sold in bakeware shops or by mail order (see page 240).

SIFTERS/STRAINERS

In theory, a sifter has from one to three screens of medium-fine wire mesh. It is used for dry ingredients (flour, baking powder, confectioners' sugar). A sieve has a slightly coarser single-screen mesh and is used for draining fruits and straining sauces. For most of the sifting operations in this book, I use a 6- to 8-inch diameter single-screen sifter with medium-fine mesh. None of the recipes in this book requires a triple-tier sifter or an electric model. I do find handy a 3-inch diameter, medium-fine sifter with a 3- or 4-inch handle, or a shaker with a wire mesh sifter top (see Mail-Order Sources and Suppliers, page 240). I use either of these for sifting/dusting flour or cocoa onto greased pans; the small sifter or shaker-sifter can reach into a tube pan to direct powder onto the sides of the greased tube, normally a difficult task.

GRATERS

I recommend a stainless steel box grater or a flat mandoline with a variety of hole sizes. For grating citrus zest I use the finest holes; for grating carrots or apples I use the medium-size holes. I also have a 4 × 8-inch flat panel grater with a handle at one end; this is useful for citrus zest and hard cheese. Fresh ginger can be grated on the panel grater or on a Chinese porcelain ginger grater sold in Asian markets. You can also remove citrus zest with a zester-stripper, a tool sold in hardware stores or bakeware shops, with one or several tiny scoops that scrape long strips off the peel. After using the zester, finely dice the pieces with a knife.

CAKE TESTERS

One of the tests for a cake's doneness is to stick a cake tester into its center; if it comes out clean, the cake is done, but if it is covered with batter, the cake needs more baking time. Theoretically, this is a fine test, but you need to watch for other signs as well because an overbaked and dried-out cake will also produce a clean testing pick. My favorite cake tester is a thin bamboo saté skewer. Buy an inexpensive package of them at Asian food markets or gourmet shops. A wooden toothpick can also be used.

CARDBOARD CAKE DISKS

Corrugated cardboard rounds are invaluable for supporting cakes and cake layers. They are sold in bakers' or restaurant supply or party and paper goods shops in disks ranging from 6 to 14 inches in diameter in plain brown paper or with one side covered with white, gold, or silver foil. Bakers' supply houses carry disks with fluted edges. If you cannot find cardboard disks, ask at a local bakery or make your own by drawing around a cake pan on a piece of stiff or corrugated cardboard. Cut out the shape and cover it with aluminum foil.

PASTRY BRUSHES

A pastry brush is used for applying egg washes to pastry and pie crusts, glazes to fruit tarts, and spreading syrups and preserves on cake layers. For the most delicate tasks, I prefer an imported European goose-feather brush with a handle of braided quills. This lovely tool, available from cookware shops and catalogues (see page 240), lasts a long time, is amazingly cheap (under two dollars), and can be washed in warm water and air-dried. Or, you can use a soft, pliable natural bristle pastry brush, better for baking than nylon or other synthetic bristles. The best are well made (so the bristles don't fall out on your pie) and come in 1- to 1½-inch widths (see Mail-Order Sources and Suppliers, page 240).

For brushing oil or shortening on baking pans, I use a sturdier nylon or synthetic bristle brush, available in sizes from 1 to 2½ inches wide. No matter how thoroughly you wash them, brushes tend to hold traces of past flavors. To keep cake icing glaze from smelling like garlic, reserve the goose quill brush for pastry only and use an indelible pen to mark other pastry brush handles "sweet" or "savory." In a pinch, a new, absolutely clean sable or soft-bristle paintbrush can be used for a pastry brush.

COOLING RACKS

When a baked cake or sheet of cookies comes from the oven, it should be set on a raised wire rack so it can cool with air circulating all around it. The rack prevents condensation of moisture on the bottom of the baked goods and promotes even cooling. Most cakes have a fragile structure and need to cool in the baking pan about 15 minutes before unmolding. After unmolding, cakes should continue cooling on a wire rack so air circulation will draw off the moisture or steam. If the steam remained inside the cake, it would become soggy. Other baked products benefit from cooling on a rack for the same reasons.

Racks range from thin wire to heavy-gauge, and from 8-inch rounds, perfect for a single cake layer, to broad rectangular racks made for the professional kitchen, holding a dozen layers. Select racks slightly bigger than you think you will need; the best are the sturdiest, with the mesh close enough together to prevent cookies from slipping between the wires.

PASTRY BAGS AND DECORATING TIPS

Pastry decorating bags are used for piping icing, meringue, or soft doughs. The simplest and handiest decorating bag is a heavy-duty plastic freezer storage bag with a small hole cut in one corner. Add the icing, or melted chocolate or other ingredient, close the top, and squeeze the contents out through the hole. Discard the bag when done; there's no clean-up. To achieve a finer piped design, drop a metal decorating tip into the bag so the tip protrudes from a small hole you cut in one corner (or attach it to the bag with the plastic coupler so the tip can be changed from the outside). Save the tip before discarding the used bag. The plastic bag method is ideal for children to use when decorating cookies.

Coated cotton and nylon pastry bags are available in sizes from 7 to 24 inches long. Select the bag fitted to the task: small bags for delicate designs and melted chocolate, large ones for piping meringue and batter. For all-purpose use, I use a 16-inch nylon bag. I prefer the nylon for ease in cleaning. It is also flexible, comfortable in the hand, and will not leak fat from the fabric as cotton will. Wash the bags in hot water and air-dry them after use.

To fill a decorating bag, fold back a 4- or 5-inch cuff and set the tip down into a 2-cup measure for support. Fill the bag, then squeeze the icing down into the tip and twist the bag closed. To use the bag, hold the twist-closure between the thumb and fingers of one hand. In this way, you hold the bag closed while applying pressure to squeeze out, the icing. The other hand guides the bag and helps support its weight.

Decorating tips made of metal are the best; avoid flimsy plastic tips because they crack easily. Tips and bags manufactured by such companies as Ateco and Wilton are available from cookware shops. Select tips that fit the bags—small tips for small bags, extra-large tips for the long bags. Drop the decorating tip into the bag, allowing the nose to peek out or use a 2-piece coupler (sold with the tips) which allows you to fasten the tip on the outside of the bag, so you can change it for another design without changing the bag.

To make your own paper decorating bag, see page 198.

THERMOMETERS

Specialized thermometers are important for accuracy at different stages of baking and in general food preparation. Take care of your thermometers. Do not put a cold one directly into boiling liquid, but rather warm it in hot water first; thermal shock can crack the glass tubes.

For instant read-out temperatures for sauces, meringues, melting chocolate, and so forth, I use an instant-read thermometer with a stainless-steel stem and a large round dial mounted on top; this has a shorter temperature range than a regular thermometer and is not meant to be left in the food throughout the cooking time. Instead, it is inserted just to check the temperature; the thermometer reacts within seconds, then is removed. Available as instant bi-therm or battery-operated digital read-out types, these instant-read thermometers are available in hardware stores, cookware shops, and from mail-order sources (see page 240).

OVENS AND OVEN THERMOMETERS

Even heat is essential for accurate baking. Both electric and gas ovens produce good results, but you must know your oven well and watch it carefully, for even the best seem to lose accuracy easily and often. While it is a good idea to have the calibration checked occasionally, and certainly if you suspect it is off, it is also important to be sure the doors close tightly, that their gaskets are still flexible, the vent filters are clean, and hot spots (which most ovens have) are monitered. Hot spots mean that baked goods color more in one spot than another on the oven shelf. If this happens, rotate the item or transfer it to another shelf or move it front to back on the same shelf halfway through the baking time.

The safest way to guarantee proper baking temperatures is to *always* have an auxiliary oven thermometer sitting on your oven shelf. The two most widely available oven thermometers are the spring type, which has two metal strips that expand or contract to move a dial, and a mercury-type thermometer, which is more accurate. I prefer the latter, available mounted on a metal stand or in a folding metal case. Both are sold in hardware and cookware shops. Set the thermometer in place on the oven rack, then adjust the outer oven thermostat so the interior thermometer is correct. Don't rely entirely on the exterior heat indicator—whether it is a manual dial or a digital readout on a brand new oven. If a recipe fails, don't blame the cookbook, or yourself, until you have your oven temperature checked.

For accuracy when baking, always preheat your oven at least 15 to 20 minutes before placing the baked goods inside. Ingredients will react in unexpected ways if set into the wrong temperature and results can be disastrous. Check the interior auxiliary thermometer before adding the baking pan.

The recipes in this book specify the position of the oven shelf upon which the food is to be baked because the heat circulation varies within the chamber. Different types of baked goods bake better in different temperatures; some prefer the hottest area on the bottom or next hottest on the topmost shelf (heat rises), most do best in the middle with moderate heat. Single-layer cakes can be baked in the lower third of the oven or the middle, where the heat is moderately hot. Thicker cakes, with more than 2 inches of batter, or cakes with a delicate structure, should also be baked in the center. If you have doubts, use the middle. If you are baking cookies or several cake layers at one time, position two racks to divide the oven evenly in thirds. Allow 1 or 2 inches between pans so heat can circulate. When baking several cakes at one time, stagger them on two shelves so they are not directly in line with one another.

CONVECTION AND MICROWAVE OVENS

Convection ovens contain an interior fan to blow the heat around. This constant circulation causes them to cook about 25 percent faster than regular ovens and produces a nicely browned crust on pies and breads and a fine interior crumb in breads. However, the rush of air produced by the fan is too gusty for fragile meringue cookies and some other baked goods, for example.

When converting ordinary recipes for regular ovens to use in a convection oven, lower the baking temperature about 25 degrees. If your home oven has a convection fan on/off button, shut it off when baking delicate cakes and cookies.

I use my microwave for melting butter and chocolate and for defrosting and warming baked goods. For actual baking, I find that a conventional oven gives more control and produces a better texture.

Special-Use Recipe Index

*Look in the Index for specific page numbers.

Where a category is indicated, for example, all brownies, see the Index for specific listings.

Specially Fun For Kids

All recipes in chapter "Kids in the Kitchen" • All brownies and bar cookies • Write-Your-Own Fortune Cookies • Clown Cupcakes; Ice Cream Cone Cupcakes • Halloween Spider Web Cupcakes • Mocha Kisses • Thumbalinas • Old-Fashioned Sugar Cookies and variations • Gingerbread Cut-Outs and variations • Favorite Chocolate Chip Cookies • Cowboy Crunch Chocolate Chip Cookies • Cookie Jar Oatmeal-Raisin Cookies • Classic Peanut Butter Cookies • Impossible Peanut Butter Cookies • Picnic Raisin Squares • Fresh Fruit Fool • Old-Fashioned Chocolate Pudding • Creamy Stove-Top Rice Pudding • Fluffy Tapioca Pudding • Elmira and Mary's Walnut Date Balls

Old-Fashioned Comfort Foods

Creamy Stove-Top Rice Pudding • Fluffy Tapioca Pudding • Clara's Noodle Pudding • Grandma's Apple-Raisin Bread Pudding with Warm Maple Sauce • Harvest Pumpkin Bread Pudding • Pennsylvania Dutch Baked Apple Pudding with Warm Nutmeg Cream • Chocolate Bread Pudding with White Chocolate Cream • Old-Fashioned Chocolate Pudding • Fresh Fruit Fool • New England Corn Bread • Charley's Jam Snacks • Peach-Plum Cobbler • Apple-Pear-Cranberry Crisp

Good Picnic or Lunch-Box Treats

Picnic Raisin Squares • Elmira and Mary's Walnut Date Balls • All muffins and scones • All chocolate brownies • Peanut Butter Brownies • Cookie Jar Oatmeal-Raisin Cookies • Old-Fashioned Sugar Cookies • Favorite Chocolate Chip Cookies and variations • Classic Peanut Butter Cookies • Impossible Peanut Butter Cookies • Triple Chocolate–Nut Biscotti • Pumpkin Bread • Chocolate Walnut Bread • Cape Cod Coffee Cake • Banana Crumb Cake • Gladys Martin's Sour Cream Coffee Cake • Blueberry Buckle

Winter Holiday Gifts from Your Kitchen

All cookies, bars, brownies, and squares • Triple Chocolate–Nut Biscotti • Chocolate Truffles • Caramel Nut Turtles • Butter Mints • Dipped Chips and Pretzel Pops • No-Bake Chewies • No-Bake Apricot Snowballs • Carol's Holiday Stollen • Pumpkin Bread • Poppy Seed Lemon Loaf • Cranberry-Orange Loaf • Cinnamon-Apple-Raisin Loaf • Cranberry Gingerbread • Applesauce Gift Cake with Icing Glaze • Chocolate Walnut Bread • Glazed Orange Bundt Cake (or lemon) • Swedish Almond Butter Cake • Black and White Pound Cake and variations • All-American Hot Fudge Sauce • Butterscotch Sauce • Peanut Butter Sauce

Autumn Holidays/Rosh Hashanah/Thanksgiving/Halloween

Three-Nut Thanksgiving Pie and variation • Pumpkin Chiffon Pie with Gingersnap Crumb Crust • Pumpkin Bread • Cranberry Pizza • Apple Pie Pizza • Golden Harvest Apple Honey Cobbler • Apple-Pear-Cranberry Crisp • Pear-Cranberry Upside-Down Cake • Mocha Walnut Tart with Walnut Pastry • Irra's Zucchini Loaf • Cranberry Gingerbread • Sour Cream Spice Cake with Honey Frosting • Carrot Cake with Cream Cheese Frosting • Pumpkin Roulade • Pumpkin 'n' Spice Muffins • Southern Sweet Potato

Biscuits • Halloween Spider Web Cupcakes •
Persimmon Pudding • Harvest Pumpkin Bread Pudding

Jewish Holidays

Cocoa Walnut Torte • Plain Walnut Torte •
Passover Chocolate Mousse Cake • Golden Harvest
Apple-Honey Cobbler

Gala Party Desserts/Valentine's Day

Old-Fashioned Coconut Layer Cake • Three-Layer
Chocolate Raspberry Romance Cake • To-Live-For
Chocolate Mousse Cake • Chocolate Sponge Roll with
Toffee Cream Filling • Lemon Sponge Roll with Lemon
Curd Filling and variation • Lemonade Cheesecake with
Honeyed-Blueberry Topping • Kristin's Key Lime
Cheesecake • Blue Ribbon Cherry Pie with Quick Lattice
Topping • Lemon Meringue Pie • Three-Nut
Thanksgiving Pie • Mocha Walnut Tart with Walnut
Pastry • Favorite Fresh Fruit Tart • Chocolate
Truffles • Mocha Kisses

Special for Springtime/Easter/Purim and Passover

Blueberry Shortcakes and variations • Classic 1-2-3-4
Cake, lemon variation • Orange Angel Cake and
variations • Glazed Orange Bundt Cake (or
lemon) • Swedish Almond Butter Cake • Cocoa
Walnut Torte • Plain Walnut Torte • Passover
Chocolate Mousse Cake • Lemon Sponge Roll with Lemon
Curd Filling • Basic No-Bake Cheesecake • Lemonade
Cheesecake with Honeyed-Blueberry Topping
• Strawberry-Rhubarb Streusel Pie • Strawberry Angel
Pie • Favorite Fresh Fruit Tart • Lemon Cream
Sherbet • Lemon Meringue Pie • Lemon Cloud
Pie • No-Bake Berry Pie

Bake Sale Favorites

All muffins • All scones • All quick breads • All
cookies (except Lemon Squares if weather is very hot) •
Fruit pies • Three-Nut Thanksgiving Pie • Peanut
Butter Pie with Chocolate Icing • Cobblers and
crisps • Mocha Walnut Tart with Walnut Pastry •
Blueberry Buckle • Cape Cod Coffee Cake • Banana
Crumb Cake • Gladys Martin's Sour Cream Coffee Cake
• Classic 1-2-3-4 Vanilla Cake and variations •
Cupcakes: Clowns, Ice Cream Cone Cupcakes, Halloween
Spider Web Cupcakes • Sour Cream Spice Cake with
Honey Frosting • Cranberry Gingerbread (omit whipped
cream topping) • Easy Devil's Food Cake • Ginnie's
One-Pot Chocolate Sheet Cake • Three-Layer Chocolate
Raspberry Romance Cake • To-Live-For Chocolate
Mousse Cake • Orange Angel Cake • Glazed Orange
or Lemon Bundt Cake • Swedish Almond Butter
Cake • Carrot Cake with Cream Cheese Frosting •
Applesauce Gift Cake with Icing Glaze • Black and White
Marble Pound Cake and variations • Cheesecakes (only if
can be kept refrigerated) • Chocolate Haystacks •
Caramel Nut Turtles • Butter Mints • Dipped Chips
and Pretzel Pops • No-Bake Chewies • No-Bake
Apricot Snowballs

Mail-Order Sources and Suppliers

Bridge Kitchenware

214 East 52nd Street
New York, NY 10022
(800)274-3435 Fax: (212)758-5387
Catalogue
Domestic and imported baking pans, equipment, and utensils, including wire pastry blender
www.bridgekitchenware.com

The Broadway Panhandler

477 Broome Street
New York, NY 10013
(212)966-3434
(no catalogue)
Wide variety of baking and cake decorating utensils

Chukar Cherry Company

320 Wine Country Road
P.O. Box 510
Prosser, WA 99350
(800)624-9544 Fax: (509)786-2591
Wide variety of excellent dried cherries, berries, and cranberries
www.chukar.com
e-mail: chukar@chukar.com

Dean & DeLuca

560 Broadway
New York, NY 10012
(212)226-6800
Catalogue (800)221-7714
www.dean&deluca.com
Wide variety of baking equipment and utensils, dark and white chocolate and cocoa, dried fruits, dried berries, cranberries, cherries, nuts, flour

Dean & DeLuca

3276 M Street, NW
Washington, D.C. 20007
(202)342-2500
(800)925-7854

King Arthur Flour Baker's Catalogue

P.O. Box 876
Norwich, VT 05055
(800)827-6836 Fax: (800)343-3002
Catalogue
Baking equipment and utensils (including nonstick baking pan liners, baking parchment, feather pastry brushes, instant-read thermometers, rotary-style nut mills), baking ingredients (including variety of flours, chocolate [dark and white], cocoa, nuts, seeds, pure extracts, coarse and pearl sugar, orange oil, Key lime juice, meringue powder, dried buttermilk powder, nuts, chocolate-covered coffee beans)
www.kingarthurflour.com

Penzeys, Ltd.

P.O. Box 933
Muskego, WI 53150
(414)679-7207 Fax: (414)679-7878
Catalogue
Exceptional selection of herbs and spices (especially good cinnamon), pure extracts, Tahitian and Madagascan vanilla beans and extracts, Dutch-processed and natural cocoa
www.penzeys.com

Revival Confections, Inc.

126 Fremont Place
Los Angeles, CA 90005
(323)936-4241 Fax: (323)937-3036
Giant chocolate-coated raisins
e-mail: revivalcon@aol.com

Simpson and Vail

P.O. Box 765
3 Quarry Road
Brookfield, CT 06804
(800)282-8327 Fax: (203)775-0462
Catalogue
Key lime juice, Tahitian vanilla beans and extract, flavored
citrus oils, Venezuelan El Rey chocolates (dark and white),
hazelnut and walnut oils, honey
www.svtea.com

Sweet Celebrations Division of Maid of Scandinavia

7009 Washington Avenue South
Edina, MN 55439
(800)328-6722
Catalogue
Cake baking and decorating equipment and utensils, cardboard cake disks, pastry bags and tips, dark and white
chocolate
www.sweetc.com

Sweet Expectations

8 Crafts Avenue
Northampton, MA 01060
(413)585-8965
Old-fashioned candy store, stocks over 300 varieties (sold by
piece or pound), including gummy fish, sharks, octupuses,
seashell candies, pebbles
www.sweet-expectations.com

Williams-Sonoma, Inc.

Mail-Order Department
10000 Covington Cross
Las Vegas, NV 89134
(800)541-2233
Wide variety of baking equipment and utensils, baking ingredients
www.williams-sonoma.com

Wilton Industries

2240 West 75th Street
Woodridge, IL 60517
(800)794-5866; (630)963-7100
Wilton Yearbook
Wilton Meringue Powder, full line of cake decorating products
and utensils
www.wilton.com/

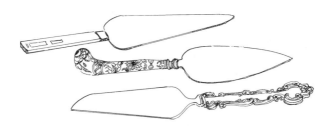

Index

Index